# AMERICANGREATS

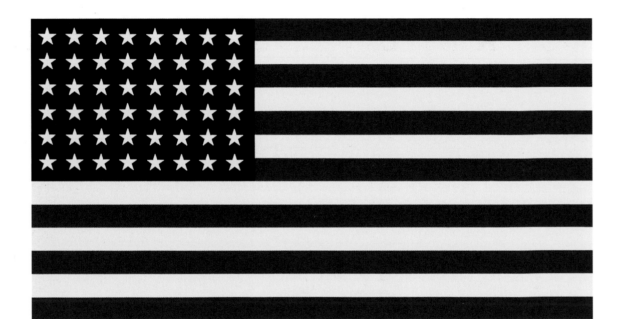

**GIVE IT YOUR BEST!**

DIVISION OF INFORMATION
OFFICE FOR EMERGENCY MANAGEMENT
WASHINGTON, D.C.

# AMERICANGREATS

EDITED BY ROBERT A. WILSON AND STANLEY MARCUS

PublicAffairs

NEW YORK

Library of Congress Cataloging-in-Publication Data
American greats / edited by Robert A. Wilson and Stanley Marcus. — 1st ed.
    p. cm.
Includes bibliographical references and index.
    ISBN 1–891620–48–7
1. United States—Civilization Miscellanea.
2. National characteristics, American miscellanea.
I. Wilson, Robert A., 1941– . II. Marcus, Stanley, 1905– .
E169.1.A471985 1999
973—dc21 99–29276
    CIP


FIRST   EDITION

10 9 8 7 6 5 4 3 2 1

Facing title page: Charles Coiner created this

World War II poster commissioned by the

U.S. Office for Emergency Managment, c. 1942.

*For all that counts,*
*Laura, Andrew, Owen, Luke*

# contributors

Kevin Baker is the author of the best-selling novel *Dreamland* and *Sometimes You See it Coming*.

Allen Barra is a sports columnist for *The Wall Street Journal*, and a frequent contributor to *The New York Times* and *American Heritage Magazine*.

Michael Beschloss, a leading presidential historian, wrote the bestsellers *Taking Charge: The Johnson White House Tapes, 1963-1964,* and *The Crisis Years: Kennedy and Khrushchev, 1960-1963.*

James L. Brooks is a three-time Academy Award winner and fifteen-time Emmy Award winner. He co-created for television *The Mary Tyler Moore Show, Rhoda, Taxi, The Tracy Ullman Show,* and *The Simpsons.* Among the films he wrote, directed, and produced are *Terms of Endearment, Broadcast News,* and *As Good as it Gets.*

Gail Buckland, Associate Professor of the History of Photography at The Cooper Union, was the photo historian for *The American Century.* She has authored eight books on photography and its history.

Christopher Buckley is the author of such *New York Times* Notable Books as *Thank You For Smoking, God Is My Broker*, and *Little Green Men*. He is the founding editor of *Forbes FYI* magazine and the son of William F. Buckley.

Marina Budhos is the author of several novels. Her latest book is *Remix: Conversations with Immigrant Teenagers.*

Joan Ganz Cooney is co-founder of the Children's Television Workshop (CTW) and originator of *Sesame Street*. Her work has been recognized with numerous honorary degrees and awards including the 1995 Presidential Medal of Freedom, the nation's highest civilian honor.

Nicholas Dawidoff has written for *The New Republic, The New Yorker* and *Sports Illustrated*. He wrote *The Country of Country* and *The Catcher Was a Spy*, a biography of former White Sox catcher Moe Berg.

David Douglas Duncan was a *LIFE* photographer from 1946 until 1955, when he left to become a freelancer. He chronicled for *LIFE Magazine* in both words and pictures the French and U.S. involvement in Vietnam. Thousands of images and numerous books came out of his friendship with Pablo Picasso.

Gary Giddins is a staff writer at *The Village Voice*. His book, *Visions of Jazz,* was awarded the 1998 National Book Critics Circle Award for Criticism.

Roy Grace, now chairman of Grace & Rothschild Advertising, worked on the original Volkswagen campaign. Four of the seventeen commercials in the Museum of Modern Art's permanent collection are his.

A.C. Greene is a Texas historian and author of more than twenty books, including *A Personal Country* and *The Santa Claus Bank Robbery.*

David Halberstam first went to Vietnam in 1962 at the age of twenty-eight. He won the Pulitzer Prize for his reporting from there in 1964. His sixteen books include *The Best and the Brightest, The Powers That Be, The Fifties, The Reckoning,* and *The Children.*

Jack Hitt is a former *Harper's* editor and journalist who writes frequently for *The New York Times Magazine*, *GQ* and *Lingua Franca*.

Marvin Kalb, Edward R. Murrow Professor of Press and Public Policy at Harvard University's John F. Kennedy School of Government, was the director of the Joan Shorenstein Center on the Press, Politics and Public Policy.

John Keegan, a distinguished British military historian, is the author of many acclaimed books, including *The First World War*, and *The Face of Battle*, selected as one of the Modern Library's 100 Best Nonfiction Books of the 20th century.

Jeff Kisseloff's work has appeared in *American Heritage*. He is the author of *You Must Remember This*, a book of oral histories of New York and *The Box*, a book about the early days of television.

Charles McGrath has been the editor of *The New York Times Book Review* since 1995; before that he was deputy editor of *The New Yorker*.

David McCullough won the Pulitzer Prize for *Truman* and is twice winner of the National Book Award. His book *The Great Bridge,* was selected by the Modern Library as one of the 100 Best Nonfiction Books of the 20th century. He is the host of PBS's "American Experience" series.

Ruth Reichl is the editor in chief of *Gourmet* and formerly the *New York Times* restaurant critic. She is the author of the critically acclaimed memoir, *Tender at the Bone*. As the chef and co-owner of The Swallow Restaurant from 1974-1977, she played a part in Berkeley's culinary revolution during that period.

David Remnick is the editor of *The New Yorker* magazine. He joined *The New Yorker* in 1992, after ten years at *The Washington Post*. His book on the former Soviet Union, *Lenin's Tomb,* won the 1994 Pulitzer Prize for nonfiction.

Mike Ritchey, a former Neiman Fellow, is a journalist and former publisher of *The Daily Planet* in Telluride, Colorado.

Gay Talese is the author of a number of critically-acclaimed best-sellers including *Unto the Sons, Honor Thy Father* and *Thy Neighbor's Wife*. His book *The Kingdom and the Power* chronicled *The New York Times's* influence and history.

John Updike was a member of the staff of *The New Yorker* from 1955 to 1957, to which he contributed short stories, poems, essays, and book reviews. His novels have won the Pulitzer Prize, the National Book Award, the American Book Award, the National Book Critics Circle Award, and the Howells Medal.

Other contributors include Robert Wilson, Jackie McElhaney and Mike McFarland.

## a note from Robert A. Wilson

From the beginning, I was helped by the encouragement and judgment of Stanley Marcus who, still in the prime of his youth, backs what he believes in; he believed in *American Greats* from the start. American Airlines's Mike Gunn and his enthusiasm for the idea resulted in support, which was crucial to our going forward. Our gratitude goes also to his colleagues, Susan Williams and Tom Morris.

I appreciate the generosity and support we received from Carl Yeckel and the King Foundation, as well as from Lee and Amy Fikes and the Fikes Family Fund. We also received support for the book in memory of David Nathan Meyerson.

My team in Dallas who worked most closely with me on the book—the little engine that could—included Joe Goodwin whose distinctive design for the book you can see for yourself, Jackie McElhaney who coordinated everything required and whose grace, high intelligence, and indefatigability never flagged; Staci Teague who tracked down images and deftly managed the permissions and credits required for their use; and Barbara Hawn whose spirit, temperament, and superb organizational skills held us together.

Kevin Baker was most encouraging and enthusiastic; his help and counsel were invaluable. Mike Ritchey, longtime steadfast friend, came through completely when I needed help most. Gail Buckland whose taste and knowledge of photography made her an ally of distinction.

My gratitude also goes to Robert Kimzey and Peter Osnos of PublicAffairs who wanted the book to be the best we could make it. To Mark McGarry of Texas Type & Book Works. And to Della Mancuso whose experience and savvy in production conquered all problems.

All the way I was lifted by the enthusiasm and judgment of Laura, my wife, and our sons Andrew, Owen, and Luke; my sister, Beth Floor; and Pam and Tom Luce. Finally I cannot overestimate the inspiration provided by the friendship and example of Rosalee and David McCullough.

## a note from Don Carty

*American Greats* celebrates America's character and courage. The book includes essays by some of America's most recognized and respected citizens. These men and women of distinction share their perspective on the achievements and ideas that have shaped America. From the Pony Express to *The New York Times*; from the Brooklyn Bridge to West Point; from *Sesame Street* to the Smithsonian—all, individually and collectively, help define this nation at its best.

American Airlines is pleased to have participated by underwriting the development of what is truly a book of distinction. We hope you enjoy the essays and pictures that so vividly portray one of this country's greatest assets: the ingenuity of its people. Please consider this book a reminder of not only how far we've come, but how far we can still go.

Sincerely,

Chairman and CEO of American Airlines

**AmericanAirlines**®
**American**Eagle®

## contents

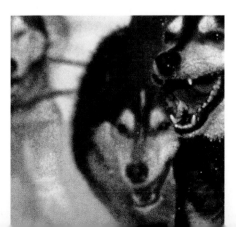

# preface

PHONE CALL from a friend, winter 1996: "I have an idea for a book and the more I work on it, the more enthusiastic I get. Do you have a minute?"

Me: "Come on over."

The conversation didn't take long. Because it was, after all, about books, which I've been writing and publishing since 1930. And it was, perhaps, a chance to help, which always gives a life a lift, especially a life in its tenth decade.

When my friend, Bob Wilson, came over, he laid out his ideas for a book with a title I liked, *American Greats*. The book would be an appreciation of America at its best. He began to talk about them. The dimensions of the baseball diamond, miraculously still intact since Alexander Joy Cartwright laid them out in 1845. The G.I. Bill, as enlightened a piece of legislation as ever conceived, creating as it did a middle class with an affordable chance for a college education. The small, no nonsense book, *The Elements of Style*, by William Strunk with an introduction by his student, E.B. White is a book that has helped generations understand and use the full power of our language. Tom Paine's *Common Sense,* which gave us the resolve to revolt. The Wright Brothers's concept of genius.

As he talked, I began thinking of my own concepts of an American great. My first idea was the self-starter, not the human variety, although that certainly is an American great, but the actual self-starter that replaced the crank on early automobiles. It's a good story.

Back to the conversation.

Bob: "So what do you think?"

Me: "Count me in. Just make sure the book rewards the reader and isn't jingoistic."

From the very start we were on the same wavelength. And the chance to offer guidance, direction, and ideas has been a pleasure. But the true pleasure has been the reaction of friends. They listen to the idea and some of the stories comprising *American Greats*. Then, to a person, they say, " I hope you're going to include . . ." or "Have you thought of . . . ?" As we expected, just about everyone has their own ideas about what exemplifies an American great.

The book jacket went through several versions until its designer, Joe Goodwin, separated the title by "American's" syllables, revealing in dazzling white, one of America's significant, most defining attributes—"I CAN."

That can-do spirit runs throughout the book. Just give us a chance, we can do it. Whether a bridge, a skyscraper, or a flying machine.

We do not view our book as definitive. Or absolute. The book is deliberately not called "America's Greatest." The book is our opinion, which we hope will trigger your own opinions, your own definitions of American greats. If someone's imagination and ambition are somehow ignited by examples of these American greats to create something that expands America's possibilities, that brings us to our feet, then this book will have succeeded.

We hope this book will help spark the beginning of a national conversation about what makes America great. The time seems right, don't you think?

*Stanley Marcus*

STANLEY MARCUS

# A M E R I C A N G R E A T S

WHEN THE FOUNDING FATHERS signed the Declaration of Independence in July 1776, it was an accepted fact that most colonists favored full separation from England. But only six months before, it was not so. There had been skirmishes with British soldiers. A variety of discontents had been diplomatically voiced by colonial leaders. But the Continental Congress was silent on the matter of New World indignation, and there was still

## common sense    'tis time to part

a sense that Parliament in London could resolve the various disputes in a satisfactory way. If anything, the colonies vibrated with unarticulated emotions and buried hopes—poised for someone to bring the scattered opinions into focus.

Clarity arrived in Philadelphia on January 10, 1776, when an English corset-maker—who had only been in the colonies about a year—published a pamphlet called *Common Sense*. In stunningly clear and moving prose, Thomas Paine gathered up the random unspoken thoughts of the average smithy or farmer, shook them in his face, and gave him the courage to accept a radical idea.

"The sun never shined on a cause of greater worth," he wrote. "'Tis not the concern of a day, a year, or an age; posterity are virtually involved in the contest . . . Now is the seed-time of continental union, faith, and honour.

"The least fracture now will be like a name engraved with the point of a pin on the tender rind of a young oak; the wound will enlarge with the tree, and posterity read it in full grown characters."

History would be made now or never, Paine wrote, "The present winter is worth an age if rightly employed, but if lost or neglected the whole continent will partake of the misfortune."

Then came the words from which there would be no turning back, "Every thing that is right and reasonable pleads for separation. The blood of the slain, the weeping voice of nature cries, 'TIS TIME TO PART."

For the first time, the notion of independence was on the lips of every yeoman in the colonies and a new idea of a separate nationality was in their heads. Thomas Paine was the first man to string together these five words: "The United States of America."

However, the brilliance of *Common Sense* extends far beyond its brash call for revolution. The document is bound in emotion and plays off of it. Every chord of discontent in the colonies was plucked by Paine in *Common Sense*. To the Tories who defended the monarchy, Paine wrote with a poet's control of language and a passionate willingness to burn

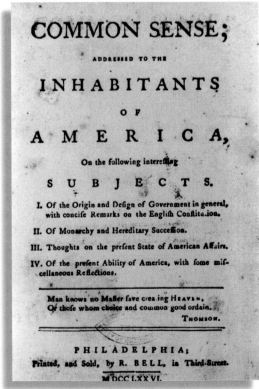

all bridges. He treasonously mocked King George as a "hardened, sullen-tempered Pharaoh" and a descendent of William the Conqueror, "a French bastard landing with an armed banditti and establishing himself King of England against the consent of the natives."

by Jack Hitt

A great fear among American commoners was a fear they had learned as subjects of the Crown: That the absence of an established, flourishing aristocracy meant that the colonists would lack the courage to govern themselves and would quickly dissolve into anarchy. Paine laughed away British "superstitions" about monarchical hierarchy, noting that in London "the rich are in general slaves to fear, and submit to courtly power with the trembling duplicity of a spaniel."

Still, might not the old tranquillity and diplomacy between England and her American colonies somehow be restored? Paine replied, "Can ye give to prostitution its former innocence? Neither can ye reconcile Britain and America . . . As well can the lover forgive the ravishers of his mistress as the continent forgive the murders of Britain." Act now, Paine implored, lest the time pass and we realize that "a little more, a little further, would have rendered this continent the glory of the earth." Then Paine adds, "since nothing but blows will do, for God's sake let us come to a final separation, and not leave the next generation to cutting throats. . . . "

When Thomas Jefferson wrote the Declaration of Independence six months later, he knew what his readers would hear when he declared his purpose "to place before mankind the common sense of the subject in terms so plain and firm as to justify ourselves."

*Common Sense* is a brilliant piece of propaganda from the American Revolution. It insulted the enemy, explained the reasons for revolt, implored the masses to act, and reached for the noblest explanations for a fight. Paine once said of his own writing that he would "avoid every literary ornament and put it in language as plain as the alphabet." And that is Paine's lasting contribution to American belles lettres. Like Franklin, he avoided the prolixities of Fleet Street and the clotted prose of the clergy. He pioneered a voice and style that is quintessentially American. Unadorned and plain, the American voice of simple declarative sentences set off by vivid imagery is the pioneering literary achievement of *Common Sense*.

By urging Americans to "let us come to a final separation," *Common Sense* stiffened the resolve to revolt. It set the stage and prepared the nation for Thomas Jefferson's Declaration of Independence six months later.

the automobile self-starter

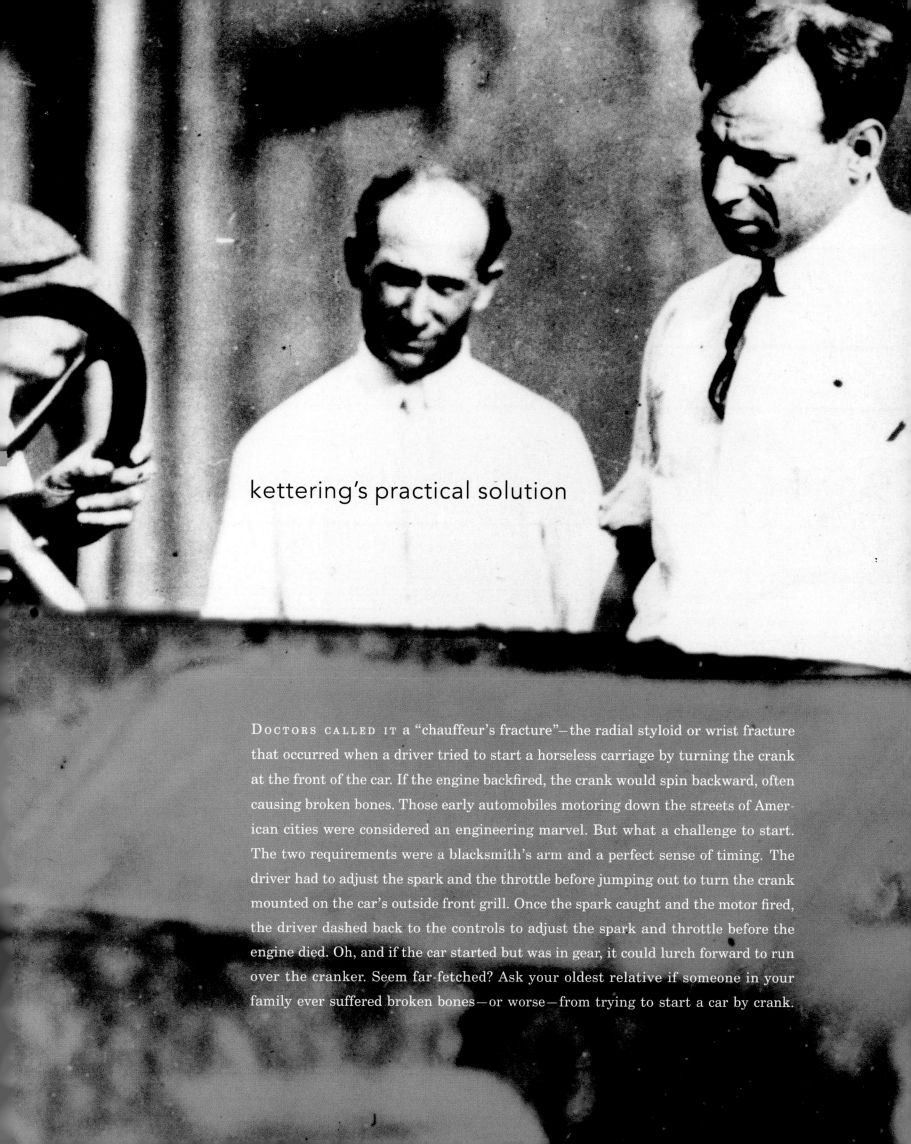

# kettering's practical solution

DOCTORS CALLED IT a "chauffeur's fracture"—the radial styloid or wrist fracture that occurred when a driver tried to start a horseless carriage by turning the crank at the front of the car. If the engine backfired, the crank would spin backward, often causing broken bones. Those early automobiles motoring down the streets of American cities were considered an engineering marvel. But what a challenge to start. The two requirements were a blacksmith's arm and a perfect sense of timing. The driver had to adjust the spark and the throttle before jumping out to turn the crank mounted on the car's outside front grill. Once the spark caught and the motor fired, the driver dashed back to the controls to adjust the spark and throttle before the engine died. Oh, and if the car started but was in gear, it could lurch forward to run over the cranker. Seem far-fetched? Ask your oldest relative if someone in your family ever suffered broken bones—or worse—from trying to start a car by crank.

The danger spelled opportunity. New Yorker Clyde J. Coleman secured a patent in 1899 for an electric self-starter. But his was a theoretical solution and never marketed. The big winner was the inventor Charles F. Kettering who, in 1910, developed a self-starter small enough to fit under the hood of a car and run off a small storage battery. After graduating from Ohio State's College of Engineering, Kettering had gone to work for the invention staff of the National Cash Register Company (NCR). There he created a high-torque electric motor that would supply power to drive a cash register, allowing a salesperson to ring up a sale without turning a hand crank twice each time. This small motor would inspire future inventions.

After five years at NCR, Kettering set up his own laboratory in a barn behind the E.A. Deeds's home at 319 Central Avenue in Dayton, Ohio. There Kettering, Deeds, and a group of engineers, mechanics, and electricians began work in 1908 on a new ignition system for the Cadillac Motor Cars Company. By 1910 they had formed the Dayton Engineering Laboratories Company, which became known as Delco Products.

Charles Franklin Kettering, Boss Kett to many, became head of research for General Motors after World War I. above left: Preliminary sketch of the design, which became the basis for Kettering's ignition patent, made July 23, 1908.

preceding page: Charles Kettering starts a 1913 test Buick fitted with his self-starter prototype, as other members of the Dayton Engineering Laboratories (later Delco Products) watch.

facing page: Promotional stunt in Dayton, Ohio, to advertise the new Cadillacs with self-starters.

Conventional thinking held that an electric self-starter was impossible; a motor powerful enough to crank an engine would have to be as large as the automobile engine itself. So much for conventional wisdom. But Henry Leland, then head of Cadillac, believed Kettering, whom he called an "absolutely unknown electrical genius," and his "Barn Gang" could devise a small motor that could crank the engine. The small motor developed for the cash register illustrated, as Kettering stated, that "more than once, we have seen research accomplishments fit together, like the words of a crossword puzzle, to aid us in solving other problems." They worked day and night for more than six months to the strains of the only record they had—"When You and I Were Young, Maggie." By January 1911, they tested an electric starter in a Cadillac; the Cadillac was then taken to Detroit for Leland to try out personally. Kettering returned to Dayton with an order for 12,000 units to be installed on every 1912 model Cadillac.

Within a year, the system was installed in six other makes of cars: Hudson, Packard, Cole, Oldsmobile, Oakland, and Jackson. In five years the self-starter helped increase sales more than sevenfold. This was the breakthrough the young motor car industry needed. The self-starter became a liberator, expanding the country's romance for the road. It came into general use as the final campaign for woman suffrage began. Women could now easily start and drive a car alone, prompting an editor of the *Detroit Free Press* to write that "Kettering's self-starter did more to emancipate women than Susan B. Anthony."

# barbed wire

ALLIS'S BLACK HILLS RIBBON. May's Pigtail. Shellabarger's Snake Wrap. Along with dozens of other varieties of barbed wire with equally exotic names, they all did the same thing: make a fence that even the toughest longhorn steer could not destroy. Robert Frost wrote long after the West understood, "good fences make good neighbors." But good fences in the Northeast

## the devil's hatband

and along the Eastern seaboard were comparatively easy to build. There were plenty of rocks and trees. As Americans began to migrate westward to the prairies and plains, however, where trees were in short supply, barbed wire allowed farmers and cattlemen to fence in their property.

Just who invented barbed wire has been hotly contested. Although the idea for a fence of twisted strands of sheet metal had been patented in France in 1860, American inventors, who seemed to know nothing of the French patent, perfected the concept of twisting two or more wires to hold barbs. The first three American patents were issued in 1867, but barbed wire was not a commercial success until 1876 when the wire manufacturing firm of Washburn & Moen of Worcester, Massachusetts, joined forces with Joseph Glidden and Isaac Ellwood of DeKalb, Illinois, two of the earliest patent holders.

Ellwood believed the greatest potential for sales of barbed wire was in the Southwest, especially Texas. He sent a salesman named John W. Gates to San Antonio to drum up business. Gates encountered dubious cattlemen and farmers, but he found a way to convince them. He built an eight-strand barbed-wire corral in the middle of the Military Plaza and told dubious onlookers: "The cattle ain't born that can get through it. Bring on your steers, gentlemen." The crowd gathered—at a distance—since no one believed the barbed wire was going to stop the Longhorns. When the cattle were driven in, they charged the fence again and again, but it held. By sunset John W. Gates had sold hundreds of miles of barbed wire at 18 cents a pound.

It was simple in design, inexpensive, unlimited in supply, and could be easily moved, mended, or rebuilt. Sellers of barbed wire believed their product made the opening of the West successful. Others argue that it was the opening of the West that made the success of barbed wire possible. Either way, the "devil's hatband," as it was called, left an indelible mark on the West.

# the baseball diamond

FAME AND SIGNIFICANCE do not necessarily equate. Asked to name the most famous diamond of all, most would reply "the Hope." But the truly significant diamond in our national life, the one with the magical ninety-foot dimensions, is the baseball diamond created by Alexander Joy Cartwright in 1845.

Those ninety-foot distances between bases have maintained a fragile balance between offense and defense for over 150 years. Red Smith wrote: "Ninety feet demands perfection. It accurately measures the cunning, speed and finesse of the base stealer against the velocity of the thrown ball." He also said, "the world's fastest men cannot run to first base ahead of a sharply hit ball that is cleanly handled by an infielder; he will get there only half a step too late. Let the fielder juggle the ball for one moment or delay his throw an instant and the runner will be safe."

The nation's pastime is played on fields reflecting a belief older than baseball, as old as the nation itself: the belief in freedom of expression. Build the fields as big as you want, the walls as high or short or as irregular; they are not the secret of this game.

The diamond's dimensions determine the nature of the conflict: base to base and across the diagonals, first to third, second to home, and home to the rubber on the elevated pitcher's mound. The magic derives from the ninety-foot borders that make the diamond of our national pastime seem like it could last forever.

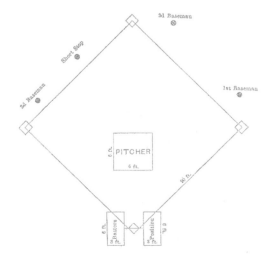

left: Wrigley Field, Chicago. right: A diamond that could last forever. While the layout of Cartwright's gem from the 1887 Spalding Guide includes a pitcher's box, the dimensions of the field have remained intact since he created them in 1845.

# the berlin airlift

## "we stay in berlin. period."

### by Kevin Baker

PRESIDENT HARRY S. TRUMAN, as David McCullough wrote, "had little time to dwell on the Republicans and their convention. On the day Dewey was chosen, Thursday, June 24, 1948, the Russians clamped a blockade on all rail, highway, and water traffic in and out of Berlin.... Clearly Stalin was attempting to force the Western Allies to withdraw from the city. Except by air, the Allied sectors were entirely cut off. Nothing could come in or out. Two and a half million people faced starvation." Asked whether American forces would remain in Berlin or pull out, Truman answered: "We stay in Berlin. Period."

Four days later, on June 28, as Thomas Dewey rallied voters to look past the war—and the Democrats—and toward the future, Truman ordered a full-scale airlift to Berlin. The same day he sent two squadrons of B-29s to Germany, the giant planes known to the world as the kind that dropped the atomic bombs on Japan. However, these particular planes were never modified to carry atomic weapons, a detail the Russians were not to know.

Truman consulted neither the White House staff nor his political advisors in making the decision. He and General George C. Marshall, his secretary of state, were convinced that the future of Western Europe was at stake in Berlin and that the situation with the Russians also being in Berlin could lead to war. The numbers were grim: the Allies had 6,500 soldiers in the city; Russia had 18,000. Those 18,000, however, were backed by 300,000 more in Germany's Eastern Zone. Politicians and newspaper editorialists thought it would be impossible to supply 2.5 million people with food, clothes, and other essentials by air, particularly when winter came.

But by the fourth week of the airlift, American and British transports were roaring in hundreds of times a day. More pilots were training in Montana, flying blind-folded through extremely narrow mock routes, similar to the Berlin routes. The efforts of pilots and ground crews prompted *The New York Times* to write: "We were proud of our Air Force during the war. We're prouder of it today." The effort was heroic, but it was not enough. Truman increased the number of planes, and 30,000 Berliners volunteered in the building of a new airfield.

By October, the airlift was clearly succeeding, and Truman sent yet another twenty-six C-54 transports into the rotation. The increase in flights guaranteed winter supplies for the city. The Russians, realizing their blockade had backfired, signaled a change in attitude. Stalin backed down.

"To do more would have been a direct threat to peace. To have done less would have been an abdication of our American honor and traditions," said General Lucius Clay, the top U.S. official in occupied Germany during the Airlift, adding "Once we accepted the challenge, the problem was attacked with characteristic American ingenuity."

Harry Truman, re-elected by the slimmest of margins, called off his airlift on May 12, 1949, fourteen months after it began. The 277,804 flights had delivered 2,325,809 tons of food and supplies, almost one ton for every man, woman, and child in Berlin, then the world's third-largest city, behind Chicago and New York. On that same day, May 12, 1949, the Allied powers approved the establishment of a new German Federated Republic, whereby the Germans would rule themselves with their own government, at Bonn.

# the birds of america
## audubon's great idea

HE ESCAPED THE CURSE of talent without will because he had both. He also had inexhaustible energy, which a late start sometimes furnishes. But it was the clarity of his focus that gave the lift to what John James Audubon called his great idea. He would paint, using watercolors, all America's birds actual size in authentic backgrounds. The result was 435 plates, containing 1,065 individual birds. More than 175 five-volume double elephant portfolios were produced. The North American Review accurately called *The Birds of America* Audubon's "imperishable monument."

As so often happens, posterity's collectors, not the artist, would reap the financial rewards. Audubon estimated the project's costs over the twelve years it took to complete exceeded $115,000 (not including living expenses for his family). He probably received over $140,000 from his 160 subscribers to the portfolio. Finances were always a problem for Audubon, and he wrote when *The Birds of America* was finished, "I find myself very little the better in point of recompense for the vast amount of expedition I have been at to accomplish the task."

So how did Audubon do it? His project had such magnitude: from the number of birds to be painted to the geography to be covered. His background as an expert woodsman, like his friend Daniel Boone, helped. Audubon was a good hunter and killed many of the birds he painted himself; later he also bought skins and skulls and entire birds and animals from trappers and hunters and taxidermists around the country.

At first, in preparation, he would hang the birds up by their feet, spreading the wings so he could get every minute bone or vein or ruffle just right. He raised their heads, wings, and tails with threads and soon constructed a bird "manikin" out of wood, cork, and wires. It was, he wrote, "a grotesque figure," and he "demolished it to atoms" in embarrassment and anger when a friend saw it and laughed. He then composed a system of thin, sharp-pointed wires to animate the freshly killed birds and set them in lifelike poses against a grid background he had drawn on a soft board. With an identical grid on his drawing paper, he could accurately repro-

preceding page: White-headed Eagle left: Great Blue Heron right: Blue Jay

17

duce the details and "attitudes" characteristic of specific birds. He had learned those unique mannerisms as only a dedicated woodsman could, by studying live birds.

America, especially the academic world, ever suspicious of the self-taught, largely scorned him and his work. The French and English, however, recognized his genius. "My God, I never saw anything like this before!" was the response of William Home Lizars, one of Britain's foremost engravers. Audubon's first subscriber, in fact, was King George IV. What must Audubon have felt with that affirmation? He was, after all, born Jean Rabine (or perhaps Jean-Jacque) Fougere Audubon in 1785, the illegitimate son of a French sea captain and a Haitian Creole woman; later adopted by his French stepmother, his illegitimacy had to be kept secret because French law would have stripped him of any inheritance.

The body of his work, including *The Quadrupeds of North America* (many of which had to be painted by Audubon's gifted son, John), would place him among the elite of the American Romantics. Before he died, the "Audubons," as the books would come to be known, were recognized in America, his adopted country, as "the greatest monument yet erected by art to nature."

Grey Fox

black baseball

the bumpy, begrudging road

## by Allen Barra

THEY WERE THERE almost from the start. Though now unverifiable, vague but credible stories attest that slaves played a game identifiable as baseball. Then, as the Civil War ended, blacks in northern cities began organizing teams. In 1867, the Uniques of Brooklyn played the Excelsiors of Philadelphia in the first "championship of colored clubs." The teams were segregated, but the crowds were not.

Not long after, another all-black Philadelphia team applied for membership in the inaugural meeting of the National Association of Base Ball Players (NABBP); they were rejected by the unsettling logic of race, with the explanation that "If colored clubs were admitted there would be, in all probability, some division of feeling, whereas by excluding them no injury could result to anyone." No one, of course, consulted the colored clubs as to whether they felt injured by the exclusion.

Still, black teams persisted. In 1869, the Philadelphia Pythians, the team that had originally applied for membership in the NABBP, got some measure of satisfaction by becoming the first black team to play and beat an all-white squad with a 27–17 victory over another Philadelphia team, the City Items.

In 1876, the National League was born and, with it, an unspoken agreement among its officials to exclude black ballplayers. But the National League was only a small part of the dynamic swirl of American professional baseball leagues that existed in the mostly Northern and industrial Mid-Eastern parts of the country in the late nineteenth century. Several black players—estimates range from fifty to perhaps one hundred—were able to make some kind of living in the disorganized professional leagues.

The most famous of those were a second baseman named Frank Grant and a catcher, Moses Fleetwood Walker. The former was light-skinned and often passed, despite his name, as a "Spaniard." Statistics are hard to come by, but it is known that he challenged for the 1887 International Association batting title while playing for Buffalo. Walker is generally recognized as the first black catcher in major league ball. If catcher's equipment truly includes "the tools of ignorance," then Walker was a wise man: He caught without a glove or protector and paid the price in the form of numerous injuries.

In 1887, Grant, Walker, his brother Welday, the legendary pitcher George Stovey, and other black stars flocked to the International League (which had integrated teams), causing an editorial in *Sporting Life* to ask "How far will this mania for engaging colored players go?"

Not very far, as it turned out.

There were numerous on-field confrontations with racist white players and off-field protests by angry fans. Cap Anson, manager of the National League's Chicago White Stockings, refused to field a team in an exhibition game if the Newark team played either Welday Walker or Stovey. More protests against blacks followed, prompting league officials to announce a ban on the signing of new black players. Welday Walker told a reporter that "the law is a disgrace in the present age." But other leagues soon followed suit, and by the end of the century, practically no blacks were left in the higher leagues.

So the era of segregated baseball began. Fabled black players would come to be known to white fans by the stories they inspired or by their nicknames, often the result of comparisons with the great white players. Oscar Charleston, considered the greatest black outfielder of the 1910–1920 period, was called the "black Ty Cobb," a tag that must have infuriated the racist Cobb. Shortstop John Henry Lloyd was known as "the black Wagner," after the great Pittsburgh Pirate Honus Wagner who, after watching Lloyd play, called the comparison "an honor and privilege."

Ironically, the half century or so leading up to Jackie Robinson's major league debut featured more games with black and white players than ever before, but they were always in the form of exhibitions and barnstorming tours. The most publicized of these were teams put together by Babe Ruth and, later, Dizzy Dean, who often matched up with his great black counterpart, Satchel Paige. When Paige beat Dean 1–0 in a 1934 exhibition game, Bill Veeck called it the "greatest pitching battle I have ever seen."

The play of Paige and other stars like Josh Gibson and Buck Leonard kept the integration issue alive. In 1943, 50,000 fans attended the Negro League's East-West All Star Game; as Satchel Paige said, "Even white folks was coming out big." The next year, baseball Commissioner Kenesaw Mountain Landis—strict opponent of integration—died. A moderate, A. B. "Happy" Chandler, became the new commissioner, and the bumpy, begrudging road to Branch Rickey and Jackie Robinson, Bill Veeck and Larry Doby, was cleared at last.

above: Poster announcing 1934 exhibition game featuring noted pitchers Leroy "Satchel" Paige and Dizzy Dean.
right (from left to right): Satchel Paige, Josh Gibson, and Cy Perkins played for the Trujillo team in the Dominican Republic in 1937 when the photo was taken.

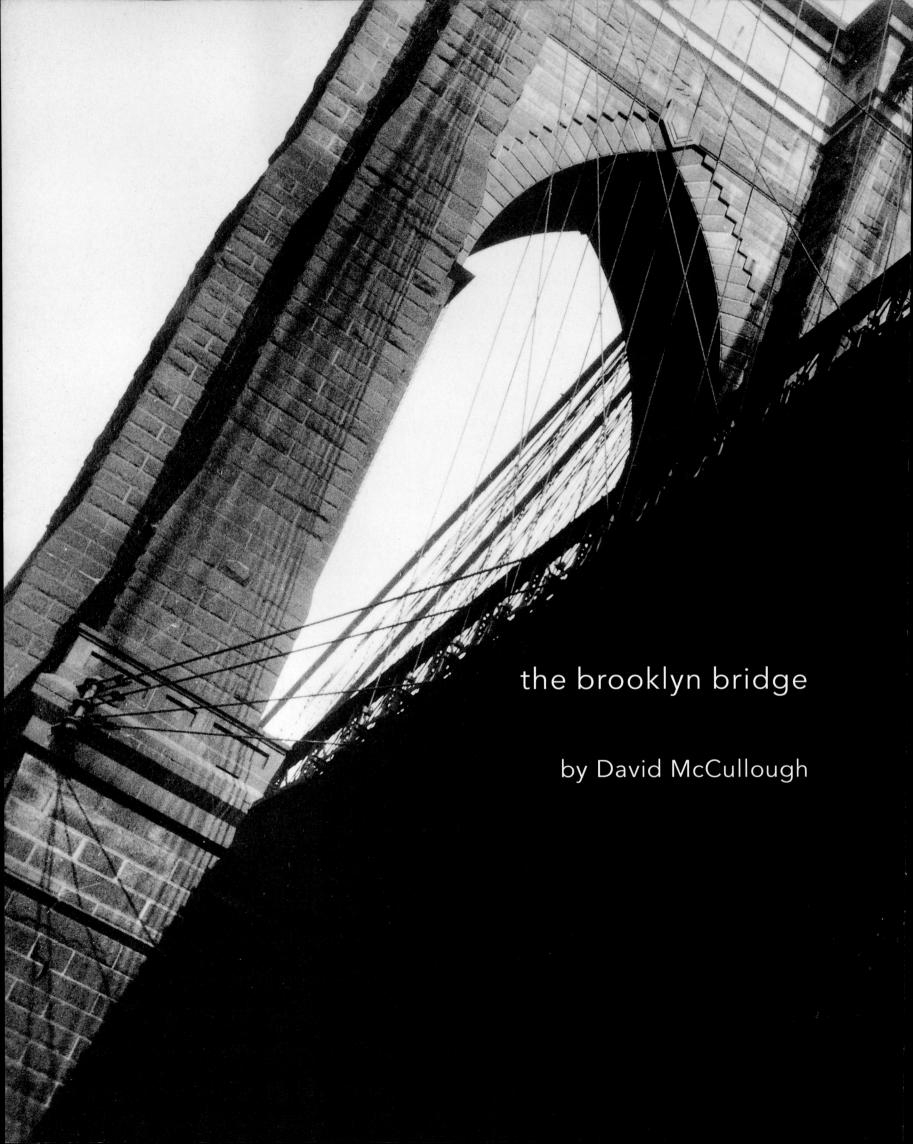

the brooklyn bridge

by David McCullough

There is something particularly appealing about a bridge, almost
any bridge, but the Brooklyn Bridge surpasses all.

In its day, it was the biggest, most famous bridge in the world, the most
beautiful of suspension bridges, and the most dramatic testament yet to American
technical ingenuity and daring. More than a mile long, it spanned New York's East River
with "one great leap," as was said. Its enormous granite towers loomed higher than anything
anyone had ever seen, higher than the topgallant sails of the square-riggers coursing the river,
higher than any building in New York, or any structure then on the North American continent.

"You see great ships passing beneath it," wrote a visitor from abroad "and you will feel that the engineer is the
great artist of our epoch and you will own that these people have a right to plume themselves on their audacity. "

It was the thing everyone from the hinterlands was told not to miss seeing ("if ever you get to New York"), and the
first New World spectacle beheld by tens of millions of immigrants as their inbound ships came up the harbor. As nothing else ever had, the bridge indicated that there was no place like New York, no place like America in the wondrous
nineteenth century.

The heroic story of its construction is well known. Its position in American life is unrivaled, and as
remarkable as anything about this infinitely unprecedented structure is that it has never lost
that position. It remains not only the proudest symbol of America's greatest city and a
thrilling work of architecture, but an enduring symbol of much that is best about
America. And this, it happens, was just as its designer, the brilliant John
A. Roebling, had promised from the start with characteristic
immodesty.

If built according to his plans, he said, the
bridge would stand down the ages as a
stunning example of engineering
and a great work of art.

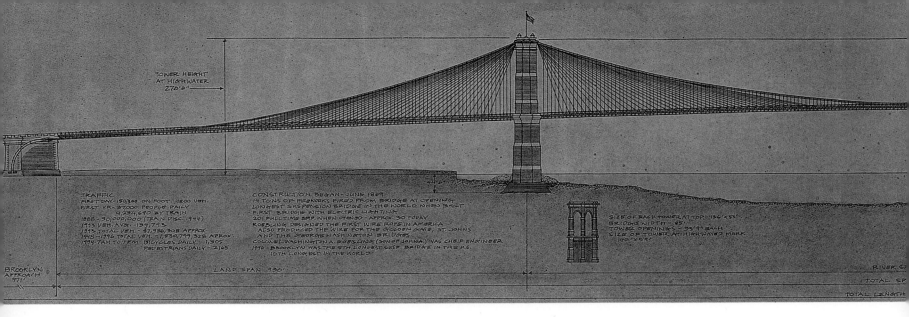

That the bridge rose out of the Gilded Age, with its rampaging corruption, its infamous Tweed Ring and the Grant administration, the very heyday of shoddy in nearly everything, makes the promise and its fulfillment all the more outstanding.

Himself an immigrant, Roebling had left Germany in the 1830s to find his destiny "in all that space" of America, and on arriving, he had taken the multitude of projects he saw under construction—highways, railways, canals—as the natural expression of an enlightened, self-governing people. It was John A. Roebling who perfected the suspension form, with bridges at Niagra, Pittsburgh, and Cincinnati. The bridge over the East River was to have been his crowning work, his masterpiece, but he died of tetanus in 1869, after a freak accident while making the initial surveys on the Brooklyn shore.

Only his son, Col. Washington Roebling, a Civil War hero, was qualified to take up the work in his place, and if dedication, high intelligence, decisiveness, and extraordinary courage are qualities to be especially admired, he was the most admirable of men. He carried on in the face of trials and setbacks never foreseen by his father, and with the ever-present knowledge that if the bridge succeeded, it would be his father's triumph, while should it fail, it would be his failure.

Washington Roebling had a gift for being always where he was needed, no matter the danger. In the crucial first stages, he was in and out of the great caisson foundation beneath Brooklyn tower, down below the river more often than anyone, to the point where he was stricken by the "bends," the dreaded caisson disease. The pain was excruciating and caused, as no one yet understood, by coming out of compressed air too rapidly.

As a result, he spent the better part of fourteen years in confinement, watching over the work with a telescope from a window in his house in Brooklyn Heights. To see that his orders were carried out, and to appraise progress on the bridge for him first hand, his wife, Emily Warren Roebling, went back and forth to the site several times daily. It was she who dealt with the press and the trustees of the project. In little time, she was conversant with every detail and became Washington's most valuable and trusted aide.

preceding page: Photographer Walker Evans shot the bridge in 1929. above: Contemporary drawing of bridge with measurements included.

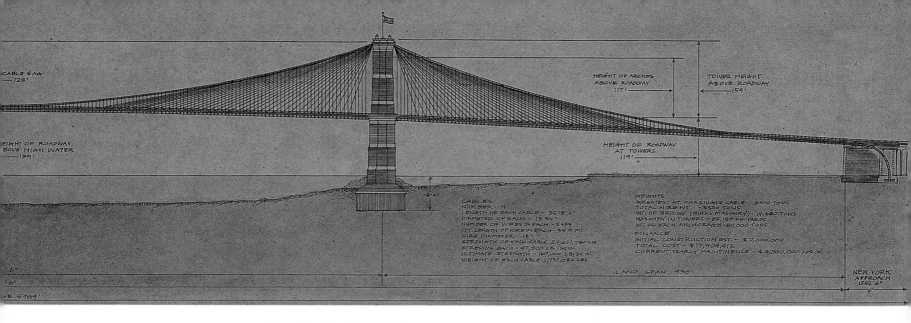

Nearly all of the work was exceedingly dangerous. How many others were eventually felled by the bends, how many were killed or maimed in building the towers or stringing the steel cables is not known—it is a measure of the time that nobody bothered to keep such records. But the cost in suffering and loss of life was considerable. Probably twenty-five or more were killed before the work ended.

The labor force was the epitome of "diversity," as we would say. Men of every color and kind, from every corner of the globe would later boast that they helped build the Brooklyn Bridge—New England farm boys new to the city, African Americans up from Maryland and Virginia, Irish and Italian immigrants in droves, English, Welsh, Swedes, Germans. Sailors proved particularly adept at the high-wire work.

Further, it was an enterprise led by youth, as suited a project that in concept and detail was virtually all pioneering and where physical stamina and creative energy counted for more than experience. Roebling, the only one who knew from experience how his father's bridges were built, was all of thirty-two when he took charge as chief engineer. The average age of the assistant engineers was thirty-one. Emily Roebling was twenty-six.

Because Roebling was never seen, rumors spread that he had lost his mind, and that if truth be known, this greatest, most daring of projects was in the hands of a woman.

The towers were completed the summer of 1876, the summer of the Centennial and the Battle of the Little Big Horn. The "spinning" of the cables commenced at once.

When the long span over the river was far enough finished for the first horse and carriage to cross, it was Emily Roebling who rode in it, carrying a rooster, as a symbol of victory, while from the rigging overhead the men waved their hats and cheered. If ever I could go back in time to witness an event, it would be this.

Construction ended, the bridge was opened on May 24, 1883. It had taken fourteen years. The fireworks in celebration that night were the most spectacular ever seen.

On reflection, some saw this clearly as an achievement of far-reaching importance.

"It so happens," wrote the architectural critic Montgomery Schuyler, "that the work which is likely to be our most durable monument, and to convey some knowledge of us to the most remote posterity, is a work of bare utility; not a shrine, not a fortress, not a palace, but a bridge."

Like other ambitious projects then under way in New York, such as the Metropolitan Museum and Central Park, the bridge was an emphatic commitment to the ideal of the city, intended as a grand-scale enhancement to city life.

On Sundays and holidays, people could escape from the narrow, congested streets of the city to walk the bridge, to go up and out over the river, higher than they had ever been, to take in the spectacular panorama and breathe air fresh from the sea. Thousands came, year in, year out, to stroll the famous pedestrian promenade, a boardwalk unlike any to be found on any bridge ever built. By design, it was placed above the vehicular traffic so as not to impede the view, the Roeblings being what might be called civilized civil engineers.

Initially, the bridge had been launched by Brooklyn people who saw that Manhattan was running out of space in which to expand. If a connection could be made, they thought, then surely the overflow would come Brooklyn's way. No one had yet imagined that a city might grow upward instead of out.

As it happened, it was the bridge itself, with its immense scale and use of steel, that marked the start of high-rise New York. Steel for girders and steel rope or cable for elevators would make possible the skyscraper and the vertical city of the twentieth century.

Though dwarfed by modern New York, and by the colossal Verrazano Bridge down the harbor, the Roebling masterpiece is still an American treasure beyond compare, beloved in a way nothing else built in America has ever been. Its towers are still the loftiest towers of stone to be seen. (The towers of the larger suspension bridges built since are of steel.) It is still acclaimed by architectural critics and figures time and again in movies, advertisements, and television commercials. Photographers find it irresistible. It is photographed, without cease, from every angle in all seasons, in every kind of light.

It remains a reminder of other days, yet serves still as an indispensable main artery. Trucks and automobiles, as unimaginable to the builders as were skyscrapers, stream across in both directions twenty-four hours a day.

And on good days, the crowds still come to walk the promenade and experience the thrill of the view, the same lift of spirits felt by so many for more than a century. It remains what it was, the greatest of bridges, the Brooklyn Bridge, made in America, its appeal defying time, a symbol now no less than ever of brave work nobly done.

29

Gertrude Elion in the laboratory with George Hitchings.

THERE MUST BE MILLIONS: Millions of people who owe their lives to Gertrude Elion yet have no idea they are in her debt. This one woman went so far and created so much: the first drugs to successfully treat acute leukemia; the immune suppressant azathioprine made kidney transplants between unrelated donors possible; acyclovir, the world's first successful antiviral drug; a system for designing new drugs that led to the development of the AIDS-fighting medication AZT. As President George Bush put it in 1991 when he awarded her the National Medal of Science, she "transformed the world."

But the odds, the times, and her gender were all stacked against her. One meeting changed everything. What's luck got to do with it? You decide.

# burroughs-wellcome and gertrude elion

In today's hyper-competitive scientific climate, anyone—regardless of gender— who comes out of school with credentials such as Gertrude Elion's is intensely recruited. Companies and universities hoping to secure such prized talent, wage human-resource warfare using all the influence deep pockets can deliver. But not in 1937. That year, at the age of nineteen after graduating summa cum laude from Hunter College, Elion went on to receive her masters degree in chemistry from New York University, the lone woman in her class. No research labs would hire her—they called her a "distracting influence." When the country went to war in 1941, though, the nation's workforce was so depleted that companies began employing women and minorities out of sheer necessity. Even then, Elion's chemistry degree meant nothing.

She worked for the A&P grocery chain and Johnson & Johnson, where she measured the acidity of pickles and tested the strength of sutures. But, in 1944, Ms. Elion walked into Burroughs-Wellcome's New York headquarters. And after a brief interview there with George Hitchings, a man too aware of and involved with the promise of science to believe in misguided gender-superiority theories, she was hired as his research assistant for $50 a week. So began a forty-year relationship with the company whose reputation she would enlarge and help to define; a company that gave her the only thing she needed: a chance. In igniting her diligent genius, Burroughs-Wellcome helped fulfill its responsibility to its founders.

Silas Burroughs and Henry Wellcome, both Americans, traveled to Europe in the late nineteenth century representing American pharmaceutical companies; they changed medical standards in the United Kingdom with their introduction of "compressed medicine," or pills. With their fortune secure, the two men formed Burroughs-Wellcome in 1880. The company thrived and after Burroughs's death in 1895, Wellcome channeled the company's focus toward becoming a research company first and profit-maker second, a move that led to the establishment of the pharmaceutical industry's first research labs. In 1936, Wellcome died and his will declared that the company was to divert all of its income toward research. The will set the stage for Elion's arrival, eight years later.

During their four decades together, Gertrude Elion and George Hitchings turned Wellcome (which became Glaxo-Wellcome in 1995) into one of the world's most prolific pharmaceutical research and invention factories. Together, in 1953, they invented the

## the perfect chemistry

tools of modern chemotherapy and successfully treated acute leukemia by creating drugs that interfered with the way cancer cells metabolized nucleic acids. In 1957, they modified those same drugs to develop anti-rejection drugs that made skin grafts and kidney transplants more possible. They discovered acyclovir, still the only effective antiviral agent against herpes, in 1973. In 1988, Elion and Hitchings shared the Nobel Prize.

In these fame-besotted times, when anonymity seems to be the worst of all possible fates, Gertrude Elion, who died on February 1, 1999, could not have cared less; save for the tributes from her scientific colleagues, her passing was barely noted. She made her position clear about the value she placed on fame and recognition in her answer to the reporter who asked if winning the Nobel Prize was the crowning moment of her career. "Of course not," she said. "If you worked all your life for an award and then didn't get it, your life would be wasted."

Gertrude Elion used up her life, all of it, on what counted most. She was never preoccupied with the spotlight. What mattered was her work, which gave her the opportunity to move the world nearer to answers, discoveries, and cures. She found her place at Burroughs-Wellcome, where her work was honored by the respect of colleagues she admired and patients whose lives she lengthened and saved, but who never knew her name.

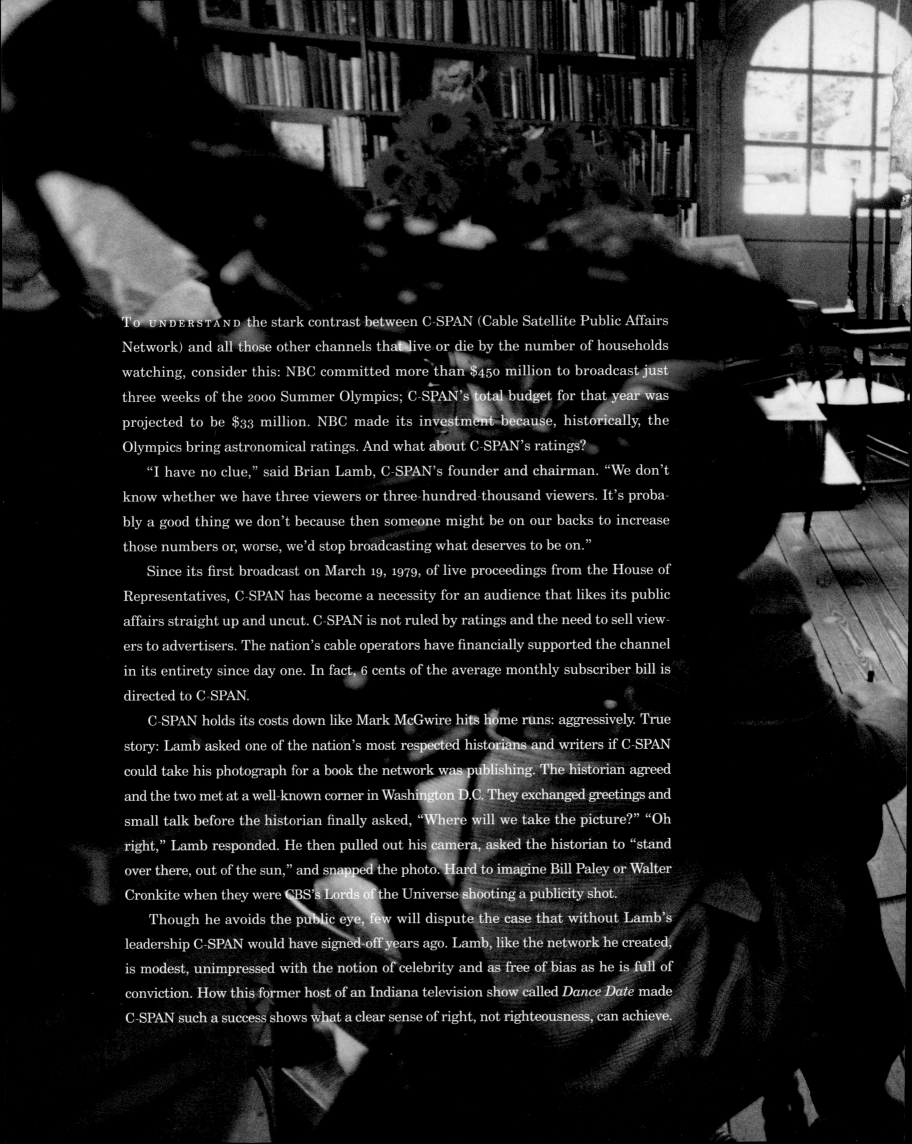

To UNDERSTAND the stark contrast between C-SPAN (Cable Satellite Public Affairs Network) and all those other channels that live or die by the number of households watching, consider this: NBC committed more than $450 million to broadcast just three weeks of the 2000 Summer Olympics; C-SPAN's total budget for that year was projected to be $33 million. NBC made its investment because, historically, the Olympics bring astronomical ratings. And what about C-SPAN's ratings?

"I have no clue," said Brian Lamb, C-SPAN's founder and chairman. "We don't know whether we have three viewers or three-hundred-thousand viewers. It's probably a good thing we don't because then someone might be on our backs to increase those numbers or, worse, we'd stop broadcasting what deserves to be on."

Since its first broadcast on March 19, 1979, of live proceedings from the House of Representatives, C-SPAN has become a necessity for an audience that likes its public affairs straight up and uncut. C-SPAN is not ruled by ratings and the need to sell viewers to advertisers. The nation's cable operators have financially supported the channel in its entirety since day one. In fact, 6 cents of the average monthly subscriber bill is directed to C-SPAN.

C-SPAN holds its costs down like Mark McGwire hits home runs: aggressively. True story: Lamb asked one of the nation's most respected historians and writers if C-SPAN could take his photograph for a book the network was publishing. The historian agreed and the two met at a well-known corner in Washington D.C. They exchanged greetings and small talk before the historian finally asked, "Where will we take the picture?" "Oh right," Lamb responded. He then pulled out his camera, asked the historian to "stand over there, out of the sun," and snapped the photo. Hard to imagine Bill Paley or Walter Cronkite when they were CBS's Lords of the Universe shooting a publicity shot.

Though he avoids the public eye, few will dispute the case that without Lamb's leadership C-SPAN would have signed-off years ago. Lamb, like the network he created, is modest, unimpressed with the notion of celebrity and as free of bias as he is full of conviction. How this former host of an Indiana television show called *Dance Date* made C-SPAN such a success shows what a clear sense of right, not righteousness, can achieve.

c-span where content is the star

Lamb had been nursing an idea for long-format public affairs television for a few years when in 1977, Congress seemed close to a decision about televising its debates. Reporting on Washington for a magazine that covered the cable business, Lamb met John Evans, then in the process of building the first cable system in the Washington area. Knowing that neither PBS nor the commercial networks would want congressional telecasts, Lamb sought Evans's opinion on another idea: What, he wanted to know, was Evans's reaction to televising Congress, uncut, on cable television? Evans was encouraging.

As it happened, Speaker of the House Tip O'Neil, already had his colleagues's support to televise their sessions. Lamb was in the right spot when luck and homework converged and told the speaker about his plan. Cable television, still in its formative stage, had been seeking a public affairs network, Lamb said, and wanted the chance to broadcast the House hearings in their entirety, five days a week.

Raising the money to fund the plan wasn't easy. The CEO of Columbia Cablevision, Bob Rosencrans, took the initiative and wrote a check for $25,000 and arranged for C-SPAN to share a satellite transponder. It took a few months, but twenty-two other cable operators committed $400,000 and a satellite uplink was also secured. By the day Congress first went on television, C-SPAN's potential reach was 3.5 million American homes, nine hours a day, Monday through Friday.

Today, content remains the star on Lamb's 24-hour, 365-day conglomerate of three diversified channels and on an FM radio station. While gavel-to-gavel congressional coverage remains C-SPAN's staple, U.S. Senate proceedings, the British House of Commons, eclectic lecture series, and historical reenactments also energize the schedule. Programming has further expanded into the discussion of nonfiction books. Based on a hunch in 1989, Lamb sensed that a new nonfiction book on the Vietnam War sixteen years in the making, by *New York Times* correspondent Neil Sheehan, *A Bright Shining Lie*, was important. If Sheehan was lucky, Lamb thought, he'd get five minutes on the *Today Show*. So he invited Sheehan to join him on C-SPAN and together they discussed the book . . . for two-and-a-half hours. The audience reaction was attentive and enthusiastic. C-SPAN networks have gone on to become a powerful, enlightened influence on the fate of serious books.

Surprisingly, the editorial relationship between C-SPAN and Congress has been relatively smooth. The few who originally voiced opposition came around. Though edits of hearings and speeches are occasionally requested, they are politely but firmly turned down. C-SPAN understands, as America's network of record, its obligation to history.

preceding page: C-SPAN's Book TV executive producer Connie Brod, left, talks with Tom Baldwin, owner of Baldwin's Book Barn in West Chester, Pennsylvania. Since 1982, C-SPAN has devoted significant airtime to nonfiction books. left: Columbia UA Cablevision president Bob Rosencrans and C-SPAN CEO Brian Lamb at the site of the network's first uplink in 1978. above: House Speaker Dennis Hastert adresses the 106th congressional session.

# calder mobiles

"Supremely friendly sculpture." That's the phrase art critic Robert Hughes has used to describe the brand, spanking-new art form created by American artist Alexander Calder in 1931. Mobiles, Marcel Duchamp called them, and the name stuck. Calder's inspiration had come from a visit to Piet Mondrian's Paris studio in October 1930. On one wall were tacked "rectangles of cardboard painted yellow, red, blue, black and a variety of whites, tacked upon it so as to form a fine, big composition." Calder's response to the sight was the genesis for his mobiles: He wanted to see the cardboards move, "to oscillate in different directions and at different amplitudes," as he put it in a letter to Mondrian.

Alexander Calder said, "The visit to Mondrian gave me the shock that converted me. It was like the baby being slapped to make his lungs start working." His initial mobiles were powered by motors, and the movements were predictable and repetitive like those of our planetary system, another source of Calder's inspiration. Those initial mobile experiments moved him in the direction of his dreams: mobiles whose movements, like life, would be more spontaneous and less predictable. He came to depend on the energy of the air itself, a perfect partner for the power of his whimsy.

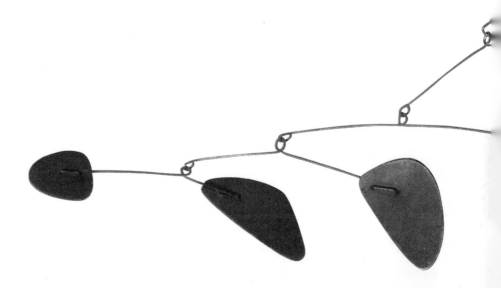

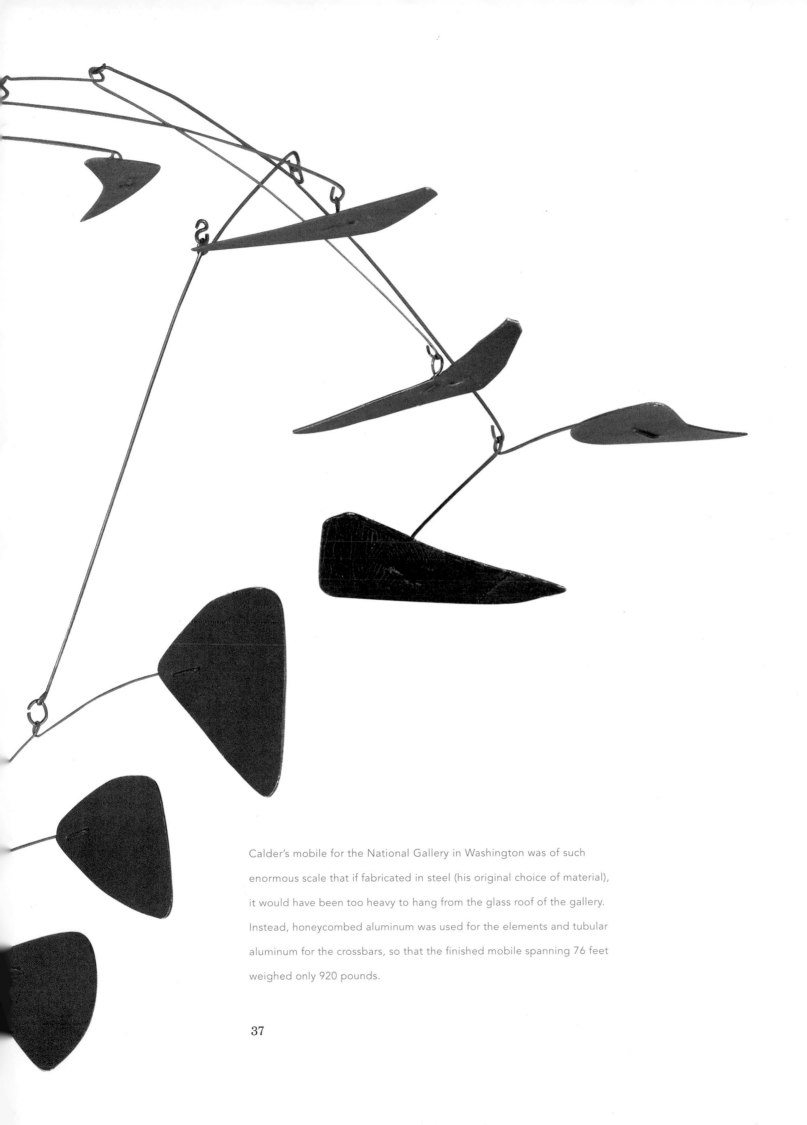

Calder's mobile for the National Gallery in Washington was of such enormous scale that if fabricated in steel (his original choice of material), it would have been too heavy to hang from the glass roof of the gallery. Instead, honeycombed aluminum was used for the elements and tubular aluminum for the crossbars, so that the finished mobile spanning 76 feet weighed only 920 pounds.

37

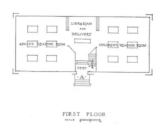

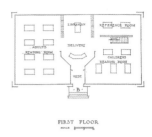

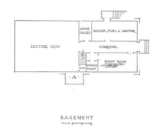

FIRST FLOOR          BASEMENT          FIRST FLOOR          BASEMENT

# carnegie libraries

ANDREW CARNEGIE was that rarest of multimillionaires: He believed that a man who died rich, died disgraced. Motivated by this belief, the enormously wealthy Scottish immigrant gave the nation one of the most remarkable gifts in its history: 1,689 public-library buildings in 1,421 communities. The value of his gifts, made between 1886 and 1917, would equal more than half a billion dollars in today's economy. It was the largest single philanthropic gesture—up to that point—in American history.

Carnegie-funded libraries were located in cities you'd expect, Pittsburgh, his adopted hometown, and New York; but more often, they were built in places like Ishpening, Michigan; Jennings, Louisiana; and Dillon, Montana. The "Patron Saint of Libraries," as Carnegie was often called, insisted that each community share in the establishment and maintenance of its own library. He would give money for a library building, only if the local taxing authority agreed to provide the site, then furnish and maintain the library with an annual pledge equal to 10 percent of the gift. This requirement, he reasoned, would involve citizens more readily than an outright donation. He was right.

The money was dispensed and administered by one person, Carnegie's personal secretary, James Bertram, who reviewed all written requests before granting approval—hard to imagine in this era of large foundation staffs and richly endowed headquarters. Bertram continued to correspond with grantees, for example, when a town might report that the funds were insufficient to complete, furnish, or buy books for its library. Bertram invariably informed those communities that the Carnegie gift was not meant for furnishings or the purchase of books, that it was up to local public opinion to prevail on local governments to fund the library's contents and to decide what books should be purchased.

Despite Carnegie's wish not to be involved, questions of library design often occurred, for many communities had no sense of how a library should be designed. To meet those requests, Carnegie engaged leading consultants from the library and architectural professions to produce a leaflet entitled "Notes on Library Buildings."

Communities that received funds to construct libraries often sought guidance from Carnegie on what their buildings should look like. Carnegie's secretary prepared a guide, which included these suggested floor plans; he also reminded communities that Carnegie funds were to cover the cost of the structure, including furniture, fixtures, and architect's fees, not cost overruns. The guide did not suggest a particular exterior, in order that "the community and architect may express their individuality."

BASEMENT

BASEMENT

BASEMENT

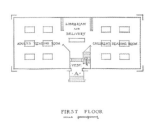

FIRST FLOOR

But the leaflet did not solve the problem of towns trying to stretch the definition of a library to get the Carnegie money. In a letter to the library committee in Anthony, Kansas, Bertram wrote: "It is all very well for you to plan your building as a dance hall, club, YMCA, dining room kitchen, etc., but remember Mr. Carnegie is paying for a Library Building and not for this kind of miscellaneous general convenience."

To one architect in Centralia, Washington, who submitted plans for approval, Bertram wrote: "A school-boy could do that better than the plans show. If the architect's object had been how to waste space instead of how to economize it, he could not have succeeded better." But Bertram was not always critical. In a letter to the chairman of the Mount Vernon, New York, Carnegie Library Building Committee, for example, he noted: "You have broken the record this morning by your note. In all my experience, having provided funds for about thirteen hundred and fifty libraries, I have never had a Chairman of a Building Committee report a surplus."

Carnegie simply believed that a citizen who read would be a better citizen and that a free, public library could offer the greatest opportunity for self-advancement. His philanthropy came at a crucial time in the development of our country's free libraries. Before 1880, there were few public libraries in America. Furthermore, the publicity surrounding Carnegie's gifts dramatized the importance of libraries, provided an incentive for towns to obtain a library, and reinforced the necessity for local governments to take responsibility for their libraries.

The Carnegie Corporation took over the funding of libraries after 1911, then terminated funding for new libraries in 1917, as World War I occupied the country's time. At the war's end, the corporation began to endow library schools, assist the Library of Congress, and fund studies to find ways to bring books to citizens in rural areas. Carnegie liked to boast that the sun never set on the Carnegie free public libraries. His great gift to American literacy backed that boast to the hilt.

# :CHEZ:PANISSE:

## CAFE MENU

: OPEN :

TUESDAY - SATURDAY, 11:30 AM TO 12:00 PM ; SUNDAY, 10:30 - 10:30

| | | | | |
|---|---|---|---|---|
| Mineral Water | .50 | | Caffe Latte | .60 |
| Italian Soda | .50 | | Cappucino | .40 |
| Milk | .25 | | Espresso | .30 |
| Tea | .45 | | Cafe | .25 |

| | |
|---|---|
| Melon & Prosciutto | 1.50 |
| Pate du Chef | 1.75 |
| Cheese Plate | 1.50 |
| Croissant, Butter, Jam | .50 |

| | |
|---|---|
| Homemade Pastries | .75 |
| Fruit | .50 |
| Ice Cream | .50 |
| Sundaes : Chocolate & Almonds, Ginger Caramel | .85 |
| Special : Sunday Brunch ( when available ) | 1.75 |

COMPLETE BEER & WINE LIST AVAILABLE

8-18-72 :: PC-JM

Chez Panisse Cafe menu from 1972 is the restaurant's oldest surviving menu.

# there is only one chez panisse

by Ruth Reichl

ALICE WATERS lies in bed at night worrying about what to feed you. She knows that she can make you happy. She also knows, in her hidden heart, that if she can find the perfect dish to feed each person who comes to her door she can change the world.

Every great cook secretly believes in the power of food. Alice Waters just believes this more than anybody else. She is certain we are what we eat, and she has made it her mission in life to make sure that people eat beautifully. Waters is creating a food revolution, even if she has to do it one meal at a time.

Alice didn't set out to change the way America eats. She just wanted to feed her friends. Having been to France, Alice had seen the way a good bistro could become the heart of a neighborhood, a place where people went for comfort and sustenance. She was not a professional cook, but she enjoyed feeding people, and she envisioned a cozy little cafe that would be open every day for breakfast, lunch, and dinner, a place where every-one from the dishwashers to the cooks would be well-paid, a sort of endless party where everyone would have fun. Reality soon set in. Faced with financial ruin, Chez Panisse was forced to become a real business. Still, the dream did not die. It just changed.

"I was more obsessed," is how Alice herself explains what happened. If she was going to have a restaurant, it was going to be the very best one she could possibly man-age. Even if that meant rethinking the very concept of what a restaurant might be.

She began with the ingredients. Every chef dreams of great products, but most make do with what is available in the market. Not Alice. Disgusted with the fish that was sold in stores, she bought a truck and sent someone down to the port to find fishermen as they docked their boats. When she could not find the baby lettuces she had loved in France, she tore up her backyard and grew her own. She found foragers

41

to hunt for mushrooms. She persuaded farmers to let their lambs run wild through the hills. She demanded better bread. Before long she had developed an entire network of people producing food just for her.

The results were electric. Chez Panisse served only one meal a day, but people reserved months ahead of time and took their chances. You would find them shaking their heads over the menu, wailing, "Chicken? I've come all the way from Maine for chicken?" Then the dish would arrive, and they'd look down with dismay and say, "It's just a piece of chicken," as if they had somehow expected the poor bird to turn into a swan as it cooked. But they'd waited months for the reservation, so they would take a bite of the chicken and a sort of wonder would come over their faces. "It's the best chicken I have ever tasted," they'd whisper reverently. "I never knew that food could taste so good."

And Alice, walking by, would smile her secret little smile. Because once again, she had done it. She had given them food that they would remember, a taste that would linger long beyond that night. And they would know, ever after, how a chicken raised in the open air, fed on corn, and cooked with care, could taste.

She knew that they would carry that flavor away with them, and that every time they ate a chicken, no matter where it might be, they would remember.

And if Alice had her way, they would go looking for that chicken—or that tomato—or that strawberry—until they found it. Because she had given them more than a meal—she had given them a memory.

There is only one Chez Panisse. In this age of multiple restaurants, it has no clones in London, Las Vegas, or Tokyo. Because Alice Waters has more than money on her mind, and she has now turned her attention to the next generation. Her latest project? Feeding the children. She wants every school in America to have a garden and every child to have an opportunity to discover the taste of fresh food.

Her fight goes on. Her revolution continues. She knows that all it takes is one taste. It just has to be the right one.

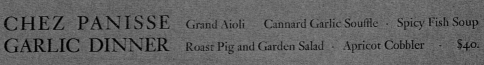

**CHEZ PANISSE** Grand Aioli · Cannard Garlic Souffle · Spicy Fish Soup
**GARLIC DINNER** Roast Pig and Garden Salad · Apricot Cobbler · $40.

Bastille Day 1987

### MENU FOR JULIA CHILD

Watercress salad with green garlic

Baked whole fish with fennel oil

Garbure with goose confit cooked in the hearth

Blood orange sherbet and fruit compote

*With affection from Chez Panisse*
*February 25, 1993*

Chez Panisse has a tradition
of creating menus for special
dinners. A dinner honoring
Julia Child, one for Bastille
Day, and one for New Year's
Eve, are shown here.

the chicago defender

# aiding and abetting the great migration

He wasn't crippled, but whether Robert Abbott walked Chicago's poorest streets or perused chic European shops, a gold-headed cane steadied his stride. On sunny afternoons the publisher rode in his Dusenberg convertible; other days, a Rolls Royce limousine. He appeared on every 1920's A-list, but avoided the social circuit. Vintage Jazz Era excess? Maybe. Gatsbyesque? Hardly.

Abbott was the son of former slaves, an African American who excelled in extravagance. He was a lawyer and America's first black millionaire publisher. The newspaper he created—*The Chicago Defender*—brought personal wealth and prestige, but Abbott's knack for flair had appeared in the *Defender*'s pages before he amassed his fortune. The paper perpetuated the Great Migration, a movement between 1916 and 1950 when millions of African Americans headed north to forge a better life.

From his landlady's kitchen, Abbott wrote, designed and distributed the *Defender*'s first issue in 1905. He labeled it "a fearless, honest champion of the people," and set out to report the news blacks witnessed everyday but never saw in print. No other publication described the African-American condition during the early 1900s with such precision and scope. All the lynchings and oppression overlooked by "white" dailies were regular *Defender* features. Abbott extended the *Defender*'s reach into the deep south where 90 percent of America's black population lived, by striking distribution deals with sleeping-car porters, entertainers, and other blacks traveling the country who could sell his paper nationally. By the late teens, circulation exceeded 50,000.

Abbott sowed the Great Migration seed after the World War I draft and a slowed immigration tide siphoned labor forces and brought industry in northern cities to a standstill. For the first time, employers hired African Americans en masse. What seemed like unlimited opportunity awaited. In the North, blacks could vote. They could send their children to better schools and work for higher wages. Abbott emphasized those benefits as early as 1916 by pasting headlines like "Farewell, Dixie Land" and "Millions to Leave South" atop the *Defender*'s front page. One-way train schedules, dos and don'ts for Northern migrants ("Don't promenade on the boulevard in your hog-killing clothes.") and want-ads appeared in each weekly issue.

"The *Defender* let blacks know that they didn't have to be satisfied living in the South. There was a place they could move to and live their lives to the fullest," wrote historian Christopher Reed.

By 1940, over 1 million Southern blacks had moved north. The *Defender*'s circulation broke 250,000, but its true readership was estimated to be five times that. Abbott's influence was undeniable. The Southern establishment tried—albeit in vain—to rid the region of his paper. When some Southern cities established laws making it illegal to read black newspapers, Abbott instructed the sleeping-car porters to toss their *Defender* bundles along the countryside instead of placing them at city limit train stops. The *Defender* could not be kept out of the South; Abbott would see to that.

"With the exception of the Bible, no publication was more influential among the Negro masses," Roi Ottley, Abbott's biographer, said of the *Defender*. "Abbott did everything to aid and abet the migration. He argued, pleaded, shamed and exhorted Negroes to abandon the South."

When Abbott died in 1940, his twenty-one-year-old nephew John Sengstacke manned the *Defender*'s helm. Sengstacke guided the *Defender* through World War II, when its circulation exceeded 400,000. He printed weekly columns by Langston Hughes and Gwendolyn Brooks. He accompanied Eleanor Roosevelt on her Tuskegee trip when she met the pilots who would soon be called the Tuskegee Airmen. He withstood J. Edgar Hoover's claims that the black press was seditious. He sent Ethyl Payne to Vietnam in 1973, making her the first African-American woman war correspondent.

In 1998 Sengstacke died. His granddaughter, Myiti, took his place, becoming only the third publisher in *The Chicago Defender* history. She also became its first woman publisher, for a newspaper that continues to make progress front-page news.

# coca-cola's recipe

## the greatest secret ever kept, told by the man who keeps it

by Christopher Buckley

IN THE SUMMER OF 1981, if you want to be precise about it, I was eating a take-out quesadilla—that's Spanish for cheese sandwich, basically—on a bench in Peachtree Plaza in Atlanta, when I was approached by a man who identified himself as "Max," but whom I knew to be Dimitri Blotkin, chief *rezident* in Atlanta. He knew me only as "Bob." What he did not know was that my real name is "Fred," and that I was part of a sting operation mounted by the FBI. I was posing as a disgruntled bank employee of the Sun Trust Bank in Atlanta.

"Lovely weather for ducks, is it not?" he said, sitting down beside me. I recognized the coded greeting as coming from Chekhov's *The Seagull*. Dimitri loved his little literary games.

"Yes," I replied, according to plan, "'though personally, I detest ducks. Indeed, how much happier I would be if we lived in a world without ducks." This was the signal that I had it on me—the object that had triggered alarms from corporate headquarters, to the Atlanta FBI field office, the CIA, all the way on up to the White House. At least, so I heard. What Dimitri was after, of course, was the formula for Coca-Cola, which is kept in the vault of the Sun Trust Bank, where I am employed.

In 1981, you may recall, the Cold War was still raging. Russia was having difficulty competing with the United States, militarily and economically. It needed hard currency. And, one night in the Kremlin, it was decided that the best way to get hard currency was to steal the formula for a soft drink.

49

The formula for what became Coca-Cola was of course created by an Atlanta pharmacist, Dr. John Styth Pemberton, in his backyard on May 8, 1886. He called his invention a "brain tonic and intellectual beverage." He died two years later. Although the official records indicate that there was no foul play, Mr. Asa Chandler, a shrewd businessman, had by then bought out Dr. Pemberton's interest. Sales of the stimulating "brain tonic" were through the roof. Not long afterwards, it was learned that the secret ingredient was cocaine, the stuff that—well, you know about cocaine, surely. The company removed the narcotic, but by then, its allure had taken hold of the American imagination. Since then, sales have steadily increased throughout the world; I think because the Coca-Cola company always managed to sound cagey when talking about how they took out the cocaine. Adding to the big mystery is the fact that the company refuses to say anything about what's in the formula and that they keep it under twenty-four-hour a day guard in the vault of the Sun Trust Bank in Atlanta. At night, the vault is partially flooded and filled with giant snapping turtles. I personally think that's part of the "mystique."

Anyway, a CIA agent, posing as a Kremlin cleaning woman, overheard the Kremlin big shots talking about their plan to steal the formula and rule the world with hard currency. So the CIA told the Atlanta FBI and they, being the FBI, set up a sting operation. (Did you see that movie, *The Sting*? I thought that was a great movie.) And that's where I came in. I'm the person the bank hires to handle the snapping turtles.

I hung out at a nearby bar called The Disgruntled Employee. Night after night, I pretended to drink too much, and loudly criticized the bank, the Coca-Cola company, the company that was allegedly threatening to repossess my car, the United States, capitalism, Adam Smith, the whole deal, and, of course, the snapping turtles, whom I especially pretended to hate, though the fact is that I love my snapping turtles. They're even cuddly, if you know how to cuddle them. I wouldn't just grab them and start cuddling.

Sure enough, Dimitri noticed me in time and made his approach. He bought me drinks, told me that he too hated capitalism and snapping turtles and even offered to kill the people trying to repossess my car. (Needless to say, I didn't take him up on that.) We struck up a friendship, went to massage parlors together, where he always picked up the tab. These could be awkward moments, because it meant taking off my clothes and revealing the "wire," or concealed FBI microphone, taped all over my body. And Lord did it hurt taking that tape off every night.

Eventually, Dimitri "popped the question." Would I steal the formula? In return, he promised me a new life in the Soviet Union, where there weren't any capitalists or snapping

51

turtles. He even said he would get me a special pass so that I didn't have to stand in line for eight hours to buy stale bread, the way Russians did. On top of it all, he promised to introduce me to his cousin Natayla, who was a real "party girl" in Sverslovsk. I took the "bait."

And that's how I found myself in Peachtree Plaza that hot morning. The plan was that as soon as I handed him the formula, the FBI would swarm in and arrest Dimitri and expose the Kremlin's evil plan to steal our most secret, secret. Every person in the Plaza, and there must have been a hundred of them, was an undercover FBI agent. Boy, would this have been the wrong place to mug someone.

The formula itself was written, in Dr. Pemberton's shaky handwriting, on the back of a broadsheet that had to do with the May 1, 1886, Haymarket Massacre in Chicago. I thought that was interesting, Dimitri being a communist and all, and this broadsheet saying that rich people and police were evil. As I sat there waiting for Dimitri, I couldn't resist peeking at where he'd written down the formula, even though it went against my training. If you're one of the Coca-Cola guards, you get this incredible training. My heart was pounding in my chest as I read: "May 8th. Haven't slept or ate in eight days. Those coca leaves sure are sumpthin, but they leaf you kinda jitterry. Plus my mouth is really dry. I hope this next batch works cause I am right thirsty." Then just below that it said, "Finally! Breakthrough at last! Hoooo-weeeee! Now I truly have a 'brain tonic' that the world will pay dearly for. And all that was missing was a couple of drops of . . ."

And that's when I heard Dimitri going on about ducks.

I folded up the formula and handed it over. Dimitri read it sort of intensely to himself, nodding and repeating the same word, "Da. . . da!" Which I guess is Russian for "Yeah, why didn't I think of that?" or something along those lines.

Then he folded it up and stuck it in his pocket and told me Natalya really wanted to meet me when I got to Sverslovsk. Then he walked away, and before you knew it, the FBI were on him like—well, you know the expression, like bees on molasses.

I read in the paper, later, that he jumped out of that window on the twelfth floor of the FBI building while they were interrogating him. Maybe that really is how it happened. All I know is, I'm glad I never did get to see the formula. I made a point of telling every FBI person who talked to me that I didn't see the formula. Maybe it's one secret that's best left alone. Maybe it's the only secret we really have left, now that I see how the Chinese are stealing our nukular missiles. Anyway, it's time to gather up my snapping turtles. They get kind of squirrelly round this time of morning, and if I don't get them now, there's the devil to pay.

53

coney island

by Kevin Baker

THE HUDDLED MASSES arriving on America's Eastern shore at the turn of the century, saw first not the Statue of Liberty, nor the Brooklyn Bridge, nor even the newborn skyscrapers, pushing their way up past the church steeples. Greeting them, instead, was a welcoming beacon of bright wonders spread along the sands on the southern tip of Brooklyn.

That star of light was "The City of Fire," and like the bush Moses encountered on Mount Horeb, it burned but was not consumed. This was Coney Island, three great amusement parks—Steeplechase, Luna Park, and Dreamland—each outlined and adorned with yet another fresh and wondrous sight, the electric-light bulb. When the sun went down, what appeared to those new Americans, pressed against the rails of their ships, was the whole island, strung with frozen pearls of fire, spinning and plunging and whirling in place.

Coney Island in 1910 was a stunning experience, even in broad daylight. Just inside Luna Park's main gate—two crosses plunged into a red heart in some transplanted bit of Catholic iconography; Pilgrims entered a fairy-tale ramble of minarets and onion domes, turrets and colonnades, lagoons and trellises. It was Frederick Thompson's architectural jungle; grossly extravagant amusement created just for the hell of it.

55

Thompson, the moody, alcoholic Frank Lloyd Wright of the American amusement park, built what would today be a gold mine for personal injury lawyers.

He designed many of Coney Island's rides to help men and women "meet"—by throwing them together. Other surprises simply reflected the rather rough and insensitive humor of the day. Visitors climbing off the Steeplechase ride—a relatively mild jaunt on mechanical horses over a mile-and-a-quarter track—were suddenly challenged by an obstacle course that included a dwarf in a harlequin suit, taking a swing at their legs with a cattle prod. Amusement? The crowd of New Yorkers, watching and laughing from a neighboring bleacher, got a charge out of it.

Still other exhibitions reflected the era's wider, less politically correct, sense of entertainment. One area, for example, allowed revelers to watch the country's first incubator babies struggling for life; and to visit a permanent, year-round village, filled with dwarves and midgets; or to view African tribesmen living in actual grass huts. Even the furies of the latest global disasters were introduced on huge stages—hurricanes, floods, volcano eruptions, and war.

Product of a time when Americans liked their entertainment spicy, tinged with a taste of danger, Coney was more than a Sunday outing. It was a place where immigrants were literally assimilated, in the roiling, holiday mobs; a place where they could watch the pageant of their lives displayed like a movie. A conductor-driven roller coaster called the "Rough Rider" once went ripping through the retaining walls, killing four passengers. The roller coaster was up and running again later that same day. There was a seamy underside of the boardwalk, including Coney's own, miniature "Bowery," and a rundown, elephant-shaped hotel that served as the local whorehouse.

To its wide-eyed audiences, Coney Island was very close to real life. Was it any wonder that one of the most popular attractions was a fake tenement building that was set on fire and the fire put out by fake firemen—every day, day after day—for a viewing public that itself lived in fire-trap tenements and so lived in constant fear?

Coney Island finally played with fire too long. Dreamland burned down in 1911, Luna Park in 1946, Steeplechase in 1964. Little more than an abandoned parachute jump and a ragged old roller coaster remain. But the Coney spirit lives on, imitated by world's fairs in Chicago, 1933; New York, 1939–40 and 1964–65; in the Disney theme park; in the names of deteriorating amusement parks on the outskirts of cities throughout the United States. None, though, can hold a candle to that world of frozen fire, that once burned so brightly along the sands of Long Island.

above: Shooting the chutes, 1903

left: Luna Park at night

57

the corvette

# like a bat out of hell

HIS NAME, Zora Arkus-Duntov, seemed better suited for the ruler of one of our neighboring planets than for the father of the Corvette, our true American sportscar. All that we admire in a car, however secretly, the Corvette provides: power for its own sake, speed, acceleration, and style. Sweden has the Volvo; we have the Corvette.

The first Corvette rolled off the production line in Flint, Michigan, on June 30, 1953. Duntov joined Chevrolet's research and development group in 1953; he would not, however, devote his full attention to the Corvette until 1955. Those first cars were six cylinder two seaters and white, Polo White, to be exact. Only 300 were produced in 1953. The next year 10,000 sales were projected; only 3,640 were made, and only two-thirds of those were sold by year-end. Then, in 1955, sales sank to 700. The trend was foreboding, even to those who believed in the destiny of a car with the Corvette's aspiration.

59

Duntov was born in Belgium to Russian parents. He was raised in Russia and in retrospect, the signs of where he was headed were clear. He loved motorcycles and at fourteen, designed a motor-driven ice sled. The family moved to Germany, and at the university, he wrote his thesis on supercharging.

When he left the Chevrolet research and development team for Corvette, he could see the car wasn't quite right: "The first time I saw Corvette I think 'beautiful, beautiful car.' I was disappointed with what was underneath but visually it was superb." But he believed in its future as did the man who created the Corvette, Harley Earl. Earl's 1927 LaSalle had placed him in the forefront of Detroit's great stylists. But it was Duntov who would transform the Corvette into a bat out of hell.

The 1956 Corvette was the first model to feel the impact of Duntov's influence. The 210-horsepower engine could be cranked to 225 with the optional twin, four-barrel carburetors. Then "for racing purposes" you could have, with the addition of Duntov's cam, 240 horsepower. This one, which reached 163 mph, got the automotive world's attention. If that wasn't enough, in 1957, you could get 283 horsepower in a Corvette. If you were a seventeen-year-old male, you knew the time it took a Corvette to go from 0–60 mph as well as you knew your own name: 6.4 seconds.

Yet in spite of the Corvette's improvements and acclaim, the car nuts in charge were still restless. Bill Mitchell, who succeeded Harvey Earl in 1958 as head of design, had the Corvette bug bad—and that was good. He was looking for something; he knew he had it when he saw the design ideas of Larry Shinoda who had recently joined the team. The young Japanese American created his first car designs when he was in a World War II internment camp with his family.

above: Euphoria surrounding the Corvette's introduction in 1953 led to the development of a series of Corvette prototypes, none of which saw production. right: Advanced sketches created by Larry Shinoda in 1960 for the "Stingray," which was introduced at the 1963 Detroit Auto Show. bottom right: The 1963 "Split-window" Corvette Stingray, classified then and now as a "milestone" in sp0rts car history, since its performance reached a level of sophistication equal to that of its design.

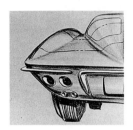

Shinoda's design resulted in what would become the most striking of all Corvettes: the 1963 Sting Ray. This all-new Corvette was introduced to the press in June of 1962. *Motor Trend*'s Roger Huntington's excitement showed: "This is a *modern* sportscar. In most ways it's as advanced as the latest dual-purpose sports/luxury cars from Europe—and this includes the new Jaguar XK-E, Ferrari GTO, Mercedes 300-SL, and all the rest. The new Corvette doesn't have to take a back seat to any of them, in looks, performance, handling or ride."

This marked Corvette's true arrival. Because now what was under the hood, Duntov's domain, could measure up to anything "out there," and even the sleekness of the design could be mentioned, at last, in the same breath as the Jaguar. Corvette would lose its way at times during the ensuing years. But a sense of heritage and resiliency always enabled it to come back. It was *Motor Trend*'s 1998 Car of the Year (after only its fifth major remake) and called "the best Vette ever." However, General Motors, Corvette's parent, has had troubles for a generation. If General Motors can be helped by the power of a good example, it need only look to its own Corvette team and their spirit and love of the game. Corvette's example will remind General Motors that the cars we admire most derive from passion and a strong singular vision.

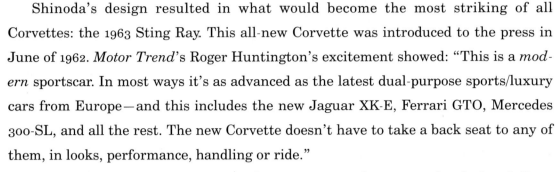

# country music

## the bristol sessions                    by Nicholas Dawidoff

TOWARD THE END of JULY 1927, Ralph Peer, a shrewd talent scout for the Victor Talking Machine Company of New York, drove into the Tennessee/Virginia border town of Bristol with his wife, a couple of engineers, and a heavy load of modern recording equipment. He was looking for singers.

Peer chose the railroad junction town because it was the largest city in Appalachia. He'd made an earlier trip, tacking up placards, making contacts, and putting an advertisement in a newspaper. Now he rented space in a hat company warehouse on State Street, hung some blankets on the walls, and hoped for the best. When a local reporter wrote that a man from New York was paying $50 per record side to anybody with talent who'd sing into his talking machine, pickers and crooners began pouring in from all over. What made the session one of the signal moments in the history of American popular song, however, was the persistence of A. P. Carter.

Carter was a quixotic carpenter, an erratic sort whose mother claimed he'd been "marked" since birth. His wife Sara was a practical woman who knotted quilts with the same skill that she handled her end of a crosscut saw. When A. P. suggested they go to Bristol, though, she was of a different mind. It was a miserable trip over bad roads, and as Sara told A. P., "Ain't nobody gonna pay that much money to hear us sing." A. P. persisted and finally packed Sara, his pregnant sister-in-law Maybelle, and two young children—one of whom Sara was still breast feeding—into a borrowed Ford Model A. Many hours—and many flat tires—later they got to Bristol.

63

They were the Carter Family: Maybelle, a nimble guitar player with a lovely voice; A. P.'s rich, sonorous bass; and Sara. As soon as Peer heard Sara's voice, he said he knew "it was going to be wonderful." On this day, they sang "Bury Me Under the Weeping Willow," "The Wandering Boy," and "The Storms Are on the Ocean," and when Southern country people heard them, they agreed with Peer: it was, indeed "wonderful." The Carters' wistfully melodic sound became the benchmark for the traditional strain of country music. In a day when the industrial transformation of the South was already making many working people nostalgic for a vanishing rural ideal, the Carter Family hit them where they'd lived. Over the years, their better songs, like "Little Darling Pal of Mine," "Wabash Cannonball," "Keep on the Sunny Side," and "Worried Man Blues," became American classics. And when Maybelle's daughter June married Johnny Cash, the Carter Family's place as the true mandarins of country music was assured.

Peer's next $50 was also well-spent, paid to Jimmie Rodgers, a street-wise former Meridian, Mississippi, railroad worker who'd lately been singing with a group of men in Asheville, North Carolina. But that day, Rodgers went solo, singing a couple of decidedly old-timey numbers, "The Soldier's Sweetheart" and "Sleep, Baby Sleep." Peer liked his smooth, drawling tenor, he was taken with the extraordinary yodel that Rodgers appended to the lullaby, and he also admired his pluck.

Later, Rodgers headed north with a passel of new material: "Blue Yodel," which began memorably: "T for Texas/ T for Tennessee/ T for Thelma/ The girl that made a wreck out of me." He was a sensation: "America's Blue Yodeler," "The Singing Brakeman," and country music's first great recording star—a bright, bawdy entertainer who appeared to be a hard-drinking, hard-loving rascal. For all of the honky-tonk trappings, Rodgers was really only modestly dissipated—and very sick in the lungs. As he sang in one of his most affecting songs, "Ain't nobody ever whipped the TB Blues." In the six years before the infection killed him, he recorded over one hundred songs.

Country has always been a hybrid genre, and blending styles was Rodgers's way. His musical dexterity, coupled with a winning smile and personality, made the cheerful rounder "The Father of Country Music."

As for country music today, Daddy would be proud. Country has come a long way since Bristol. So many Americans are buying country records and listening to country on the radio that it has become the most popular music in the—well, in the country.

above: Jimmy Rodgers, the "Father of Country Music."

right: Detail from a poster for a Carter Family concert.

the duke ellington orchestra

## by Gary Giddins

DUKE ELLINGTON liked to claim he won his job at the Cotton Club, in December 1927, because he showed up three hours late for the audition, as did the owner, who heard only Ellington and none of his rivals. After five years of touring or working in arson-prone saloons, it was the luckiest of breaks. Radio broadcasts transmitted from the mob-owned, segregated (blacks on stage, whites at the tables) Harlem nightclub were relayed across the country and ultimately the world, bringing him instant recognition. The long engagement enabled Ellington to double the size of his band, encouraged a daring prolificity, and provided him with a unique apprenticeship working with top-flight choreographers, songwriters, dancers, singers, comics, set designers, and other professionals involved in developing the Cotton Club's slick and sexy reviews.

Ellington responded with a wry, insinuating music—erotic, exotic, ironic, ingenious. He invented his own instrumental voicings and found uncanny soloists whose virtuoso embellishments seemed to burble from the dreamy brew like nightmare chatter. Some considered Ellington's music as salacious as the serpentine dancing it accompanied, but music lovers in and out of the academy heard in it a fresh, audacious, musical language and a genius for sultry melodies and startling harmonies. Ellington tapped into something recondite, almost occult, yet accessible—unshackling characters as shadowy as "The Mooche" or as seductive as "Black Beauty" while issuing injunctions on the order of "Rockin' in Rhythm" or "It Don't Mean a Thing If It Ain't Got That Swing."

By the time I discovered Ellington's music, in 1963, he had been leading his orchestra for forty years, few of which found him just marking time. That became evident when I bought my first Ellington albums and realized that immersion in his music generated a mystery that could be solved only through obsession; the variety was overwhelming. Knowing nothing about him except that he was a key figure in a music with which I was newly fascinated, I began with the gorgeously expansive arrangements of the 1950's *Ellington Masterpieces*, thinking "masterpieces" was a good place to start in anyone's education. Wanting to hear more, I picked up RCA Vintage compilations from the '20s and '40s, Columbia LPs from the '50s, collaborations with modernists John Coltrane and Charles Mingus, suites, symphonies, dance records, collections drawn from his pop standards (from "Mood Indigo" to "Satin Doll"), and the then new monuments, like *Far East Suite* and *His Mother Called Him Bill*, the Sacred Concerts. Here's the punch line: Even after accumulating a hundred Ellington LPs, it seemed to me that each revealed something the others did not.

Yet none conveyed the adventure of hearing the band live. In addition to the extraordinary charm and practiced wit of Ellington himself, his concerts displayed intricacies in his music that the highest of hi-fidelity re-creations failed to capture. The Ellington Band appeared in the mid-60s one summer afternoon in New York's Central Park, on a

provisional stage in the unceremonious setting of a few hundred folding chairs. No one seemed to mind that a few of us wandered right up to the raised apron. Standing there, a few feet from the reed section, I heard something I've never experienced with any other orchestra—something that gets to the heart of the Ellington mystique. While all five saxophones performed in perfect unison, I could simultaneously hear each distinct voice. They blended and yet did not blend. I heard perfect organ-like chords and at the same time, the distinct virile edge of Harry Carney's baritone saxophone, the piping center of Johnny Hodges's alto, and the foggy burr of Paul Gonsalves's tenor, among others. It was magic, a unified front that honored the individual—an Ellington epiphany.

That same year, coincidentally, the Pulitzer Committee rejected the unanimous recommendation of its music jury to present Ellington with a special prize honoring his life's work. Ellington's much quoted quip was, "Fate is being kind. Fate doesn't want me to be too famous too young." One of the singular ironies of his career is that his matchless fame never compromised his tenaciously protected privacy. He was omnipresent, playing one-nighters in every conceivable venue, from 4-H clubs to the way stations of the fine arts to palaces, but when he died, in 1974, at seventy-five, obituary writers for the newspapers didn't know if he was married or to whom. He was as unknowable as Salinger or Pynchon, but without making a fuss. Perhaps he maintained the veil so successfully because his music was so elegantly illuminating of himself, of the rest of us lost in its glistening rhythms, and of the country it vigorously honored.

Ellington wrote, "I live in the realm of art and have no monetary interests," yet there was nothing monastic about his art. He eschewed ivy tower experiments and inside curves, yet innovated ceaselessly, attempting every idiom, including opera and musical theater. He wrote for and about people, shrewdly assessing their responses on the dance floor or in the concert hall, yet he was also the first to break the three-minute tyranny of the 78 RPM record; the first to compose specifically for the LP; one of the first to create a television oratorio. He belonged to no particular fashion or epoch — the Swing Era was a ten-year blip in a fifty-year road trip. During a few months in 1959, he wrote the austere *Queen's Suite* and the driving score to Otto Preminger's *Anatomy of a Murder.* The film score revved up a popular film and was heard by millions. The suite, a gift to Elizabeth II, was for her ears only; Ellington privately pressed two copies, delivering one to the Queen, and no one outside his inner circle

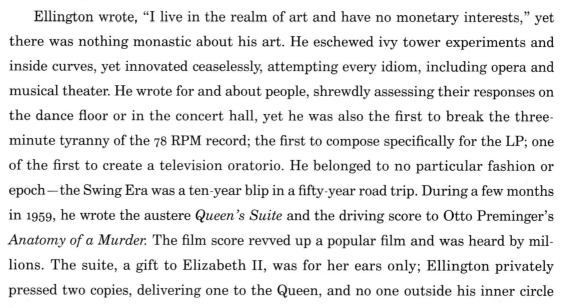

knew of its existence until two years after his death, when it was acclaimed a masterwork. Imagine being that certain the tap would not run dry. Ellington was that certain, and it never did.

# edison's invention factories

## "stick-to-itiveness"

THOMAS EDISON'S invention factories were not torn by debate over the merits of applied research versus basic research. They were about applied research with a vengeance. "I find out what the world needs. Then I go ahead and invent it," Edison said. Did he ever. And when he finished, he would have 1,093 patents in his own name alone, more than any other American in history.

His second patented invention, a stock market ticker, sold for $40,000 in 1869. That sale provided the money for a workshop in Newark, New Jersey, where he and a small group of workers produced stock tickers, ink recorders, and typewriters for automatic telegraphy. Yet Edison was eager to leave the city and its high expenses. So in 1876, he moved the workshop twelve miles south to the village of Menlo Park, where the first of the invention factories was built. The laboratory and workers were just a hundred yards up the hill from the Edison home.

These workers came from all over the world: a German glass blower, a Swiss clock-maker, an English mechanic, mathematicians, carpenters, and draftsmen. At the time, Menlo Park was the best-equipped private laboratory in the country. The atmosphere Edison created encouraged independent, inventive thinking. When a new employee asked him about the company rules, Edison replied, "There ain't no rules around here. We're trying to accomplish something."

He could be authoritarian and cranky and set impossible deadlines, yet he was there shoulder to shoulder with his employees one eighteen-hour day after another. Balance between work and personal life was not an issue; creation was. His approach toward failure was the antithesis of that taken by so many well-known corporations that have flourished and faded. He put it this way, "If I find 10,000 ways something won't work, I haven't failed. I am not discouraged, because every wrong attempt discarded is another step forward. Just because something doesn't do what you planned it to do doesn't mean it's useless."

The indefatigable nature of Edison and his workers was exemplified by the search for a material that could make a durable filament essential to an incandescent light bulb. Edison and his team tried numerous materials including platinum, palladium, broom corn, boron, and silicon. Then on October 22, 1879, they tested carbonized cotton thread. It would glow for thirteen-and-a-half hours without bursting into flame. The problem that plagued early light-bulb developers—filament materials that burned up too quickly—was solved.

And what a difference those invention factory ideas meant to the young nation:

> The first commercially viable incandescent light bulb
> The cylinder phonograph
> The nickel-iron-alkaline storage battery
> The electric pen, forerunner of the mimeograph
> The Edison Business Phonograph later the ediphone,
>    competitor of the dictaphone
> The kinetoscope

Edison even created inventions that improved other inventions: a simple carbon-button transmitter for the mouthpiece of Alexander Graham Bell's telephone, eliminating the need to shout into the phone to be heard. He was part of that American self-taught, if this doesn't work, we'll try something else, plain-spoken tradition that believed genius was simply "hard work, stick-to-itiveness and common sense."

left: Edison, seated in the middle holding his hat, with his laboratory workers at his Menlo Park laboratory, where the phonograph was invented in 1877. The first recorded words were "Mary had a little lamb." left above: Edison's drawing for the patent application for the first successful incandescent lamp. He and his workers solved the fifty-year-old problem of what material could be made to glow in a vacuum for an extended period of time instead of bursting into flame.

# The Elements of Style

## William Strunk, Jr. & E. B. White

Macmillan Paperbacks ᴧᴧρ 107 $.95

# parvum opus

SINCE 1918, standing alone against the marauding armies of the prolix and opaque has been a little book titled *The Elements of Style*. This terse manifesto of clarity was written by a professor of English at Cornell, William Strunk, Jr. More than four decades later, a Strunk student who took his class, English 8, in 1919 gave a boost, if not a guarantee, to the immortality of *The Elements of Style* by enlarging and revising it while keeping its soul intact. The student's name was Elwyn Brooks White, or E.B., White as his readers came to know him.

The book is to the English language what a firebreak is to a prairie fire. It's a book of unassailable rules and principles that protect the power and primacy of our language. The book scorns "the vague, the tame, the colorless, the irresolute." Once taken to heart—which is the only way *The Elements of Style* should be taken—readers will be equipped to fight the good fight on behalf of the clear, the brief, the bold; and for the rest of their lives, all sentences they read and write will be measured against Will Strunk's enduring credo:

> Vigorous writing is concise. A sentence should contain no unnecessary words, a paragraph no unnecessary sentences, for the same reason that a drawing should have no unnecessary lines and a machine no unnecessary parts. This requires not that the writer make all his sentences short, or that he avoid all detail and treat his subjects only in outline, but that every word tell.

farm security administration photographers

*I see one third of a nation ill-housed, ill-clad, ill-nourished.*

FRANKLIN DELANO ROOSEVELT, 1937

PRESIDENT ROOSEVELT understood it was not enough for him to see the Great Depression's grip on the nation. The American people would have to see for themselves the faces of their fellow citizens, especially those in the West and South, their backs against the wall, drained by the struggle to hold families and farms together. The documentary photographs of those whose livelihood depended on the land would be taken by some of the finest photographers in our nation's history. Those photographers, Dorothea Lange, Lewis Hine, Walker Evans, and others would create the consciousness necessary to mobilize the government's resources. Their photographs would create the necessary sense of urgency.

The small, nimble government agency that would support and encourage their photographic mission was the Resettlement Administration—later to be called the Farm Security Administration (FSA)—under the leadership of Rexford Tugwell. Tugwell was an original member of FDR's brain trust, and still assistant Secretary of Agriculture. Importantly, neither the Resettlement Administration nor the FSA had congressional oversight.

Thanks to their boss, Roy Stryker, these photographers had the freedom to tell the truth as they saw it; their photographs, taken from 1935 to 1943, are now housed at the Library of Congress. Their pictures bore witness to what people were enduring, refuting what newspapers called "moochers" or "an invading hoard of idle."

Looking at these portraits now, we can see the compassion of the photographers and the dignity in the portraits of Americans on the edge. To those who thought these pictures were propaganda, Dorothea Lange replied with anger years later, "Everything is propaganda for what you believe in, isn't it. . . the harder and more deeply you believe in anything, the more in a sense you are a propagandist."

In discussing the work of Dorothea Lange and her husband, Paul Taylor, the photography curator Therese Heyman summed it up: "They clung to the hope that what they were doing might be part of a solution." That could be said, as well, about all members of that band of photographers who, in their own way, honored those whose photographs they took.

## by Gail Buckland

Dorothea Lange took this 1940 photograph of a migrant worker taking a break from picking cotton in Eloy, Arizona. His hand, according to Lange, hid his bad teeth. He could earn about two dollars a day for ten hours work.

75

FDR's fireside chats  holding us together

FDR spoke from a small room without a fireplace in the White House basement to millions of Americans. In his calm and reasoned conversational manner, he re-assured the nation in the depths of the Great Depression and through a World War.

Saul Bellow described his own experience of listening to President Roosevelt, an American aristocrat, Groton and Harvard educated, hold the nation together, using only a radio and the power of his personality: "I can recall walking eastward on the Chicago Midway. . . drivers had pulled over, parking bumper to bumper, and turned on their radios to hear Roosevelt. They had rolled down the windows and opened the car doors. Everywhere the same voice, its odd Eastern accent, which in anyone else would have irritated Midwesterners. You could follow without missing a single word as you strolled by. You felt joined to these unknown drivers, men and women smoking their cigarettes in silence, not so much considering the President's words as affirming the rightness of his tone and taking assurance from it."

The nation needed the assurance of those Fireside Chats, the first of which was delivered on March 12, 1933. Between a quarter and a third of the work force was unemployed. Every bank in America had been closed for at least eight days. It's hard for us to imagine. It was the nadir of the Great Depression.

The "Fireside" was figurative; most of the chats emanated from a small, cramped room in the White House basement. Frances Perkins, Roosevelt's Secretary of Labor, described the change that would come over him just before the broadcasts: "His face would smile and light up as though he were actually sitting on the front porch or in the parlor with them. People felt this, and it bound them to him in affection."

In that first radio visit, Roosevelt began by explaining how the banking system worked: "when you deposit money in a bank the bank does not put the money into a safe-deposit vault. It invests your money in many different forms of credit—bonds, mortgages. In other words, the bank puts your money to work to keep the wheels turning around."

He went on to announce that the banks would reopen the next day, and that those who chose to participate would have most of their deposits guaranteed by the federal government. This was not the end of the depression, the president said, but surely the end of the downward spiral that had brought the economy to a standstill.

Roosevelt's Fireside Chats and, indeed, all of his efforts to communicate contrasted with those of another master of the airwaves, Adolf Hitler. Hitler fueled the rage in the German people via radio and encouraged their need to blame while FDR reasoned with and encouraged America. Hitler's speeches were pumped through cheap plastic radios manufactured expressly to ensure complete penetration of the German consciousness. The appropriation of this new medium by FDR for reason and common sense was one of the great triumphs of American democracy.

by Kevin Baker

freedom of expression

by Marvin Kalb

For me, there is a direct and historic link between the First Commandment of the Old Testament and the First Amendment of the U.S. Constitution—that one leads inexorably to the other. The First Commandment explains the origins of freedom, and the First Amendment defines the scope of freedom. Both point unmistakably to freedom as America's greatest contribution to humanity. Not the automobile, jazz, or Hollywood; not the word processor or even the Internet, all these are often described as America's unique assets; but rather it is the awesome concept of freedom that is America's ultimate symbol, attraction—and export!

The First Commandment reads: "I am the Lord thy God, who brought thee forth out of Egypt, out of the house of bondage; and thou shalt have no other God before me." In this way God sanctions an escape from bondage and puts people on a path toward the "promised land," toward freedom. In Chapter 16 of Deuteronomy, it is written: "They went through a change from being enslaved to being free people. They were reborn and redeemed." This is a powerful message, ricocheting through history until it finally found a permanent home in colonial America.

In the early eighteenth century, the Trustees of Yale, many of whom were scholars who read Scripture in the original Hebrew, designed a coat of arms for the college in the shape of a book open to two Hebrew words—"Urim" and "Thummim," which have come to mean "light" and "truth" in English. The book, of course, was the Bible. Not too far north, Harvard graduates had to master three languages—Latin, Greek, and Hebrew. Gentlemen in those days had to have more than a passing familiarity with the Old Testament. It was then not mere coincidence that carved into the Liberty Bell in Philadelphia, which tolled a brave message to a people overthrowing British rule, was an uplifting phrase selected from Chapter 25 of Leviticus: "Proclaim liberty throughout the land, unto all the inhabitants thereof."

The commandment that blessed an escape from oppression and embraced the pursuit of freedom led, or should have led, the founding fathers to pen the Bill of Rights. They had much on their minds, many interests to satisfy, but they agreed that the delineation of freedom was to be their primary responsibility. It was to become the First Amendment, inspired in part by the First Commandment, and it read: "Congress shall make no law respecting an establishment of religion, or prohibiting the free exercise thereof; or abridging the freedom of speech, or of the press; or the right of the people peaceably to assemble, and to petition the government for a redress of grievances." Throughout American history, these freedoms have become intertwined with American life, one indistinguishable from another.

Freedom of religion, of speech, of assembly—these are crucial and central to democracy; but, for me, freedom of the press is the key to an open mind and an open market, the twin foundations of a free society. In governmental and politically philosophical terms, it is distinctly an American idea.

Years ago, in the late 1950s and early 1960s, when I was a CBS correspondent in Moscow, I was frequently struck by the fact that the Soviet Constitution of 1936 also stressed the centrality of "freedom of the press," but its words meant nothing. The press was the handmaiden of the ruling Communist Party—it echoed the party line with absolute fidelity. In Western Europe, the press was free, or relatively free, and still is, but it was not protected by parliament and, unlike the Soviet example, no piece of parchment ever spoke of a need to honor and protect the press.

"Only in America," once the title of a book by a transplanted North Carolinian journalistic legend named Harry Golden, does the press have a constitutional guarantee that it will be free. Must it be socially responsible? Not necessarily. Indeed, Alan Barth, who once wrote the most elegant editorials for *The Washington Post*, touched off a tidal wave of controversy in the late 1970s by advocating a "right" for the press to be "irresponsible." Those were the days after Vietnam and Watergate when the press, heady with hubris, was attempting to prove that its disillusionment with the war and disappointment in Nixon did not mean that its coverage of both was "irresponsible."

With the end of the Cold War in the early 1990s, journalists from Eastern Europe, who had always marched to their Party's drummer, converged on Cambridge for a series of seminars to proclaim their sudden devotion to this American notion of "freedom of the press"—and, in a broader sense, to freedom and democracy. They and so many others associated America with freedom in all of its many untidy formulations. It was to America that millions from all over the world came for the opportunity to enjoy personal freedom and economic opportunity, the same explosive message that attracted my own father and mother here almost a hundred years before.

I have always been proud to be an American journalist, teacher, and writer. All of my life, I assumed, correctly, that I was protected by the First Amendment, which defines my freedoms, and the First Commandment, which affirms in magnificent simplicity that God considered His finest work to be the liberation of humanity from bondage with the promise that one day they will reach the "promised land" of freedom.

May it be so.

freedom riders

"we are prepared to die"

by Kevin Baker

SOMETHING WAS NOT RIGHT that morning of May 20, 1961. John Lewis sensed it the moment he led the Freedom Riders into the Montgomery bus station. The terminal was deserted, save for a pack of reporters and a few figures loitering in the shadows. There was no police presence at all.

Lewis's intuition was accurate, just a little slow. He and his colleagues were ambushed by a dozen white men armed with bats, bottles, and lengths of pipe. A larger mob soon followed, led by a woman yelling, "Get those niggers!"

Even the reporters were brutally beaten to the ground. John Seigenthaler, a Nashville newspaper editor working as a special observer for Robert F. Kennedy and the Justice Department, was clubbed unconscious when he tried to push one of the Riders into the safety of a cab. Lewis, a seminary student and future Georgia congressman, was knocked unconscious. Jim Zwerg, a white student from another country, was held down while his teeth were methodically knocked out with his own suitcase. William Barbee was slugged to the ground and stomped.

The barbarous treatment was not unusual. Six days earlier, outside Anniston, Alabama, a bus had been chased down by fifty cars and firebombed and its passengers barely escaped with their lives. Inside the city limits, white Anniston thugs swarmed aboard still another Freedom Rider bus, beating Riders mercilessly, including a retired professor who sustained permanent brain damage.

Nor did the terror end there. The demonstrators who escaped the buses were often arrested and imprisoned. Others were denied sanctuary and even first-aid at local hospitals. When some were sheltered in Montgomery's "Brick-a-Day" church, a massive white mob nearly succeeded in storming and burning the house of worship, even though Martin Luther King Jr., and dozens of other civil rights leaders were inside.

preceding page: This Greyhound bus used by the Freedom Riders was set on fire by militant segregationists on the outskirts of Anniston, Alabama. The Freedom Riders challenged segregation in interstate bus terminals across the South in the summer of 1961. above (left to right): James Zwerg and John Lewis, now U.S. Representative from the 5th District of Georgia, were members of the Freedom Riders in 1961. They endured beatings as they challenged segregation in Montgomery, Alabama.

On February 1, 1961, four students at all-black North Carolina A&T, in Greensboro, took stools at a Woolworth's segregated lunch counter. In Nashville, a group of idealistic, religious, and determined individuals, headed by James Lawson, James Bevel, Diane Nash, and Lewis, led a months-long protest that brought down the city's public segregation laws.

The protestors were the backbone of the nascent Student Nonviolent Coordinating Committee (SNCC), and with James Farmer's Congress of Racial Equality (CORE), they decided to make a living test in the Deep South, of whether the Supreme Court's repeated decisions against segregated federal facilities—which included interstate bus facilities—were worth the paper they were written on.

Busloads of students and their elders put themselves on the line, enduring beatings, prison terms, and humiliations—until the more-established civil-rights organizations, the Kennedy administration, and finally much of the public, awakened and came to their aid. Theirs was the first, mass, youth-led revolt of the 1960s, and the finest. And though their movement would still be shelled and occasionally shattered, the Freedom Riders stayed in the saddle. The race was not a sprint, but victory went fairly to the sure and the right.

"We will continue our journey one way or another," said Jim Zwerg. "We are prepared to die."

In 1944, America had a difficult question to answer: what to do with the 16,354,000 men and women serving in the armed forces when they came home from the war?

The Department of Labor figured that 15 million would be unemployed. A similar post-war coincidence of lower production and returning veterans had produced a sharp depression from 1921–1923.

In response, President Franklin Roosevelt took to the airwaves, proposing a series of benefits for the men and women in uniform. The veterans' self-appointed lobby, the American Legion, grabbed onto the proposal with both hands—as did the Hearst newspapers. Legion publicist Jack Cejnar came up with the term, "The G.I. Bill of Rights," officially passed as "The Serviceman's Readjustment Act of 1944."

Returning veterans could borrow up to $2,000 to buy a house, start a business, or start a farm. They would receive $20 a week for fifty-two weeks, until they found a job. There would be lifelong medical assistance, improved services for those disabled in action, and a de facto bonus of $1,300 in discharge benefits.

The effect of the program was substantial and immediate. By 1955, 4.3 million home loans worth $33 billion had been granted. Veterans were responsible for 20 percent of all new homes built since the end of the war. Instead of another depression, the country enjoyed unparalleled prosperity for a generation.

Few veterans, though, collected their $20-a-week unemployment. Instead, they used the money for the most significant benefits of all: education and vocational training. Altogether, 7.8 million vets received education and training benefits. Some 2.3 million went to college, receiving $500 a year for books and tuition, plus $50 a month in living expenses. The effect was to transform American education and help create a middle class.

College was bliss to men used to trenches and K-rations. By 1946, over half the college enrollments in the country were vets, who often bonded into close, supportive communities within the wider campuses. Countless G.I. Bill graduates would go on to occupy the highest ranks of business, government, the professions, and even win Nobel Prizes.

The number of degrees awarded by U.S. colleges and universities more than doubled between 1940–1950, and the percentage of Americans with bachelor degrees or more rose from 4.6 percent in 1945, to 25 percent a half-century later. Joseph C. Goulden wrote, in *The Best Years 1945-1950*, that the G.I. Bill "marked the popularization of higher education in America. After the 1940s, a college degree came to be considered an essential passport for entrance into much of the business and professional world." Thanks to the G.I. Bill, a successful entrance into that world was created for millions of men and women who kept our world free, and assured its future.

by Kevin Baker

the G.I. bill                    helping create the middle class

LE OF MADISON !

ETS IN TENT

ROOMS TO RENT

YOUR SPARE ROOM !   GIVE A VET

HANCE TO USE THE 'GI' BILL.

UNIV. HOUSING BUREAU

BADGER 580

CHAPTER AMERICAN

Address delivered at the dedication of the Cemetery at Gettysburg.

Four score and seven years ago our fathers brought forth on this continent, a new nation, conceived in Liberty, and dedicated to the proposition that all men are created equal.

Now we are engaged in a great civil war, testing whether that nation, or any nation so conceived and so dedicated, can long endure. We are met on a great battle field of that war. We have come to dedicate a portion of that field, as a final resting place for those who here gave their lives, that that nation might live. It is altogether fitting and proper that we should do this.

But, in a larger sense, we can not dedicate — we can not consecrate — we can not hallow — this ground. The brave men, living and dead, who struggled here, have consecrated it, far above our poor power to add or detract. The world will little note, nor long remember what we say here, but it can never forget what they did here. It is for us the living, rather, to be dedicated here to the unfinished work which they who fought here have thus far so nobly advanced. It is rather for us to be here dedicated to the great task remaining before us — that from these honored dead we take increased devotion to that cause for which they gave the last full measure of devotion — that we here highly resolve that these dead shall not have died in vain — that this nation, under God, shall have a new birth of freedom — and that government of the people, by the people, for the people, shall not perish from the earth.

Abraham Lincoln

November 19, 1863.

WHAT ABRAHAM LINCOLN said that day at Gettysburg, November 19, 1863, has been analyzed, memorized, and explained but never emulated. The address's only flaw was its prediction, "The world will little note, nor long remember, what we say here. . . . "

The compactness and concision of the address have something to do with the mystery of its memorability. Two-hundred-and-seventy-one words. Ten sentences, the final one accounting for almost one third of the length. Two-hundred-and-five words had a single syllable, forty-six had two, twenty had three syllables or more. The pronoun "I" was never used.

In studying poetry and trying unsuccessfully to write it, Lincoln learned the role of rhythm and poetry's need to make sense fast. Rhythm, compression, precision especially as to the right word above all, were attributes of the president's most effective communications. The sound of what he wrote and said mattered to him. "He not only read aloud, to think his way into sounds, but wrote as a way of ordering his thoughts," noted Gary Wills in his unparalleled book, *Lincoln at Gettysburg.*

Lincoln had admired and seen at once the future for the telegraph, requiring as it did, getting to the point and clarity. The directness the telegraph encouraged applied to his communications with his generals in the field as this message to Grant shows: "Hold on with a bull dog grip, and chew and choke as much as possible." The telegraphic quality can be clearly heard in the address, "we cannot dedicate, we cannot consecrate, we cannot hallow this ground."

Perhaps the most overshadowed speech in our nation's history was the one the Gettysburg dedication's organizers had seen as the main event, Edward Everett's oration. He was the antithesis of Lincoln. Everett was a Harvard man (later to be its president), Phi Beta Kappa, a professor of Greek, former governor of Massachusetts, and ambassador to England. He was considered one of the great orators of the day and, in fact, the organizers had changed the cemetery's dedication date to accommodate his schedule. Everett's speech of approximately two hours was well received by an audience one estimate put at 18,000. Lincoln congratulated him on the speech.

Afterward, in a note to Lincoln, Everett wrote, "I should be glad to flatter myself that I came as near to the central idea of the occasion, in two hours, as you did in two minutes." Lincoln's graceful reply concluded, "I am pleased to know that in your judgement, the little I did say was not entirely a failure."

preceding page: The handwritten copy of the Gettysburg Address, known as the Bliss-Baltimore version, hangs in the White House. right: A November 19, 1863, parade through Gettysburg before the dedication of the cemetery. Lincoln delivered the two minute speech, but didn't expect anyone to remember it.

# a great day in harlem

The jazz greats who posed for this 1958 photo taken on 126th Street in New York City were a who's who of the jazz world. The children sitting on the curb were from the neighborhood. The jazz greats in the historic photograph on the preceding pages are numbered above for your ready reference:

1. Hilton Jefferson; 2. Benny Golson; 3. Art Farmer; 4. Wilbur Ware; 5. Art Blakey; 6. Chubby Jackson; 7. Johnny Griffin; 8. Dickie Wells; 9. Buck Clayton;  10. Taft Jordan; 11. Zutty Singleton; 12. Red Allen; 13. Tyree Glenn; 14. Miff Mole; 15. Sonny Greer; 16. Jay C. Higginbotham; 17. Jimmy Jones; 18. Charles Mingus; 19. Jo Jones; 20. Gene Krupa; 21. Max Kaminsky; 22. George Wettling ; 23. Bud Freeman; 24. Pee Wee Russell; 25. Ernie Wilkins; 26. Buster Bailey; 27. Osie Johnson; 30. Eddie Locke; 31. Horace Silver; 32. Luckey Roberts; 33. Maxine Sullivan; 34. Jimmy Rushing; 35. Joe Thomas; 36. Scoville Browne; 37. Stuff Smith; 38. Bill Crump; 39. Coleman Hawkins; 40. Rudy Powell; 41. Oscar Pettiford; 42. Sahib Shihab; 43. Marian McPartland; 44. Sonny Rollins; 45. Lawrence Brown; 46. Mary Lou Williams; 47. Emmett Berry; 48. Thelonious Monk; 49. Vic Dickenson; 50. Milt Hinton; 51. Lester Young ; 52. Rex Stewart; 53. J. C. Heard; 54. Gerry Mulligan; 55. Roy Eldridge; 56. Dizzy Gillespie; 57. Count Basie.

ON A CERTAIN August morning in 1958 (no one seems to remember the exact date), the epicenter of jazz was 126<sup>th</sup> Street, between Fifth and Madison, New York City. There, fifty-eight jazz musicians—the great and the near great—gathered at the invitation of *Esquire Magazine* to have their picture taken. The picture was scheduled for ten in the morning. One of the musicians said he "wasn't aware there were two ten o'clocks in one day." *Esquire*, under the art direction of Robert Benton, wanted a photograph for an upcoming feature in its January issue. The idea was Art Kane's, an ambitious freelance art director who also volunteered to take the photograph, in spite of his almost total inexperience. As usual, no one involved had any notion they might be making history because what becomes history, like the best jazz, can surprise you. Art Kane's photograph was and is an awfully cool picture taken on a muggy city summer day. And if you're a stickler for accuracy, don't worry if you count only fifty-seven musicians: Willie "The Lion" Smith had wandered off when the shot that became *the* photograph was taken.

However, to really understand the story behind the picture, watch the Oscar-nominated documentary, *A Great Day in Harlem*. It was directed by a first-time documentary filmmaker, Jean Bach, who in her late seventies has more gumption, style, and resilience than most of today's self-proclaimed, oh-so hip filmmakers could ever muster. She knows and loves jazz and the only city where that historic picture could possibly have been taken. She worked on the film with a great producer, Matthew Seig, and a superb editor, Susan Peehl.

They all knew what they were doing and it shows; more importantly, they all *loved* what they were doing and that shows, too, from the opening frame to the final credit. The film, Whitney Balliet wrote in *The New Yorker*, is "about the taking of the picture, and it's also about mortality, loyalty, talent, musical beauty, and the fact that jazz musicians tend to be the least pretentious artists on earth."

# huckleberry finn

by Charles McGrath

HERE'S A GOOD LITERARY rule of thumb: Any book that someone has seen fit to ban has got to be worth reading. And when a book has been banned for so long and so often and for so many reasons as *The Adventures of Huckleberry Finn* has been, that's as compelling an endorsement as you can hope for. If anything, *Huckleberry Finn* has become even more disturbing over the years since its first appearance, in 1885. It's a book that, even when you reread it, is never quite what you expect—by turns, raw, sweet, funny, affecting, deeply principled, and deliberately shocking.

It has been a lightning rod for the squeamish and for nay-sayers and prigs of every stripe. *Huckleberry Finn* was a victim of political correctness long before there was such a term. The indictment is by now tiresomely familiar, and of some of the charges, at least, the novel is clearly guilty. Yes, it uses the "n" word—215 times, to be precise. (People did back then. They still do.) And Huck—not to mention most of the book's other characters, both black and white—does engage in what we would today call racist thinking. But Huck is not Twain, remember, and early on we discover that he has a lot to learn. The story of *Huckleberry Finn* is, in part, the story of Huck's education, and he is taught by none other than Jim, the runaway slave, who is in fact the book's wisest and most humane character. Set at a time when America was still riven and corrupted by slavery, *Huckleberry Finn* is a depiction of racism at its most virulent, but it is itself among the most antiracist novels ever written.

The charge of racism is so specious, that it invites us to wonder if some other agenda isn't at work in the minds of those who raise it, and the same is true of those nineteenth-century moralists, the librarians, town fathers, and custodians of the public weal, who originally objected to the novel on grounds of vulgarity and sacrilegiousness. What really upsets people about *Huckleberry Finn*, one suspects, is that it is so deeply skeptical—subversive even—of received wisdom and official pieties of every sort. It breaks all the rules and does so right from the first sentence: "You don't know about me, without you have read a book by the name of *The Adventures of Tom Sawyer*, but that ain't no matter."

There had never been a sentence like that in American literature before. It *is* vulgar, in the way that everyday speech is vulgar, and it introduces us not to the familiar narrator of nineteenth-century fiction, with measured cadences and worldly wisdom, but to a fourteen-year-old boy—a wiseass who takes nothing on faith, especially not what he's been told by his elders. It's a voice so authentically American that it's startling that we had never heard it in books until then, and in an almost embarrassing way, it reveals as phony so much that had been written until that moment. Hemingway famously said of *Huckleberry Finn* that all American literature comes from it and that "there was nothing before"—which is a stretch, but not by much. What is certainly true is that all American comedy comes from *Huckleberry Finn*. It established in an instant the two enduring hallmarks of our national sense of humor: a deadpan delivery and a take-no-prisoners attitude.

The famous scenes on the raft, lovely though they are, are in a way the least of it. *Huckleberry Finn* takes us on a tour not just down Twain's beloved Mississippi but through an America just then in the process of becoming the country that we now live in. Along the way we meet an incomparable gallery of rogues, swindlers, hypocrites, and the occasional well-meaning dupe—people in whom we can still see ourselves. Twain's take on this nascent country is withering and exact but also fond and understanding. Nothing would please him more one suspects—or surprise him less—than to learn that his book still has the power to amuse us even as it makes us wince.

page 96: "For What I Says" was one of the illustrations created (as are the others in this essay) by Thomas Hart Benton for an edition of *Huckleberry Finn* printed by the Limited Editions Club in 1942. **above:** "It Was A Steamboat that had killed herself on a rock." **right:** "Doan' you 'member . . ."

# the iditarod
## the last great race

"I am nine. I already have four dogs. When I get to be eighteen
I am going to go crazy, too, and run this race."

From Gary Paulsen's *Winterdance: The Fine Madness of Running the Iditarod*

Being a little bit crazy helped right from the beginning in Anchorage, that first Saturday in March 1973, when thirty-five mushers and their dog teams left the starting line to race 1,151 miles across the winter-locked Alaskan wilderness to Nome. There was a compelling case to stay home and put another log on the fire. First, there was the weather: temperatures that could reach sixty-five degrees below zero with winds in excess of one hundred miles an hour. Second, there was the almost total lack of recognition; the prize money was still only an intention. Third, there was the chance that the sled dogs could be eaten alive by wolves. And lastly, there was the stretch over the Bering Sea's undependable ice. One of the participants, Bobby Vent, summed up the mood: "Nobody figured anybody could make it."

Twenty days and forty-nine hours after leaving Anchorage, Dick Wilmarth and his team of huskies led by Hotfoot crossed the finish line in Nome. Twenty-two teams (including Vent's) completed the race, with last place finisher John Schultz arriving twelve days after Wilmarth. Schultz's record still stands. Event organizer Joe Redington mortgaged his house and all the prize money was awarded.

**preceding page:** Countless attempts at crossbreeding have failed to replace the full-bred husky. With its rangy leanness, thick coat, intelligence, and innate desire to race alongside other dogs, it remains the ultimate sled dog. **above:** Considering the terrain covered and weather endured over the Iditarod's 1,151-mile route, just finishing is sometimes reward enough. One of the race's lasting traditions is the Red Lantern winner: At the start of each year's race, a lamp is hung at the finish line in Nome; the last musher to finish extinguishes it.

Today, the Iditarod is Alaska's signature event and is emblematic of its frontier spirit, which stands in sharp contrast to the television-watching lower forty-eight. Nearly five hundred mushers, as young as eighteen, as old as eighty-eight, have come from fifteen countries to compete. Today the dogs are faster, the drivers more knowledgeable, and the trail, though every bit as ominous, a little less difficult. The last four champions needed just over nine days to complete the journey (Doug Swingley set the speed record in 1995: nine days, two hours and forty-two minutes).

The Iditarod, Athabascan for "distant place," dates to 1925 when a diphtheria epidemic swept through Nome, wiping out its supply of antitoxin. The closest serum was in Anchorage but trains could only carry the medicine as far as Nenna; there, twenty sled dog teams in seven days relayed the serum over the final 627 miles to Nome. That was the inspiration for Dorothy Page to pitch a commemorative race in 1967 as part of Alaska's centennial celebration. She approached Redington, a sled-dog traditionalist, and six years later the annual trail race commenced.

Men and women compete head-to-head. In fact, the most dominant Iditarod performance belongs to Susan Butcher who won four times over a five-year stretch, from 1986 to 1990.

Each musher can field a team of between twelve and sixteen dogs. Never has a contestant finished the race with his team completely intact, though. It is not unusual for more than half the team to drop out over the course at one of the race's twenty-seven checkpoints. Some become sick, some are injured, some get dropped for strategic purposes, and a very few die.

Success, however, would be impossible without the heroic drive of the dogs. Mushers spend countless training hours learning each dog's tendencies. Trust is established by "becoming a dog," as mushers say. They spend nights together inside kennels; the musher massages dogs' shoulders and tends their feet; they share meals.

Musher Gary Paulsen wrote, "The Iditarod is not really a sled race, nor a race of people, nor of money, nor of macho idiocy, nor of feminine strength, nor intellect, nor bravery. It is a dog race. . . the base of the equation is dogs."

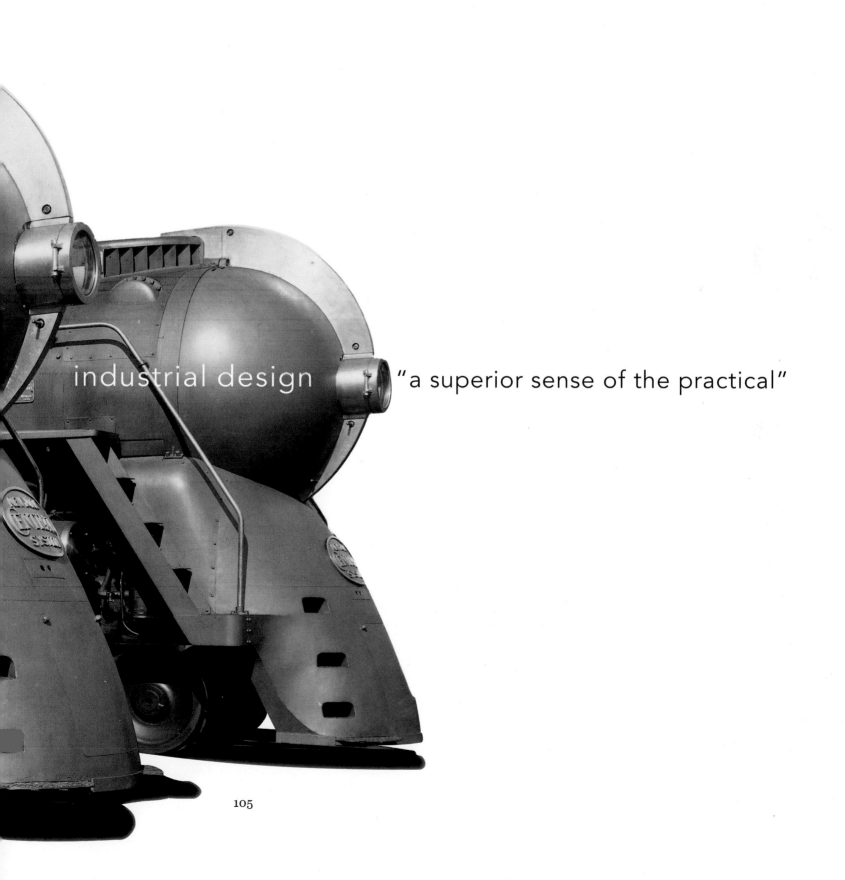

industrial design    "a superior sense of the practical"

On September 19, 1935, a *New York Times* critic wrote about a play in New Haven, "meeting the scenic requirements of the play's called for ingenuity, inspiration and a superior sense of the practical." Neither *The New York Times* critic nor the stage designer responsible, then thirty-one, knew that his stage design would be his last. Nor did the designer foresee that his design sense would have a far more pervasive effect on every day American life than he ever could have had as a stage designer. However, what the critic recognized in "Paths of Glory's" scenic design—"a superior sense of the practical"—would be evident throughout the rest of that designer's career. His name was Henry Dreyfuss, one of the pivotal figures in the emergence of industrial design.

Dreyfuss would move surely to center stage in the comparatively new discipline of industrial design. Industrial designers were energized by the belief that anything could be improved by design. Especially by *their* designs. With the exception, perhaps, of the egg. They would bring the same level of intensity to improving the design of a door handle as the interior of Air Force One. Shape, color, utility, tactility, materials, research, even whimsy. All could be brought to bear. Dreyfuss's work and thinking would influence everything from airplanes to alarm clocks, from locomotives to telephones, from thermostats to John Deere tractors.

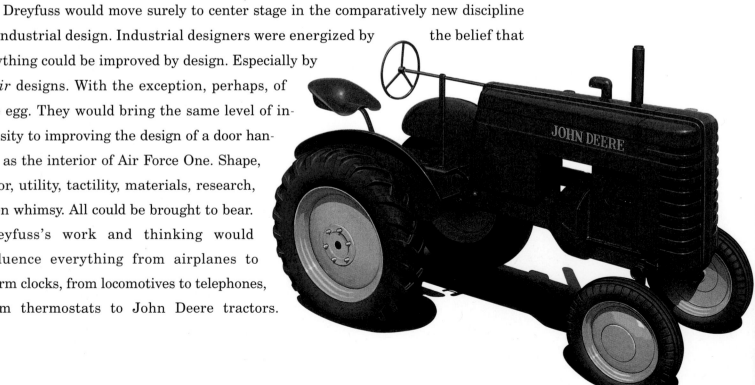

previous page: Three streamlined Hudson J-3a locomotives designed by Dreyfuss in 1938 powered the 20th Century Limited between New York and Chicago. **top left:** Consolidated Vultee Aircraft Co., Convair Car, Model 118, 1947, designed by Henry Dreyfuss and Ted Hall. This four-seater version of the Convair Car was successfully tested on April 28, 1948. **left center:** Bell telephone Laboratories, Model 500, designed by Dreyfuss and produced in 1955. **bottom left:** Dreyfuss proposed this John Deere tractor design in 1940. **right:** A 1946 DCW (dining chair wood) designed by Charles and Ray Eames. Molded seat and back and oak base painted black.

Norman Bel Geddes, a stage designer himself, and one of the seminal figures of industrial design, was an early, lasting influence on Dreyfuss. One of Geddes's precepts held that the "value of form lies in its ability to express significance clearly." While that may smack of guru talk, when truly believed, as Dreyfuss did (and other Geddes teachings as well) that precept would be, perhaps, most clearly visible in the round Honeywell thermostat. While its presence became invisible because it was—and remains—so basic to our lives, the Honeywell thermostat's longevity has more to do with the fact it plays its role so well.

Dreyfuss designs, going back to what the theater critic said, manifested "a superior sense of the practical." That's why they succeeded. Contrast that with the revered watch design in the Museum of Modern Art's design collection, featuring a blank black watch face. That watch is perhaps a protest against the esthetics of usefulness, something Dreyfuss and his generation, having been shaped by the depression, would never have thought to protest. Charles Eames, a most thoughtful and respected influence on design, talked about the difference between effect and affectation. With that in mind, we see clearly that the watch's effect—to tell time—was sacrificed for the design affectation.

Raymond Loewy, another giant of industrial design and a competitor of Dreyfuss's, made a statement whose truth remains indisputable: "The most difficult things to design are the simplest. To improve the design of a threshing machine is easy, particularly compared to, say, a scalpel or needle." The locomotive, designed by Dreyfuss, was, at least based on time required to execute, somewhat simpler than the thermostat, which took more than a decade to complete. Perhaps, the complexity of redesigning the simplest things derives from their already being so close to the essence of their purpose.

Industrial design, at its best, sends powerful signals: of speed, of desirability, of sleekness, of sensuality. Much of the energy in industrial design's defining decades was directed toward streamlining or, more accurately, to use Dreyfuss's word, "cleanlining." Raymond Loewy summed it up, "Industrial design amounts to the shaping of everyday life." The most inspired of those designs shape it for the better.

109

industrial light & magic

IT WAS THE SUMMER OF 1975 and a bizarre, vague science-fiction project was demanding all of Harrison Ellenshaw's time, effort, and thought. Late into the night, he and his colleagues would work from a Van Nuys, California, warehouse, the makeshift home of a new, special-effects outfit soon to be called Industrial Light & Magic (ILM).

"We didn't know much about the [film's] storyline or the performances because George [Lucas] was being so secretive," said Ellenshaw, a Disney animator moonlighting on the strange project as a matte painter. "Then I happened upon a storyboard featuring the Wookiee Chewbacca, and that really made me have doubts. I thought it was a huge mistake. *King Kong* had just been bashed critically, and here was some kind of monkey-thing. I thought, 'Why would you put something like that in a space film?' Shows what I know."

The movie that caused Ellenshaw to question his assignment was, of course, *Star Wars*. His discovery of that "huge mistake" was really not unlike Humphrey Bogart's and Tim Holt's wonder at the life-altering dust kicked up by a dancing Walter Huston in *Treasure of Sierra Madre*. It's the reason—that mystery, that surprise—why George Lucas was so secretive: He—as well as Ellenshaw and his doubting mates—were creating a generation's defining movie moment. How, after

## "to leap without looking"

all, could Ellenshaw know that one day he would be recognized as a trailblazing force behind a special effects studio that transforms moviemaking with each project it completes?

ILM has contributed its otherworldly effects to eight of the ten highest-grossing worldwide films. Only five times since *Star Wars'* 1977 debut has the Academy of Motion Picture Arts and Sciences *not* nominated ILM for Achievement in Visual Effects. Fourteen times the studio has taken home the Oscar (longtime ILM effects supervisor Dennis Muren owns more Academy Award statuettes than any other person alive—eight).

When directors want an effect done right or as it has never been done before, they go to Industrial Light & Magic. Spielberg, Cameron, Zemeckis, Levinson, Scorsese, Kurosawa, Coppola, Stone, Allen—many of the twentieth century's greatest filmmakers have sought ILM's talents, hoping it could make real the unreal.

No single film has had as direct an effect on the advancement of visual effects as *Star Wars*. During filming, special-effects supervisor John Dykstra introduced motion control (a computerized system that simultaneously moves camera and models), bringing special effects into the computer age. After *Star Wars*, the company's epic breakthroughs kept coming: the first digital effect ever photographed in *Star Trek II: The Wrath of Kahn* (1982); the incorporation of live-action and animation in *Who Framed Roger Rabbit?* (1988); the first computer-generated three-dimensional character in *The Abyss* (1989); the first "living" digital creations in *Jurassic Park* (1993); and historical drop-ins in *Forrest Gump* (1994). On Memorial Day weekend in 1999, nearly a quarter-century after it began, ILM again altered visual effects with its developments for *Star Wars: Episode I—The Phantom Menace*, in which 90 percent of the film incorporates digital effects and photo-realistic animation.

Steven Spielberg, who has collaborated with ILM more than any other director, said, "In the beginning, working with ILM and watching them attempting to fulfill my wish list of ideas was a little like standing on the end of a three-meter diving board, staring down into poured concrete with just a couple of puddles here and there. And yet, together, we managed to leap without looking. Leaping without looking has made Lucas's company the greatest show since P.T. Barnum; and all of us in the movie business who are fortunate enough to hear ILM say, 'Yes, we'll do your movie with you,' can bear witness to that fact."

preceding page: X-Wing fighters approaching the Death Star, from *Star Wars* (1977). **left:** Halloween flying sequence from *E.T.: The Extra Terrestrial* (1982).

## out in the garage

### where inventions begin

by Jeff Kisseloff

THE BACK SHOP, woodshed, or garage has always been to American industry and culture what the Tigris and Euphrates were to Western Civilization. Whether it was Thomas Edison or Bill Gates, great ideas taking root in unglamorous surroundings is as American as the covered wagon. Yet, while it may seem an old-fashioned notion that a lone inventor can repair to his shed and emerge with a billion-dollar idea, the daily reports of new initial public offerings and their breathtaking valuations indicate that as we near the end of the twentieth century, the tradition is stronger than ever.

California, the land of the gold rush, seems to have a special attraction for inventors. The first working model of a television receiver was born in a San Francisco loft under the direction of twenty-one-year-old Philo T. Farnsworth. It was in a tiny, hot dog stand in Santa Anita that the McDonald brothers set out to sell the first fast food.

In 1923, a young Walter Disney hustled a contract to make a small cartoon/live action feature for $1,500. He got a $500 loan from his uncle to get started. His parents took out a home equity loan for another $2,500. That allowed him to rent the back room of a local real-estate office in a cowtown called Hollywood where the first Disney film, *Alice's Day at Sea*, was made.

It hasn't changed. A Los Altos garage gave birth to the entire home computer industry in 1976, when two members of the Home Brew Computer Club, Steve Jobs and Steve Wozniak, both college drop-outs, set up shop to sell their techie friends a circuit board Wozniak had invented. Jobs was a Beatles fan, so he named their new outfit, Apple Computer, after the Beatles's record company name.

Around that time, Ben Cohen and Jerry Greenfield used a different kind of garage to garner a more low-tech fortune. The two old buddies had always prided themselves in their nonathletic abilities. Their favorite activity was snacking at each other's homes, so after they graduated from college and decided to go into business together, selling food was a natural.

They pooled their resources to take a $5 correspondence course on how to make ice cream, then moved to Burlington, Vermont, where they figured the frigid temperatures would discourage competition. There, they rented an abandoned gas station and installed a four-and-a-half-gallon freezer that would produce the first batches of Ben and Jerry's ice cream.

Of course, not every inventor stuck his hand into the tin and came out with chunky monkey. Most fail, and even those who receive patents and set up small companies don't make the kinds of fortunes that allowed Wozniak to retire at thirty-five. Look at poor Eli Whitney, who invented the cotton gin in 1793 while working as a tutor at a Georgia plantation. His was probably the most influential invention of the eighteenth century, and it got him into the history books, but had no impact on his bank book.

But that's not the point. The dream that it's possible, that an idea can come out of nowhere and with a lot of hard work can lead to success, is still alive. That kid out in the garage working away or thinking about dropping out of Harvard to start his own company can change the world.

left: Philo T. Farnsworth, seen here in his Philadelphia laboratory around 1933, stands next to his improved Image Dissector tube used to scan images for transmission. above: The background drawing depicts a design for a camera tube, which used electrons to produce a television image. Farnsworth drew this for his high school chemistry teacher in 1922.

racing as it was meant to be

IT DOESN'T HAVE THE NAME RECOGNITION of Churchill
Downs, Belmont, or Santa Anita. It's not a leg of the Triple
Crown like Pimlico. But when Queen Elizabeth II, who knows
her horseflesh, visited an American racetrack, she made the
pilgrimage to Lexington, Kentucky, and Keeneland. There they
believe the *Sport of Kings* is just that, a magnificent sport
whose traditions need protecting.

Keeneland looks like Bobby Jones used to dress. There is
taste and dignity everywhere. Ivy covered limestone buildings. No blimps. No public address system until 1997. Instead,
you find tranquillity. It's the place to go to preview future
Triple Crown and Breeders Cup contenders. It's the place
where racing's cognoscenti go to buy and sell. That explains
why Queen Elizabeth II was there.

The next time you make a serious bet on the horses, do your
homework. If you're undecided, put your money on the horse(s)
that trained at Keeneland. In 1993, all the money finishers at
the Kentucky Derby and Preakness received their spring training at Keeneland. Twenty-four Keeneland horses have gone on
to win the Kentucky Derby. Trainers believe their horses relax
and prepare themselves better by spending time at Keeneland.
And so do the distinguished crowds who appreciate the Golden
Age, now over, that Keeneland so steadfastly represents.

keeneland

Keeneland located in the Bluegrass Region of Kentucky near Lexington is a race course, training facility and the site of world famous thoroughbred sales. By intent, time seems to stand still at Keeneland but not the horses. It has retained much of the original layout created in 1916, with the grandstand facing west instead of east and the clubhouse at the head of the homestretch rather than at the first turn, as in all other American racetracks.

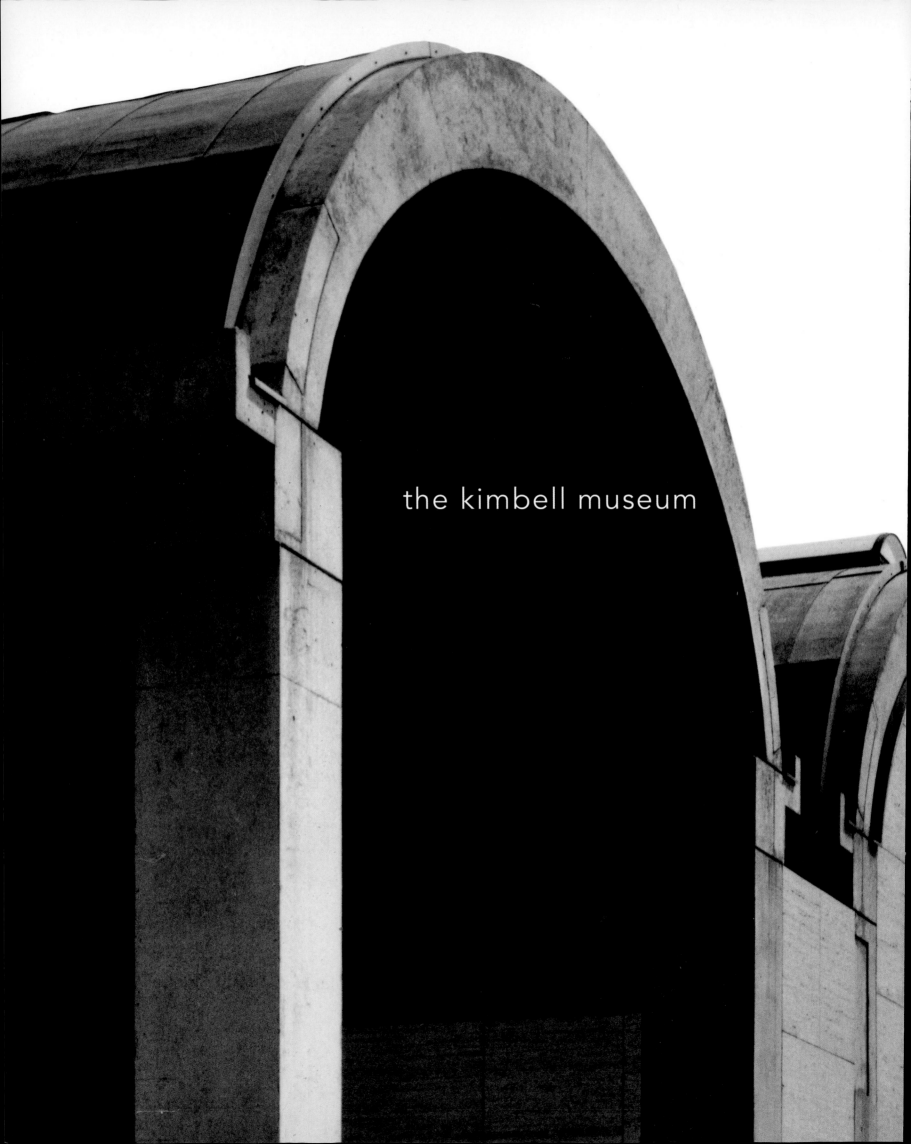

the kimbell museum

## "the client is human nature"

IN THE OPENING PARAGRAPH of his handwritten letter, dated June 25, 1969, to Mrs. Velma Kimbell, the architect Louis Kahn wrote, "I hope you will find my work beautiful and meaningful." Mrs. Kimbell and her late husband, Kay, wanted a great museum for the city of Fort Worth, Texas. They were part of that sliver of the truly rich willing to give up the power of their money to those who know best. The Kimbells would pay for the entire museum, donate the nucleus of a fine collection, and leave an endowment of such magnitude that the Kimbell would be among the handful of museums able to aggressively buy the best. What they did so well, to pay them the highest of all compliments, was on the order of a Paul Mellon gesture. Few in the history of our nation ever used their fortune so forcefully on behalf of the arts as Mellon did, the best-known example of his generosity being The National Gallery in Washington, D.C., first conceived by his father, Andrew Mellon, as a gift to the American people.

Kahn's letter, written four days before official ground-breaking ceremonies he could not attend, was politic but not entirely representative of one of his more deeply held convictions: "Even when serving the dictates of individuals you still have no client in my sense of the word. The client is human nature."

No museum has ever served that usually overlooked client better.

The director the Kimbells chose for their yet-to-be-museum, Richard Fargo Brown, director of the Los Angeles County Museum, shared their ambition. Brown was able to persuade the Kimbells and their board of directors to select Louis Kahn, initially Brown's third choice after Marcel Breuer and Mies van de Rohe. After learning more about Kahn, and spending time with him, Brown became convinced Kahn was a person he could work with. Brown had strong opinions, formed in part by having his recommendation ignored that architect Mies van der Rohe be engaged to design the Los Angeles County Museum in the early sixties. Brown valued human proportions and ease of viewing, and he sought "warmth, mellowness [remember, this was the sixties] and elegance" for the Kimbell Museum. Most importantly, he believed natural lighting is central to the viewing experience. And natural light would become the characteristic most emblematic of the extraordinary design Louis Kahn would deliver. Why such emphasis on natural light? "Because it is the light the painter used to paint his paintings," Kahn said.

Kahn wanted light to have the luminosity of silver as it reflected off the distinctive cycloidal concrete vaults. Visiting the museum today, the light reminds one of the beach on cool, dry days. Kahn believed natural light would give a sense of the time of day to museum goers and provide a mood that artificial light, because of its static nature, could not. With his natural lighting fixtures, custom designed for the Kimbell, Kahn disarmed the enemy of art: direct sunlight, particularly the light of ferocious Texas summers. Yale University's inspirational architectural historian, Vincent Sculley, describes Kahn's buildings as being full of ancient power. This is clearly evident in the Kimbell's Roman arches, which were inspired by ruins in Rome Kahn had studied. Part of the building's power also derives from the clarity of the structure and how it reveals itself at once to those who visit.

The building itself occupies almost 2.5 acres or 120,000 square feet of built space, about a third of which is for exhibitions. The scale always seems right. You never feel remote or insignificant. The materials Kahn insisted on—concrete, with all its irregularities; open-grained travertine, so different from highly polished marble (Kahn liked that it provided traction underfoot); and wood—all work together as natural materials can when their attributes are fully understood. Instead of inducing fatigue as museums often do, the Kimbell is restorative. "The feeling of being home and safe comes to mind," Kahn explained.

South gallery, which houses the permanent collection. **right:** Kahn's early sketches for the Kimbell Museum.

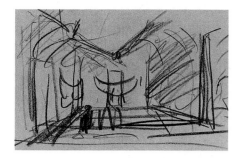

Compelling evidence of the edifice complexes of Museum directors, their boards, and architects, surrounds us. Museums seem to be constantly undergoing alterations or construction. What's good will be better bigger says the gospel of growth. But not at the Kimbell. . . so far. In 1989, when Brown's successor, Edmund Pillsbury, and the board drew up plans to enlarge the Kimbell, they made a good case for the need for additional space. And then a funny thing happened on the way to the construction drawings. Opposition, determined and reasoned, came forth, not just in Fort Worth, but nationally.

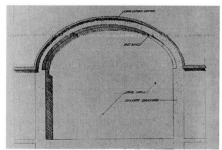

It's hard to believe a building then only eighteen years old, could inspire so many architects to mount up and do battle, some of whom may have coveted the Kimbell's commission themselves. But they did and such heat was put on, that Pillsbury felt compelled to meet with the architects and other critics in New York to, can you believe it, explain himself. *Mirabile dictu*. The Kimbell's leaders changed their mind and backed down, leaving an American architectural triumph intact.

One thing we'll never know for sure is whether the Kimbell's human proportions are due only to Kahn or to the Law of Unintended Consequences. Up the slight hill to the Kimbell's west stands the Amon Carter Museum. The guardian of the museum's

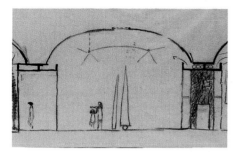

namesake and chief benefactor, Amon Carter, protected his view of Fort Worth's modest skyline to the east, requesting a height restriction of forty feet on the Kimbell Museum. Kahn and the Kimbell board honored that request. Without that restriction would Kahn have gone higher? We don't know or need the answer. The Kimbell is what it is.

The great miracle of the space created by Louis Kahn for the Kimbell is that all sense of duty associated with going to a museum is removed and replaced by a desire to be there. We are given the feeling, not that we are in a museum that is better than we are, but that we are part of a space as good as we would like to be.

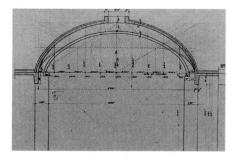

# lend lease

## "the most unsordid act"

FRANKLIN DELANO ROOSEVELT introduced his idea at a press conference on December 17, 1940, in typically homey, easily comprehensible language:

> Suppose my neighbor's home catches on fire, and I have a length of garden hose four or five hundred feet away. If he can take my garden hose and connect it up with his hydrant, I may help him put out the fire. Now what do I do? I don't say to him before that operation, 'Neighbor, my garden hose cost me fifteen dollars; you have to pay me fifteen dollars for it.' No! What is the transaction that goes on? I don't want fifteen dollars—I want my garden hose after the fire is over.

The neighbor on fire was England, facing almost alone the full ferocity of the Nazi blitz; England was the only major European power still resisting, barely, the German juggernaut. The formal cry for help, a desperate letter from Churchill to Roosevelt, had been received eight days earlier on December 9, when a navy seaplane had touched down next to the U.S. cruiser *Tuscaloosa*, waiting in the Gulf of Mexico, off Florida's southern coast. The president was on board recuperating from the rigors of his November reelection campaign, when the crew of the seaplane delivered the letter.

by Kevin Baker

125

Women.. Defend DEMOCRACY HERE NO A.E.F. NO CONVOYS DEFEAT H.R.1776
AMERICAN PEACE MOBILIZATION • N.Y. COUNCIL
A.P.M. N.Y. COUNCIL
Women.. Defend DEMOCRACY HERE NO A.E.F. NO CONVOYS DEFEAT H.R.1776
AMERICAN PEACE MOBILIZATION • N.Y. COUNCIL
DON'T LET Roosevelt SACRIFICE OUR MENFOLK Defeat H.R.1776
AMERICAN PEACE MOBILIZATION • N.Y. COUNCIL

"The moment approaches when we shall no longer be able to pay cash for shipping and other supplies," the prime minister had written, pointing out that the Exchequer was down to its last $2 billion—with $5 billion in orders from American munitions factories outstanding.

What was needed, Roosevelt knew, was some way around the Neutrality Act, an isolationist reaction to World War I; the act stipulated that any belligerents had to pay cash on the barrelhead for weapons—and that loans could not be provided at all to those nations that had not yet repaid their debts from the Great War.

Harry Hopkins, Roosevelt's man for all seasons, noted that his boss on the *Tuscaloosa* calmly went through two days of "refueling, the way he so often does when he seems to be resting and carefree."

"Then, one evening," Hopkins later recalled, "he suddenly came out with it—the whole program . . . there wasn't much doubt that he'd find a way to do it."

The "whole program" became House Resolution 1776, better known as "lend-lease." It would grant Roosevelt the authority to "lend" tanks, planes, ships, and other aid not only to England but "any country whose defense the president deems vital to the defense of the United States." Something had to be done to stop Hitler, and done quickly; leaders across the political spectrum rallied to the support of H.R. 1776.

One such leader was Wendell Willkie, the Republican candidate FDR had just defeated in the 1940 presidential campaign. Quizzed by a Senate committee over the contradictions between his support for the bill and his own, quasi-isolationist presidential campaign, Willkie simply grinned and answered, "I struggled as hard as I could to beat Franklin Roosevelt, and I tried to keep from pulling any of my punches. He was elected President. He is my President now." When Washington state's Democratic Senator Homer Bone asked, "What is worse than war?" Republican Warren Austin of Vermont told him, "I say that a world enslaved to Hitler is worse than war, and worse than death."

The isolationist opposition was organized and powerful. There was the Mother's Crusade Against Bill 1776; Col. Charles Lindbergh had assured the Senate that Britain was doomed. The Congress had more faith in FDR's idea, passing H.R. 1776 by large margins on March 11, 1941; The bill provided Roosevelt with $7 billion in appropriations for America's allies-to-be—the first of some $50 billion to be anted up by the end of hostilities in 1945.

Winston Churchill called Lend-Lease "the most unsordid act in the history of any nation." How much did it mean? Maybe everything.

# the library of america

IN THE LATE 1920s an appreciation of the need for historic preservation, fueled by the endangered architectural heritages of Charleston, South Carolina and New Orleans, began to emerge in America. Who knows how great—and permanent—our nation's losses would have been had that sense of urgency not been translated into action over subsequent decades.

A similar sense of urgency motivated the founding and formation of The Library of America. This extraordinary initiative, not nearly as well known as it deserves to be, is ensuring that America's literary heritage is preserved and remains in print in beautifully designed, affordable books.

Since its first books were published in 1982, The Library of America has reflected the good sense and good taste of the people in charge. The watchdogs of political correctness have been kept at bay. Introductions to the books are absent because, the Library's leaders say, "We present writings as the authors intended them to be presented, without someone else's explanatory interventions."

Edmund Wilson, the distinguished writer and critic, was among the first to articulate the need for the library. He argued that literature is as significant a part of our heritage as other artistic and cultural pursuits. He wrote, "It is absurd that our most read and studied writers should not be available in their entirety in any convenient form." In 1962, Wilson wrote to Jason Epstein, a foresighted editor at Random House, "The kind of thing I should like to see would follow the example of the *Editions de la Pléiade*, which have included almost the whole of the French classics in beautifully produced and admirably printed, thin-paper volumes ranging from 800 to 1,500 pages." Epstein got on board along with other intellectuals Wilson enlisted, including Lionel Trilling and Alfred Kazin. Requests for funding were made in 1963 but to no avail.

Progress was glacial until 1978 when Roger Kennedy, vice president of the arts for the Ford Foundation, promised support. Then in 1979, funding was finally approved, with $600,000 coming from Ford and $1.2 million coming from the National Endowment for the Humanities. In May 1982, the first eight books were published: Walt Whitman's *Poetry and Prose*; Herman Melville's *Typee, Omoo,* and *Mardi*; Harriet Beecher Stowe's *Uncle Tom's Cabin, Oldtown Folks*, and *The Minister's Wooing*; and Nathaniel Hawthorne's *Tales and Sketches*.

The thoughtfulness of Cheryl Hurley's leadership, The Library of America's president, is apparent just where it counts: in the books, now numbering over one hundred. The readability, thanks in part to the Galliard typeface, is particularly welcome because each book is roughly two-thirds the length of the Bible. And the books open easily and lie flat. The size of the volumes was influenced by the "golden section," a harmonious proportion from antiquity favored by the Greeks; the books feel good in the hand.

Except for its seed money, The Library of America raises its own money and pays its own way. It doesn't receive any regular government support as some mistakenly think. Few nightmares are more terrifying than imagining Congress poking its nose into The Library of America's decision-making process.

The Library of America's recent offerings demonstrate the expansive view of their mission.

Two volumes, *Reporting Vietnam: American Journalism 1959-1975*, is the most comprehensive collection of reporting on that war, 116 pieces by over eighty writers.

*Writing New York*, a collection of more than a hundred pieces celebrating the 100th anniversary of Greater New York.

Two volumes by Eudora Welty, the first living writer to have her work collected in The Library of America.

Two volumes of Gertrude Stein's work and two volumes of James Baldwin's, one of essays and one of his early novels and stories.

*Crime Novels*, two volumes worth of American noir of the 1930s, '40s, and '50s.

Two volumes of poetry, one of Wallace Stevens's work and another of Robert Frost's.

The Library of America is not coasting. Their pedal is to the metal. Yet they maintain their focus. The scope of their ambition widens, as it surely must in an America that now watches three hours and forty-six minutes of television per day per person.

# LIFE

NOVEMBER 23, 1936 **10** CENTS

# LIFE magazine

## by David Douglas Duncan

LIFE AT *LIFE* was a wild, twenty-year bronco-busting ride in the big time news rodeo after World War II. I'd been roaming the South Pacific as a Marine combat photographer who saw the war end from atop a 5-inch cannon turret overlooking a simple table where Gen. Douglas MacArthur and Baron Mamoru Shigemitsu signed the articles of surrender aboard the battleship USS *Missouri*—my home state—anchored in Tokyo Bay. At that excruciatingly silent ceremony, I met senior *LIFE* photographer Jay Eyerman—on his way to Hiroshima—who suggested that his magazine might offer a future to a trooper with my nomadic background; should I ever get to New York when out of uniform—just phone. "Offer a future!" To be a *LIFE* photographer! The possibility was simply not discussed in terrestrial terms by other photographers of that era.

Soon I was out of uniform, in New York, and on the phone to *LIFE*. We met. That same weekend I became *LIFE*'s newest staff photographer, then I was on my way overseas once again. Russia was pushing battle tank-loaded trains down through Azerbaijan, headed for the oil fields of southern Iran. Iran? I'd never heard of Azerbaijan. . . and my old school atlas still called the place Persia.

Overnight—it took three airborne days to get there—I was headed for Tehran as a brand new *LIFE* photographer.

And toward an entirely new life.

131

There was a casual aura of elitism surrounding most *LIFE* photographers when mixing with others of their newborn profession—"photojournalism." They benefited from and reflected the influence (and respect in most areas) emanating from their editorial power base, *Time/LIFE/Fortune* magazines; and that self-righteous autocrat, China-born missionary-oriented tycoon, a dreamer-turned-publisher, Henry R. Luce with whom few on the magazines's staffs had ever exchanged a single word. Or even seen!

The photographers, left mostly to themselves in that high-pressure word environment, were generally quiet men (and a few extraordinary women) with often unique camera talents. All bonded into a multinational, microcosmic, latter-day legion of Chevaliers of a Roundtable whose quest was a self-assigned search for *their* Holy Grail: that elusive ultimate image concealed somewhere within the mystery of their next picture story. For most of us, the search was our reward. That supreme print of our imagination was generally unphotographable. Or at least it was for me: such being the essence of dreams. Perhaps luckily for us, few others ever imagined or were aware of the possible effect of those celestial subjects that escaped us. Yet *LIFE*—and we—survived gloriously for years, submerged in our often less than fully realized efforts.

We came from everywhere.

Russia, Albania, Germany, England (The Isle of Mann), Latvia, New Zealand, Japan, France, Italy, Wales, Algeria, Seattle, San Francisco, Los Angeles, Boston, Brooklyn, Wichita (Kansas), Fort Scott (Kansas), and Kansas City, (Missouri)—me. I lived and saw that *LIFE* life firsthand. But never from within the states.

*LIFE* photographers were the superstars of a romantic new art form of professionals who profoundly influenced and extended the awareness of Americans (and much of the rest of a worldwide audience) to the postwar changes in everyday global existence and customs and vanities . . . forever. Yet *LIFE* photographers were mostly anonymous, a paradox of surprising portions compared to the lives their work touched. There were the exceptions, of course: Robert Capa, Alfred Eisenstaedt, Margaret Bourke-White, Carl Mydans—and the nonstaff *LIFE* photographers, Philippe Halsman (100+ covers), and a few others of uncharted depths like Gjon Mili, the strobe-flash genius and lyrical ballet sequences photo poet. While considered giant talents among their peers, even they did not enjoy (or suffer) "sidewalk" recognition and fame—quite unlike those Hollywood and Broadway stars whose trademark images they helped to create and then blazen everywhere. *LIFE* photographers were not objects of any public relations efforts by *LIFE* or Time, Inc., their parent publishing conglomerate. At any one time, we were no more than thirty—with very few based in the magazine's New York offices. We were paid probably less than many minor bank officials in the buildings surrounding Rockefeller Center, where we luncheoned at Pearl's when in town between assignments or replacing battered gear.

We pursued our photographic lives out of dedication to a rare profession, requiring love of almost endless work, unrelated to any sort of significant financial benefits. We battled ferociously for photo-page space and covers with our other *LIFE* photographer-colleagues, yet spoke with enormous pride of their achievements when they dominated an issue of the magazine. For all the competitiveness, there was always respect, even awe sometimes, for each others' work. Week after week, month after month, year by year, for nearly twenty years.

After those great editors like Edward Thompson left seeking other challenges, postal rates and production costs zoomed drastically; audience tastes probably became altered or even satiated; and photography, fine photography, became an affordable hobby worldwide including color printing at corner-drugstore prices.

Then global television captured the hearts and minds. . .

We know the rest.

Taken in 1957 in France by Jacqueline Picasso, Duncan shows Pablo Picasso how to operate a camera.

# M*A*S*H    the final episode "good-bye, farewell and amen"

## by Marina Budhos

ON FEBRUARY 28, 1983, 125 million Americans tuned in to the last episode of one of their all-time favorite shows: *M*A*S*H*. For weeks, newspapers had run contests, asking readers to write with suggestions of how the show should end. *M*A*S*H* bashes were held in every major city, and people donned old Army fatigues to watch the show in bars. Seventy-one percent of viewers watching television that night helped "Good-bye, Farewell and Amen" become the most-watched show in history. We were saying farewell, not just to beloved television characters, but to an era and the antiwar spirit that the show had captured so well.

    *M*A*S*H*, which ran for eleven years and garnered nearly one hundred Emmy nominations, is still broadcast in reruns and considered to be one of the finest efforts network television ever made. Based on Richard Hornberger's best-selling novel and the hit movie directed by Robert Altman, the story of a fictional 4077 Mobile Army Surgical Hospital unit near the front lines in the Korean War was filled with the high jinks of the book and movie, yet established its own tone of prickly intelligence, wit, and warmth. In tackling the darker subjects of war, the show perfectly echoed a conscience-stricken America, troubled by Vietnam. Weekly, 30 million Americans tuned into the familiar opening credits, featuring the sound of choppers and the theme song, "Suicide Is Painless." In reality, the book's author, Hornberger, was a surgeon from Maine who had served in a MASH unit in Korea and hated the show for its antiwar message.

Nurses running to meet helicopters carrying the wounded was part of the signature footage that opened each *M*A*S*H* episode.

137

*M\*A\*S\*H* creator, comedy writer Larry Gelbart, put the wise-cracking, womanizing, yet humane Benjamin Franklin "Hawkeye" Pierce (Alan Alda) at the center of the action. Sharing Hawkeye's flea-bitten tent were fellow surgeons Trapper John and Frank Burns, who was having an affair with Margaret "Hot Lips" Houlihan, the strong-willed head nurse. A favorite part was that of Max Klinger, the cross-dresser who would try anything to get to go home. The cast changed over time, and finally even Gelbart left, exhausted from battles with network censors.

The last episode, "Good-bye, Farewell and Amen," which ran two-and-a-half hours, was a brilliant culmination of everything the series represented: good, funny television drama that probed the ugly underside of war—in that last case, the savagery of peace in the closing and brutal days of Korea.

"What happened on the bus?" Sidney Freedman, the psychiatrist keeps asking Hawkeye, who, at the final episode's opening, is in a mental institution.

Slowly, we learn that on July 4, after a day at the beach, the unit's bus stopped to pick up refugees and wounded G.I.s who told them to drive the bus into the bushes to hide from an enemy patrol. Hawkeye keeps hissing at a refugee woman, to keep the rooster on her lap quiet. The woman complies. Eventually, the repressed memory emerges: The woman had smothered her own child.

Hawkeye shakily returns to 4077. On the night of the armistice, one of the worst rounds of casualties is brought in.

"Does this look like peace to you?" Margaret asks.

Then over the PA system comes a litany of the war's damage, ending with "two million killed and one hundred thousand Korean orphans." As the unit is broken down, each character gropes toward civilian life. After everyone exits, we are left with Hawkeye and Hunnicutt (who replaced Trapper John), who share an emotional embrace.

"I left you a note," Hunnicutt tells his friend, then mounts his motorcycle and heads off into the nearby hills.

As Hawkeye lifts off in a helicopter, he sees down below on the deserted 4077, spelled out with stones, the message: "GOODBYE." This last episode, considered the best in television history, was more than a good-bye: it was an homage to how far serious and intelligent television can go, and a reminder that it very rarely does.

The last scene from the final episode of *M\*A\*S\*H*.

# the marshall plan essentials for european recovery

## by Kevin Baker

IN HARVARD YARD, on June 5, 1947, Secretary of State George C. Marshall's fifteen-minute speech painted for graduates a grim picture of the continuing "hunger, poverty, desperation, and chaos" in a Europe still devastated after the end of World War II. It was time, Marshall asserted, for a comprehensive recovery plan. "The initiative," he said, "must come from Europe."

Marshall's words meant something more than boilerplate commencement hoo-rah to Ernest Bevin, Britain's wily foreign minister. Bevin replied to Marshall's "suggestion" almost at once, and by July 3, he and France's Foreign Minister George Bidault had invited twenty-two nations to Paris, to develop a European Recovery Plan (ERP).

Bevin had been alerted to the importance of Marshall's speech by Dean Acheson, Marshall's Under Secretary of State. Acheson was the point man for the old Eastern Establishment and he had already done a masterful job of laying the groundwork for Marshall's speech, pointing out to the public that European cities still looked like the bombs had just stopped falling, ports were still blocked, and farmers were hoarding crops because they couldn't get a decent price. Further, the Communist parties of France and Italy, their marching orders received directly from the Kremlin, were launching waves of strikes, further destabilizing already-shaky governments.

President Truman insisted that the plan be called "the Marshall Plan," honoring the man he believed to be "the greatest living American." Yet much of the reactionary Congress viewed it as "Operation Rat Hole," pouring money into a "bold socialist blueprint."

The Soviets and their Eastern European satellites, invited to participate, refused; in February 1948, Stalin's vicious coup in Prague crumpled Czechoslovakia's coalition government, and inspired speedy passage of the ERP. On April 14, the freighter *John H. Quick* steamed out of Texas's Galveston Harbor, bound for Bordeaux with 9,000 tons of American wheat. Soon, 150 ships were shuttling back and forth across the Atlantic, carrying food, fuel, industrial equipment, farming supplies, construction materials—essentials for recovery.

The Marshall Plan's most impressive achievement was its inherent magnanimity, for its very success returned Europe to a competitive position with our own country.

Winston Churchill wrote: "Many nations have arrived at the summit of the world but none, before the United States, on this occasion, has chosen that moment of triumph, not for aggrandizement but for further self-sacrifice."

The Marshall Plan, named after George C. Marshall, Army chief of staff during World War II and later President Harry Truman's secretary of state funneled nearly $13 billion to the countries of Western Europe. The aid helped prevent starvation, eliminate devastation, and laid the foundation for Europe's reconstruction.

mohawk steel workers

dealing with the fear

In 1886, the Dominion Bridge Company set out to build a cantilevered bridge over the St. Lawrence for the Canadian Pacific Railroad. The bridge would be set on land belonging to the Kahnawake Mohawks. In exchange, the Mohawks demanded jobs on the project.

The company agreed, assuming that the Mohawks would unload box cars, and perform other menial tasks. Instead, the Indians climbed all over the bridge, "as agile as goats," asking if they could try riveting. As one company official later wrote, "It was quite impossible to keep them out." Indeed, "As the work progressed, it became apparent to all concerned that these Indians were very odd in that they did not have any fear of heights."

Dominion Bridge trained a dozen or so Mohawks as riveters, a difficult, dangerous skill that entailed heating rivets until they were red-hot, tossing them thirty to forty feet through the air, then catching and forcing them through steel beams with a hammer, or a pneumatic drill—all of this some 500 feet or more above the ground.

Soon there were seventy iron and steel riveters in the Kahnawake band, working projects throughout Canada. The "Caughnawagas," as whites first called them, had always proved adroit at adapting to the vagaries of capitalist culture. They thrived as guides for French fur trappers, raft riders for lumber companies, circus performers—even patent-medicine salesmen.

Then, in 1907, came "the disaster"—the collapse of the Quebec Bridge, killing 96 workers in all, 33 of them Kahnawakes. The tragedy might have ended Kahnawake Mohawk participation in high steel right there; instead, it made Mohawk boys determined to become steelworkers—and Mohawk women determined that their husbands and sons would never work one job again in such concentrated numbers.

The Kahnawake riveting gangs continued to spread out; by the 1910s they had reached New York. There, they worked nearly all the monumental structures of greater New York: the Empire State Building and the George Washington Bridge; the Chrysler Building and the World Trade Center; the U.N. General Assembly Building; the Triborough Bridge; and the Verrazano Bridge; the Pulaski Skyway; and the West Side Highway.

## by Kevin Baker

Some believe the Mohawk's lack of fear doing difficult, dangerous work at great heights can be attributed to a genetic factor, but the Mohawks believe it's simply a matter of "dealing with the challenge and the fear."

By the 1930s, a community of 700 Mohawks was living in the old North Gowanus neighborhood of Brooklyn. Local Italian groceries carried the Mohawks' favorite brands of corn meal, and the riveters drank Canadian beers at the Spar Bar and Grill, and the Wigwam, with its picture of Jim Thorpe on the wall and the sign "The Greatest Iron Workers in the World Pass Thru These Doors." Rev. Dr. David Munroe Cory, of the Cuyler Presbyterian Church, translated the Gospel of St. Luke into the Mohawk-Oneida language and held monthly services in that tongue.

The community's center remained along the St. Lawrence. When they were working on a job, Mohawk steel workers might make the twelve-hour trip up there from the city on Friday nights, returning on Sunday nights—often driving at breakneck speeds. They always received a joyous reception on the reservation, and the gypsy-like nature of their work seemed to hold a great appeal. They would drive on, all over the United States— even arriving in time to help rivet together the Golden Gate Bridge.

What made the Mohawks such superb high-steel workers remains something of a mystery. The legends assumed some kind of genetic advantage, but there is little evidence of fact in the story. Joseph Mitchell, in his scrupulous *New Yorker* article, "The Mohawks in High Steel," thought Kahnawake children in Brooklyn "have unusual manual dexterity; by the age of three, most of them are able to tie their shoelaces." But Kanatakta, Executive Director of the Kanien'kehaka Raotitiohkwa Cultural Center, suggests that it's more "a question of dealing with the challenge and the fear."

The Mohawks were able to handle the fear, but not the changes in the construction industry. By the late 1960s, riveting had all but disappeared. The Brooklyn community dissolved, too, as crime rates rose.

The lure of high-steel work, though, would not so easily dissipate, not in a community where the graves of men who died on the job are marked with steel-girder crosses. By the 1990s, some 20–25 percent of Mohawk men were in steel construction again, and dozens of them were living in New York.

The demand will always be there. Mitchell quoted the Dominion Bridge official: "Men who want to do it are rare and men who can do it are even rarer."

TRIGGERED BY the oldest of journalism's preoccupations: the desire to be first with a dramatic story, Edward R. Murrow and William Shirer, and the Columbia Broadcasting System (CBS), their network, made broadcast journalism history March 13, 1938, 1 a.m. London time. What set the stage was CBS founder and CEO William Paley's realization that his network had just been soundly beaten again by the National Broadcasting Company (NBC) and their reporter "Ubiquitous Max" Jordan, with his eyewitness account of Austria's downfall. Worse, the fault was Paley's. Until Jordan's story and its effect on America, Paley had supported news editor Paul White's decision not to use the network employees on hard-news reporting. To their increasing

## making journalism history

chagrin, men like Murrow and Shirer were forced to cover truly soft stories like concerts, instead of Hitler and the Third Reich's actions and intentions. Paley had had enough. He had Paul White call Shirer and tell him: "We want a European round-up tonight." The broadcast would cover the European reaction to the Nazi's Austrian takeover. The players would include Shirer in London with a member of Parliament; Murrow in Vienna; and American newspaper correspondents in Paris, Berlin, and Rome.

Eight hours to put together what had never been done before. As Stanley Cloud and Lynne Olson described in *The Murrow Boys:* "Never mind that it was five o'clock, London time, on a Sunday afternoon, which meant that all offices were closed and that all the technicians and correspondents and members of Parliament they would need were out of town, off in the country, or otherwise unreachable. Never mind the seemingly insuperable technical problems of arranging the lines and transmitters, of ensuring the necessary split-second timing. Never mind any of that. That was what being a foreign correspondent was all about. It was part of the code of the brotherhood: When the bastards asked if you could do something impossible, the only acceptable answer was yes. Shirer reached for the phone and called Murrow in Vienna."

Beginning at 8 P.M., with announcer Robert Trout's words, "We take you now to London," Murrow, Shirer, and their comrades "proved radio was not only able to report news as it occurred but also to put it in context, to link it with news from elsewhere—and do it with unprecedented speed and immediacy. They set in motion with that thirty minute broadcast in March 1938 a chain of events that would lead, in only one year, to radio's emergence as America's chief news medium and to the beginning of CBS's decades-long dominance of broadcast journalism." The broadcasts by Murrow and his team during the London blitz and over the entire course of the war set the standard for broadcast-reporting style and eloquence.

Edward R. Murrow in
London around 1940.

"we take you now to london"

# n.c. wyeth's treasure island illustrations

OH, IT WAS FUN ALL RIGHT, breaking the code and learning to read for ourselves. But there were those withdrawal pains. No more being read to. Now it was about words, not pictures. We were going to have to rely on our mind's eye for pictures. Still, we couldn't deny when we borrowed books with those earliest library cards, the secret pleasure of a book's long list of illustrations in the front and the connection to seeing the pictures in our prereading past. In few books was that reading experience more intensified by the combination of illustrations and story than in the Scribner's edition of Robert Louis Stevenson's *Treasure Island* with its unforgettable illustrations (fourteen in all) by N.C. Wyeth.

Robert Louis Stevenson had written *Treasure Island* to entertain his own grandson. Why Stevenson's story would link so strongly with N.C. Wyeth's talent and ambition can partially be explained by Stevenson's belief that "illustrations should narrate, that a picture in a storybook . . . should be the handmaiden of the text, competing with it upon equal terms." N.C. Wyeth's paintings would elevate a wonderful text into a nearly perfect reading experience.

Charles Scribner's Sons, in February 1911, had asked Wyeth to consider an assignment to illustrate an "elaborate edition" of *Treasure Island*. Wyeth agreed. He would do fourteen paintings in all for the book, each measuring 47″ x 38″—one every sixteen pages or so in the finished book. Scribner's message wired to Wyeth on seeing the completed paintings has resonated with readers ever since: "Pictures great."

Wyeth's breakthrough was the perspective of his paintings: "The reader is actually the boy (Jim Hawkins) at all times." The boy was the center of the action and so, therefore, was the reader. As Wyeth's biographer David Michaelis wrote in his outstanding Wyeth biography: "Through Jim's eyes, we confront the blind beggar under a bright-as-day moon on the lane outside the Admiral Benbow Inn. Tapping with his stick, calling out in a voice 'cruel, cold, and ugly,' Pew gropes for us from the dark recesses of his cape with an enormous outstretched hand. Not only do we experience the thrill of confronting a predator up close but we have the grisly satisfaction of absorbing every detail of one who would like to catch us but cannot."

Wyeth's illustrations, like the greatest storytellers, scare us in the safety of our imaginations; those images have retained their power to scare, no matter how many decades removed we are from our first encounter with those hard, merciless men striding across the endpapers of *Treasure Island*.

The background illustration for the blind beggar, Old Pew, was inspired by N.C. Wyeth's childhood home at 284 South Street in Needham, Massachusetts, adjacent to a street called "Blind Lane."

national geographic maps

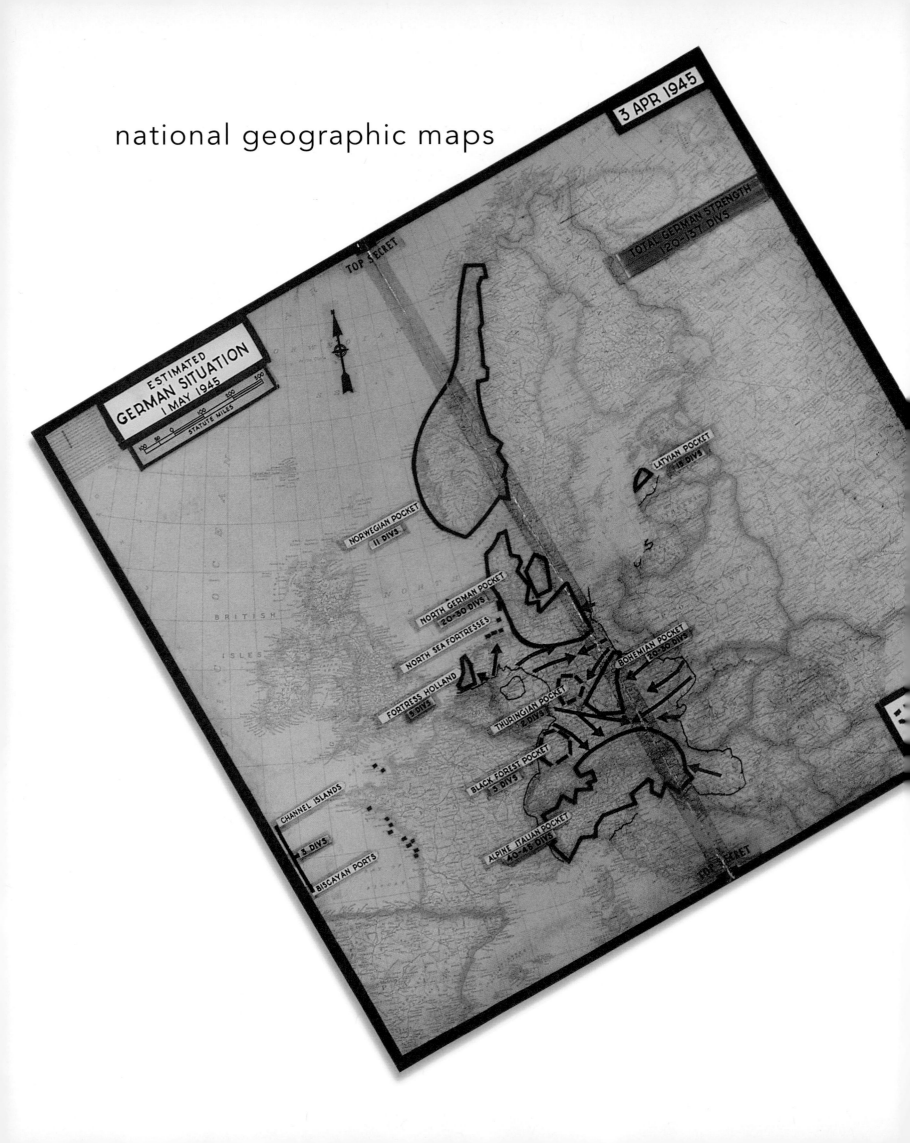

FOR OVER A CENTURY, one organization above all has given us a certain sense of where we are and where we want to go. Commanders in chief, school children, explorers, the lost, and even dedicated couch potatoes have put their justifiable faith in the splendid maps of the National Geographic Society and its cartographers. The elegant and clearly legible typefaces for place names, one source of the maps' mystique, were designed by the magazine's staff in the 1930s.

During World War II, National Geographic maps were at the epicenter of the action, thanks in part to a president who was deeply interested in geography. The Society had furnished FDR a cabinet, which was mounted on the wall behind the desk in his private White House study. Maps of continents and oceans could be pulled down like window shades by the president—and were throughout the war.

In the early winter of 1942, President Roosevelt urged the American people to try to have a map of the world available for his next Fireside Chat, scheduled for the evening of February 23. FDR told his aides: "I'm going to speak about strange places that many of them never heard of—places that are now the battleground for civilization . . . I want to explain to the people something about geography—what

## a sense of where we are

our problem is and what the overall strategy of the war has to be. I want to tell it to them in simple terms of ABC so that they will understand what is going on and how each battle fits into the picture. . . If they understand the problem and what we are driving at, I am sure that they can take any kind of bad news right on the chin."

There was an unprecedented run on maps and atlases. And that evening, 10 p.m. eastern war time, the country listened to its president, following along, absorbing the messages about what was now truly a World War. The audience, more than 80 percent of the country's adult population, was the largest for any geography lesson in history.

The National Geographic Society has gone on, expanding both its ability to map and the scope of its focus: from the amazing Mt. Everest map, to outer space, to the ocean floor. As the Geographic's former chief cartographer put it: "I like to think that National Geographic maps are the crown jewels of the mapping world!"

This National Geographic map "Estimated German Situation 1 May 1945" shows imminent Allied victory and was the last map prepared for President Roosevelt before his death on April 12, 1945. It hung in the White House Map Room until the end of the war. It was returned in 1998 to the White House by a former aide to FDR and once again hangs in the Map Room.

# navajo code talkers

## the century's best kept secret

by Jack Hitt

DURING WORLD WAR II, on the dramatic day when Marines raised the American flag to signal a key and decisive victory at Iwo Jima, the first word of this momentous news crackled over the radio in odd guttural noises and complex intonations. Throughout the war, the Japanese were repeatedly baffled and infuriated by these seemingly inhuman sounds. They conformed to no linguistic system known to the Japanese. The curious sounds were the military's one form of conveying tactics and strategy that the master cryptographers in Tokyo were unable to decipher. This perfect code was the language of the Navajo tribe. Its application in World War II as a clandestine system of communication was one of the twentieth century's best-kept secrets.

After a string of cryptographic failures, the military in 1942 was desperate for a way to open clear lines of communication among troops that would not be easily intercepted by the enemy. In the 1940s there was no such thing as a "secure line." All talk had to go out onto the public airwaves. Standard codes were an option, but the cryptographers in Japan could quickly crack them. And there was another problem: The Japanese were proficient at intercepting short-distance communications, on walkie-talkies for example, and then having well-trained English-speaking soldiers either sabotage the message or send out false commands to set up an ambush. That was the situation in 1942 when the Pentagon authorized one of the boldest gambits of the war.

Navajo Code Talker Corporal Lloyd Oliver, was a field radio operator with a Marine Artillery Regiment in the South Pacific in 1943. The Navajo Code contained 619 terms by the end of the war, all based on words used in daily life on the reservation.

The solution was conceived by the son of missionaries to the Navajos, a former Marine named Philip Johnston. His idea: station a native Navajo speaker at every radio. Since Navajo had never been written down or translated into any other language, it was an entirely self-contained human communication system restricted to Navajos alone; it was virtually indecipherable without Navajo help. Without some key or way into a language, translation is virtually impossible. Not long after the bombing of Pearl Harbor, the military dispatched twenty-nine Navajos to Camp Elliott and Camp Pendleton in California to begin a test program. These first recruits had to develop a Navajo alphabet since none existed. And because Navajo lacked technical terms of military artillery, the men coined a number of neologisms specific to their task and their war.

According to Chester Nez, one of the original code talkers: "Everything we used in the code was what we lived with on the reservation every day, like the ants, the birds, bears." Thus, the term for a tank was "turtle," a tank destroyer was "tortoise killer." A battleship was "whale." A hand grenade was "potato," and plain old bombs were "eggs." A fighter plane was "hummingbird," and a torpedo plane "swallow." A sniper was "pick 'em off." Pyrotechnic was "fancy fire."

It didn't take long for the original twenty-nine recruits to expand to an elite corps of Marines, numbering at its height 425 Navajo Code Talkers, all from the American Southwest. Each Talker was so valuable, he traveled everywhere with a personal bodyguard. In the event of capture, the Talkers had solemnly agreed to commit suicide rather than allow America's most valuable war code fall into the hands of the enemy. If a captured Navajo did not follow that grim instruction, the bodyguard's instructions were understood: shoot and kill the Code Talker.

The language of the Code Talkers, their mission, and every detail of their messaging apparatus was a secret they were all ordered to keep, even from their own families. They did. It wasn't until 1968, when the military felt convinced that the Code Talkers would not be needed for any future wars, that America learned of the incredible contribution a handful of Native Americans made to winning history's biggest war. The Navajo Code Talkers, sending and receiving as many as 800 errorless messages at fast speed during "the fog of battle" are widely credited with giving U.S. troops the decisive edge at Guadalcanal, Tarawa, Saipan, Iwo Jima, and Okinawa.

Private First Class Preston Toledo (on the left) and Private First Class Frank Toledo of the First Marine Division were cousins who served together as Navajo Code Talkers in the South Pacific.

To see this room today—its windows transparent once more, its ceiling a heavenly vault that guards against the weather and inspires all the many heads below it bowed over their textbooks and PowerBooks, their homework assignments and first drafts—to see it today in all its radiance is to be renewed. The New York Public Library's greatest single treasure, hands down, is Room 315; not merely its physical beauty, which has always been exhilarating, and never more so than now, but more its symbolic beauty. The place vibrates with feeling. It is so beautiful, that it may even distort the process of reading, making a particular book seem better than it really is. Authors should aspire to be read here.

the new york public library's
room 315

However, the most important thing to know and feel about Room 315 is that it is the most democratic room in the cultural capital of the democratic world. There are no tickets necessary here, no fees, no letters of introduction, no restrictions. The Statue of Liberty may invite the new American home; Room 315 takes them in and offers them—offers us—entry into the best of what has been thought, felt, and experienced by humankind. Nothing less than that.

There's a maxim of Schopenhauer's—never one to look on the lighter side of things—that runs: "If only, when one acquired a book, one could also acquire the time with which to read it." This room is consecrated to providing the time to read. In a land of free speech and cheap talk, the reading room isn't just a place to find knowledge and culture, but to imbibe in it. In that sense, the Reading Room is closer to an open bar than to a mausoleum. So welcoming is it that it takes discipline not to take it for granted. At the Bibliotheque Nationale, in Paris, with all its glittering glass, it takes about a week to get a book. Let us pity the poor Parisians!

## by David Remnick

As a young man—and as an old man, too—Alfred Kazin was among the many people who got their education by coming to these burnished tables and ordering up book after book, reading and staying till closing time. In one of his memoirs, Kazin recalls how he did his reading for the first great book, *On Native Grounds*. "In the midst of that endless crowd walking in and out of 315 looking for something, that Depression crowd, so pent up, searching for puzzle contests, beauty contests, clues to buried treasure off of Sandy Hook; seeking lost and dead rich relatives in old New York books of genealogy and Pittsburgh telephone books . . . there was something about the vibrating empty rooms early in the morning—light falling through the great tall windows. The sun burning smooth the tops of the golden tables as if they had been freshly painted—that made me restless with the need to grab up every book, press into every single mind right there in the open shelves. My book was building itself."

Though reading is a solitary pleasure, Kazin of course, was far from alone. The young James Baldwin, too, was one who came to 42nd Street from Harlem, frightened at first by the stone lions and the building, "unimaginably vast." But like so many others before him, Baldwin joined the others at the tables in 315, and we know what he left behind, what he, like Kazin and so many others, added to the life of the imagination, to our active shelves.

157

# the new york times

AS A YOUNG MAN from the distant dunes of South Jersey I arrived in Manhattan almost a half-century ago to embark on a vaguely defined apprenticeship within the newsroom of *The New York Times*, filling paste pots and performing other menial chores as required by my elders who each day wrote and edited without apparent effort millions of words that more or less conformed to the standards of the *Times*'s late publisher, Adolph S. Ochs, and his motto: "All the News That's Fit to Print."

Although Mr. Ochs had died eighteen years before I joined the paper in the early summer of 1953, I sensed the essence of this man constantly as I made my daily rounds carrying news summaries and memos into the offices of various executives and administrators. Framed photographs of Mr. Ochs were hung everywhere. Two bronze statues reflecting his patriarchal persona greeted visitors in the lobby and also up on the fourteenth floor where the stockholders and directors met. And his name was referred to regularly in the elevators, in the corridors, and within the nooks and crannies of the Gothic building's cavernous interior, especially when the conversationalists were veteran employees who were fast approaching retirement age and were alarmed by what they perceived to be the infiltration of undignified, modern trends threatening the venerable traditions of the *Times*: "Did you see what made Page One today?" one of them might ask, adding: "Oh, Mr. Ochs must be turning over in his grave!"

I was quite familiar with the professional reputation of Mr. Ochs long before I came to New York, having as a schoolboy in the late 1940s overheard many discussions about him between my father (who avidly read the *Times*, receiving it in the mail each day three days late), and an elderly distinguished author and journalist named Garet Garrett—for whom my tailor-father made suits—who had once been an editorial writer for the *Times* with close personal ties to Mr. Ochs.

While the seventy-year-old Mr. Garrett then lived in virtual retirement in a New Jersey farm house some miles from the island resort of Ocean City where I was born and reared, he nonetheless personified the metropolitan splendor and sophistication to which I someday hoped to escape, and his many reverential references to Mr. Ochs prompted me to borrow a book about the *Times* from the town library—then located within the Ocean City High School—in the front of which, in stone lettering, bore the name "OCHS."

by Gay Talese

above left: The legacy of the modern *New York Times* began when Aldoph S. Ochs (shown above) purchased the bankrupt paper in 1896. **top:** April 13, 1945 **center:** April 15, 1970 **bottom:** December 8, 1941

**The New York Times**

LATE CITY EDITION

VOL. CXXVIII....No.44,207

NEW YORK, FRIDAY, MAY 4, 1979

20 CENTS

PRODUCER PRICES UP BY 0.9% FOR APRIL; FOOD DOWN A LITTLE

Rises Expected to Keep Consumer Costs High and Further Harm Carter Fight on Inflation

## CONSERVATIVES WIN BRITISH VOTE; MARGARET THATCHER FIRST WOMAN TO HEAD A EUROPEAN GOVERNMENT

BIG SWING INDICATED

Tory Leader Given a Clear Mandate to Change the Country's Course

Ribicoff Decides He Won't Seek A Fourth Term

Margaret Thatcher leaving polling station after casting her vote in London yesterday.

Terrorists Bomb the Rome Offices Of the Christian Democratic Party

'Genuine' Tory Taking Charge

Margaret Roberts Thatcher

For Central Park Bird Watchers, Thrills Take Flight Every Spring

Bird watchers stalking their "prey" early yesterday morning in Central Park

---

**The New York Times**

LATE CITY EDITION

VOL. CXXII...No.42,112

NEW YORK, SATURDAY, MAY 12, 1973

15 CENTS

## PENTAGON PAPERS CHARGES ARE DISMISSED; JUDGE BYRNE FREES ELLSBERG AND RUSSO, ASSAILS 'IMPROPER GOVERNMENT CONDUCT'

White House Says Attacks Will Continue in Cambodia

GRAY CALL TO NIXON

Said to Inform Inquiry It Came 3 Weeks After Watergate

NEW TRIAL BARRED

But Decision Does Not Solve Constitutional Issues in Case

Air of Expectancy, Then Tears, Shouts, Embraces

Judge William Matthew Byrne Jr., above, threw out the Pentagon papers case and, left, defendants were freed. They are Anthony J. Russo Jr., left, and Dr. Daniel Ellsberg.

Sudan Puts Off Trying 8 Who Killed U.S. Envoys

A New Grand Jury Reported Planning To Summon Biaggi

CONNALLY TO TAKE LEAVE FROM FIRM

New Adviser to President Will Also Resign From All Corporate Boards

Congress Ascending

Watergate Seen as Altering Balance Between Executive and Capitol Hill

2-GERMANY PACT IS VOTED IN BONN

Parliament Also Approves Joining United Nations

Norton Simon Bought Smuggled Idol

The bronze statue of the Hindu deity Siva

86th St. Toonerville Tale: 3 Flee From a Police Van

NIXON AGAIN ASKS LEGAL AID TO POOR

Independent Agency Would Replace O.E.O. Unit

257

Adolph Ochs was the first of six children born to a German Jewish immigrant couple who had met and married in the American South before the Civil War; and while Adolph's father was an erudite and refined man of varied talents, making money was not one of them. And so the young Adolph—who at fourteen was a floor sweeper and clerk with *The Knoxville Chronicle*; who at eighteen was a typesetter and reporter with *The Louisville Courier-Journal*; and who at twenty (with a down payment of $250 on a total sales price of $5,750) became the owner of the declining *Chattanooga Times*—emerged prematurely as his family's patriarch, its energizer, its exemplar of a work ethic and a master planner who would bring prosperity and status to himself and to those family members whom he would attract into the newspaper business.

What Mr. Ochs did with *The Chattanooga Times* was what he would later do, on a much grander scale, with *The New York Times*—he made it into a *news*paper and not a gazette of opinion, or a showcase for star writers, or a champion of the underdog or topdog, or a crusader for political or social reform. Ochs had something to sell—news—and he intended to sell it dispassionately and with the guarantee that it was reliable, verifiable, and not deviously inspired.

In 1896, when he was thirty-eight, Adolph Ochs acquired the bankrupt *New York Times* for $75,000; founded in 1851, the newspaper was losing $1,000 a day and had $300,000 in unpaid bills when Ochs took it over and quickly transformed it: He eliminated the installments of romantic fiction that the earlier management believed would lure readers, and eschewing scandalous stories based on gossip, he expanded the coverage of financial news, business trends, real-estate transactions, the official if dreary activities of government that other newspapers of the day had long ignored. He wanted a paper of record, one that each day would publish a record of every fire in New York, the arrival time of every mail ship, the names of every official visitor to the White House, the precise moment the sun set and the moon rose. He said he wanted his paper to be impartial and complete—and "not soil the breakfast linen."

Throughout his publishing career he made brilliant business decisions—his genius had been not only in the type of newspaper he created but that he had made such a newspaper pay. And on the occasion of his seventy-fifth birthday in 1933 he issued an optimistic public statement in the aftermath of America's Great Depression in which he asserted that "we are sobering up and painfully getting our house in order. The tragic experience we are having will result in educating the people that care, caution, and conservatism are as necessary in economics as in physical health, and that the Ten Commandments and the Sermon on the Mount cannot be ignored, nor forgotten. They should continue to be our guide to a philosophy of life."

Ochs's daughter and only child, the late grand dame of the *Times* Iphigene Sulzberger, in seeking to explain the paper's greatness—and specifically why it survived while numerous other publications of merit failed—often retold the story of a traveler who meets three stonecutters along a road one day and asks each of them what he is doing. The first stonecutter says, "I am cutting stone." The second stonecutter, when the question is repeated, replied, "I am making a corner stone." But when the question is asked of the third stonecutter, he answers, "I am building a cathedral." The strength of the *Times*, said Iphigene Sulzberger, derives from a tradition in which most of its people are cathedral-builders, not stonecutters.

In 1992, Iphigene's forty-year-old grandson, Arthur Ochs Sulzberger Jr., became the publisher; and in his opening statement he emphasized that while the nation and New York City were then in an economic recession that was diminishing the newspaper's advertising revenue—and had cut the *Times*'s 1991 projected earnings to less than 60 cents a share as compared with 1990's 85 cents a share—the *Times* would not cut back on the expense of full coverage of the news at home or abroad.

While losing large sums of money is not a casual matter at the *Times,* it is a fact that for more than a century the Ochs and Sulzberger family proprietors have confronted financial crisis in every generation without ever reducing the quality of the newspaper or otherwise succumbing to the bottom-line mentality that is characteristic of so many modern American corporations. As the new publisher said, "If you have quality information, profit will follow."

The fifth publisher of *The New York Times* continued his statement on the editorial page: "It has been four generations since Adolph S. Ochs laid down the precepts that have successfully guided *The New York Times* for 96 years. Those principles have been carried forward with distinction by my grandfather, Arthur Hays Sulzberger; my uncle, Orvil E. Dryfoos; and my father, Arthur Ochs Sulzberger. Each of these men, in their message upon being named Publisher, quoted the pledge Mr. Ochs made when he took the helm of the Times: 'To give the news impartially, without fear or favor, regardless of any party, sect or interest involved . . . '"

top: October 30, 1929

bottom: December 11, 1936

Feb. 20 & 27, 1995    Price $2.95

# THE NEW YORKER

# by John Updike

GREATNESS did not come immediately to *The New Yorker,* which was founded in February 1925. But it had going for it the zeal and enthusiasm of its founder and first editor, Harold Ross, and the financial indulgence of his principle backer, Raoul Fleischmann, and the elegance of its first cover, displaying the knickerbocker dandy drawn by Rea Irvin and later dubbed Eustace Tilley. Its cover was the best thing about the first issue—"The magazine *stank*," Fleischmann is supposed to have pronounced—and until the reign of Tina Brown as editor (1992–1998), the same cover, unchanged but for the slowly rising price of the magazine (the first issue cost 15 cents), ran on every anniversary issue, the third week of February.

The first year was perilous; by its fourth month of publication, *The New Yorker*'s circulation had sunk to 4,000 (from an initial 15,000) and there were only three or four pages of advertising in each issue. Fleischmann narrowly agreed to keep things running through the summer, and by fall the magazine was finding its own tone. The liveliness of the times helped. New York was at its gaudiest in these Prohibition years; American writing, graphic art, and musical comedy were feeling their oats; and soon a host of bright, young talents was attracted to the pages of this hopeful little weekly. Some, like Robert Benchley and Ralph Barton, already had established names; others, like E.B. White, came in from the cold of advertising work (in 1926). White brought in James Thurber after him. The cartoonists Peter Arno and Helen Hokinson became regulars that first year, as did Janet Flanner, who contributed her letters from Paris under the pseudonym "Genet." Katherine Angell, later to become White's wife, came aboard as editor, and her Bryn Mawr-educated taste proved an important complement to Ross's newspaperish idea, both prim and rowdy, of a magazine. As well as getting funnier, *The New Yorker* in its fiction, reporting, and poetry got more serious. It flourished during the Depression—so much so that Ross and Fleischmann, who wanted to keep their pet in bounds, actively discouraged new subscriptions.

165

Greatness, perhaps, arrived in the years of World War II, which was excellently covered by such correspondents as A.J. Liebling and Daniel Lang. A stripped-down overseas "pony" edition introduced the magazine to G.I.s, thousands of whom became subscribers after the war. The devotion, in 1946, of an entire issue to John Hersey's account of the dropping of the atom bomb on Hiroshima, demonstrated to all that *The New Yorker* was no longer a merely funny magazine. William Shawn, the fact editor who persuaded Ross to make this striking gesture—the issue omitted cartoons and Talk of the Town—succeeded to the editorship of the magazine on Ross's untimely death in 1951.

Shawn's long reign from 1951 to 1987 saw a financial heyday and then a decline in advertising revenue; Peter Fleischmann, Raoul's son, sold the magazine to Condé Nast Publications in 1985. Shawn was, against his will, eased out two years later; the short reign of Robert Gottlieb ended in 1992; Tina Brown shook up the format and the traditional demeanor of understatement; and now David Remnick, a thirty-nine-year-old writer for the magazine, calmly leads it, its fifth editor, into an uncertain future. *The New Yorker* as I knew it, from my first acquaintance with its pages as a child of about eleven, and then as a contributor from the age of twenty-two, seemed unique—not only the best general magazine in America, but perhaps the best that America ever produced. What was great about it, from a reader's point of view, was the variety and intelligence of its written contents, the beauty and energy of its cartoons, the dependable factual and typographical accuracy, and the enclosing decorum and decency of it all. The writer's name appeared at the end, there were no bothersome, cute editor-manufactured subheads to "hook" the reader, and for a long time there was not even a table of contents, the product was so pure. Everything in the magazine was trusted to speak for itself. Take it or leave it, the pages implied: Shawn claimed that the editors merely published what they found interesting, and gave no thought to pleasing an imagined or projected readership.

facing page: Charles Addams's cartoon appeared in *The New Yorker* in 1940. top: Harold Ross was *The New Yorker*'s founder and first editor.

From a contributor's point of view, these external virtues were matched by an incomparably solicitous editing process, one that sometimes irked with its thoroughness but saved a writer from many a slip and prodded him to many an improvement. The old editors—in my dealings, Mrs. White, William Maxwell, G.S. Lobrano, Howard Moss, and Shawn himself—radiated gratitude for what they considered a worthy contribution. They had uncanny ears for a false note; they sometimes surprised you by accepting a daring or experimental piece; they manifested a cloistered virtue, in a fallen, hustling world, that made appearing anywhere else feel like a dangerous trespass. To be sure, there were quirks of editorial taste and a prudery that became anachronistic; still, your words looked better in *The New Yorker* than anywhere else. As the poet William Stafford once told me, a poem in *The New Yorker* was like a letter to your friends. For a young short-story writer, appearing there opened doors to publishing houses.

The magazine's towering integrity rested on a handful of personalities, those of Ross and Shawn foremost, and yet held for sixty years, through week after week of words and images, and set a standard that still haunts the national literary consciousness. Without *The New Yorker* in this century, everyone's sights would have been lowered.

the oklahoma land rush of 1889

"a handful of white dice thrown out across the prairie"

AT THE STROKE OF NOON on April 22, 1889, the largest one-day settlement of land in American history began. Free land for the taking! It didn't matter who you were or where you came from, just get there first and stake your claim. With the sound of "Dinner Call" from the soldiers' bugles, thousands of people at points along every border of the area fanned out across the open prairie of Oklahoma territory to claim a plot of 160 acres to call their own. When the dust settled, they had claimed 3,125 square miles, an area more than twice the size of Rhode Island. Reporters from Eastern newspapers and magazines arriving to cover the story found plenty to write about. The sheer mass of humanity, the noise, the impatient urgency of the scene came alive in one reporter's overheated account: "The long row toeing this line is bending forward, panting with excitement, and looking with greedy eyes toward the new Canaan, the women with their dresses tucked up to their knees, the men stripped of coats and waistcoats for the race to follow. And then a trumpet call, answered by a thousand hungry yells from all along the line, and hundreds of men and women on foot and on horseback break way across the prairie."

They were headed for some two million acres of United States land that had not been assigned to the Creek and Seminole Indian tribes in earlier treaties. A *St. Louis Dispatch* reporter wrote of a minister's conversation with a man driving a wagon getting set to go after his land. When the minister offered a religious tract to the driver, he was told to keep it. The minister asked, "Don't you want to go to Heaven?" The man replied, "That's just where I'm headed." When President Benjamin Harrison signed the bill that opened the land the month before in March 1889, it became known as "Harrison's Hoss Race" or simply "The Run." What had been wide-open prairie was settled almost overnight. Tents went up, businesses opened, and postal service began. *Harper's Weekly* reported that Oklahoma City, only days after the land run, looked like a "handful of white dice thrown out across the prairie."

preceding page: This photo is often identified as the start of the Oklahoma Land Rush in 1889; it's not. The picture was actually taken four years later, at the opening of another run, to the Cherokee Outlet, on September 16, 1893, by one of three associates working for the photographer William S. Prettyman. Prettyman had covered the 1889 opening, but instead of photographing the frenetic start of the biggest race for free land in U.S. history, he photographed wagons crossing the flood swollen Salt Fort River. This explains why one photo collector describes Prettyman as "a photographer by design and a historian by chance" and why no photographs of the start of the 1889 land rush exist.

Free land, lots of land, underneath the prairie skies created a powerful allure. Who made the run? Pennsylvania miners, Indiana bricklayers, Michigan lumbermen, and New York pharmacists, plus assorted butchers, tailors, and blacksmiths. A group of Mormons traveled east from Utah to stake their claims. The news of free land even crossed the Atlantic, increasing the number of immigrants who traveled in steerage from the ports of Liverpool, Bremen, Hamburg, and Antwerp.

Some arrived by train, planning simply to set out on foot, with little more than a blanket to sleep on. Others had well thought out plans. Families drove prairie schooners, huge wagons filled with furniture, household goods, farming implements, and food. Men planning to start a business brought whatever they'd need: well-drilling equipment, medicine, or a law library. Those who could afford a fast horse—some paid up to $500 for a racehorse—could count on staking their claims ahead of the wagons. To speed the process, they used willow poles, sharpened at one end, a name and claim attached to the other. They could thrust them into the ground while racing at full gallop around the perimeter of their claim.

Despite U.S. soldiers' efforts to prevent anyone crossing the line until noon on April 22, 1889, many jumped the gun to stake their claim, then went into hiding to avoid detection by patrolling soldiers. They were called "Sooners," and were initially hated by those who played by the rules. In time, Sooners became a positive, not a pejorative, term; getting there first, as the Sooners did, became part of the American grain. Although estimates of the number of people who made The Run in 1889 range from 12,000 to 100,000, the federal census of 1890 counted 53,822 inhabitants. In less than twenty years the newly settled land won statehood. Theodore Roosevelt signed the proclamation on November 16, 1907, making Oklahoma the forty-sixth state in the Union.

# the outermost house

CERTAIN WRITERS LEAVE society's center and tumult and head to the edges of the world. There they are able to write and think clearly for themselves about what should count. Thoreau's *Walden* is in that tradition and so is a less well-known book titled *The Outermost House* by Henry Beston, the story of the year from 1926 to 1927 he spent on the Great Beach of Cape Cod. Out of this sense of remove, even isolation, a writer often finds the clarity necessary to strip life down to its grain. The books that result then help us to see clearly that there is more to life than getting.

*The Outermost House* restores our sense of proportion, physically and philosophically. First there is the house Beston himself designed and built on top of a dune near Cape Cod's Eastham. Twenty feet by sixteen feet, two rooms, a kitchen-living room, and a bedroom. Displaying what he called a "somewhat amateur enthusiasm for windows," there were seventeen windows in all. Hugging the dune twenty feet above high-water mark thirty feet from the great beach, "the ocean besieged my door," he wrote. Only to the north, Nauset Light, "had I touch with human things. On its solitary dune my house faced the four walls of the world."

This was Beston's headquarters for what stretched into a year, beginning in September 1926, when the twenties were still roaring. What he recorded reminds us, if we're alert, what's there to see. New Year's Day, 1927, a flock of ruddy turnstones took flight as he approached.

Henry Beston built his little house which he called the Fo'c'sle on the dunes of Nauset Spit, on Cape Cod's outermost beach in 1926. It was swept out to sea in the fierce winter hurricane of February 1978.

I shall always remember this picture as one of the most beautiful touches of colour I have ever seen in nature, for the three dominant colours of this bird—who is a little larger than the semipalmated sandpiper—are black, white, and glowing chestnut red; and these colours are interestingly displayed in patches and bold stripes seen at their best when the bird is flying. The great dunes behind them and the long vista of the beach were cold silver overlaid with that faint, loveliest violet which is the overtone colour of the coast.

There is nothing dated about this book or its point of view. When he writes, "The world today is sick to its thin blood for lack of elemental things, for fire before the hands, for water welling up from the earth, for air, for the dear earth itself underfoot," he talks directly to us, seventy-five years later, as surely as Thoreau does from the shores of Walden Pond. Rachael Carson, whose voice sounded an early, eloquent alarm about what we were doing to our natural world, said *The Outermost House* was the only book that influenced her writing. The creation of the Cape Cod National Seashore in 1961 was motivated by Beston's book, first published in 1928.

So what of the fate of the little house where the story of "a year on the Great Beach of Cape Cod" was created? A winter hurricane of unparalleled intensity in February 1978 swept the house off its pinnings into the marsh; from there it floated out in a storm-formed inlet into the ferocity of the surf and, as one writer put it, perished. Well-meaning people have wanted to rebuild the Outermost House; many Cape Cod natives believe, however, it was a natural death, and resist the idea. Maybe they're right. For Beston's book serves as a more powerful memorial than a mere facsimile of his house.

# the paris review interviews with writers

## getting black on white

*THE PARIS REVIEW,* which is not a review and headquartered on New York's Upper East Side, was founded in 1953. From the outset the founding editors, led by its editor-in-chief, George Plimpton, were determined to "make no compromise with public taste." The compelling evidence of that determination is borne out by two facts: that its circulation in the intervening forty-six years has grown to 12,000 and that no issue has ever been profitable. The circulation, Plimpton believes, could easily be improved if more people on the *Review* masthead, one of the largest of any publication, would subscribe. Having the son of the Aga Khan as your first publisher no doubt helped the magazine avoid getting preoccupied with making a buck.

The *Review* from the outset felt a responsibility to introduce writers of promise. And they have and continue to fulfill that responsibility: Philip Roth, T. Coraghessan Boyle, Mona Simpson, Evan S. Connell, and Jay McInerney to name a few. Plimpton admits the editors have blown some. What he calls "an almost perfect story," the Pension Grillparzer section from John Irving's *The World According to Garp* was turned down by an editor because it was "too derivative of Thomas Pynchon." William Kennedy, Pulitzer Prize-winning author of *Ironweed*, also received his share of rejection slips from *The Paris Review*, Plimpton, years later, was embarrassed to learn. The review's first poetry editor, Donald Hall, rejected an early poem of Allen Ginsberg, prompting Ginsberg to write George Plimpton that Hall would not recognize a poem if it buggered him in broad daylight.

But the greatest gift of all bestowed by *The Paris Review* on its readers are the remarkable interviews with writers that have been published in every issue beginning with the first (an interview with E.M. Forster on the craft of writing). These interviews are revealing and, most significantly, they are collaborative. Unlike today when interviewers try so often to overshadow or even ambush interviewees, *The Paris Review* insists that the writer's point of view prevail. Frequently, the interviewers will send a copy of the interview to the writer and the writer can then edit or adjust their responses.

This July 1963 issue featured an interview with Norman Mailer.

Here are four examples:

*How much of a book is in your mind before you start?*

PHILIP ROTH: "What matters most isn't there at all. I don't mean the solutions to problems; I mean the problems themselves. You're looking, as you begin, for what's going to resist you. You're looking for trouble. Sometimes in the beginning uncertainty arises not because the writing is difficult but because it isn't difficult enough. Fluency can be a sign that nothing is happening; fluency can actually be my signal to stop, while being in the dark from sentence to sentence is what convinces me to go on."

*Do you think a style can be cultivated or at least refined?*

KATHERINE ANNE PORTER: "I've been called a stylist until I really could tear my hair out. And I simply don't believe in style. The style is you. Oh, you can cultivate a style, I suppose, if you like. But I should say it remains a cultivated style. It remains artificial and imposed, and I don't think it deceives anyone. A cultivated style would be like a mask. Everyone knows it's a mask and sooner or later you must show yourself— or at least, you show yourself as someone who could not afford to show himself, and so created something to hide behind.

"Style is the man. Aristotle said it first, as far as I know, and everybody has said it since, because it is one of those unarguable truths. You do not create a style. You work, and develop yourself; your style is an emanation from your own being."

*Do you keep notes, or a journal, or diaries, or write scenarios? What's your preparatory material?*

NORMAN MAILER: "That also varies with each of the books. For *The Naked and the Dead* I had a file full of notes, and a long dossier on each man. Many of these details never got into the novel, but the added knowledge made me feel more comfortable with each character. Indeed I even had charts to show which characters had not yet had scenes with the other characters. For a book which seems spontaneous on its surface, *The Naked and the Dead* was written mechanically. I studied engineering at Harvard and I suppose it was the book of a young engineer."

*What, then would you say is the source of most of your work?*

DOROTHY PARKER: "Need for money, dear."

These interviews, especially in collections that come out every few years, are a great enduring gift to the nation. Don't, for a moment longer, leave your library without *The Paris Review*.

# the pony express

UNTIL THE SPRING OF 1860, it was a long twenty days by stage-coach for mail to get from St. Joseph, Missouri, to Sacramento, California. Maybe longer in the winter. Too long in any case for businesses and merchants. Finally, the stagecoach company of Russell, Majors, and Waddell, of Leavenworth, Kansas, created an entirely new standard for delivery speed. Charging $2 to $10 per ounce, depending on the distance, their idea, the Pony Express, cut the delivery time in half. Whatever was charged, however, wasn't enough; the owners never made money. But their idea and the young, hell-bent-for-leather Pony Express riders intrigued the nation. In *Roughing It*, Samuel Clemens, aka Mark Twain, described the excitement of spotting a rider from his stagecoach:

Presently the driver exclaims: "HERE HE COMES!" Every neck is stretched further, and every eye strained wider. Away across the endless dead level of the prairie a black speck appears against the sky, and it is plain that it moves. Well, I should think so! In a second or two, it becomes a horse and rider rising and falling, rising and falling—sweeping us nearer and nearer—growing more and more distinct, more and more sharply defined—near and still nearer, and the flutter of the hoofs comes faintly to the ear—another instant a whoop and a hurrah from our upper deck, a wave of the rider's hand, but no reply, and man and horse burst past our excited faces, and go winging away like a belated fragment of a storm!

The Pony Express began on Tuesday, April 3, 1860. Every Wednesday and Saturday, one rider would leave at noon from Sacramento heading east, another from St. Joseph, at 8 A.M., heading west. Riders would cover seventy-five to one hundred miles, averaging eight miles an hour; every ten to twelve miles they would change horses at a relay station. The payload was twenty pounds of letters, all tucked into a Mexican saddlebag, known as a *mochila*. The letters were wrapped in oiled silk to keep them dry when rivers or streams were forded. At "home stations," an incoming rider would pass the *mochila* on to a new rider; then he'd bunk down until the mail returned going in the opposite direction; rested, he was off again, back the way he had come.

The dedication of the daring young riders became a staple for bedtime stories. Children heard about nineteen-year-old Jack Keetley, who rode 340 miles in 31 hours. No stops, until he was taken from the saddle sound asleep at the end of his ride.

Speed mattered to Americans even then, and the Pony Express was, in every way, about speed; even its history went by in a flash—nineteen months, two weeks, three days, and the bold experiment was finished, a victim of technology. The ride lasted from April 3, 1860, to November 20, 1861: 596,501 miles in all, 30,700 pieces of mail, and one lost *mochila*.

The Pony Express and its eighty expert riders, 400 horses and 190 relay stations all became irrelevant on October 24, 1861, with the completion of the transcontinental telegraph line. That pattern of one innovation one technology, giving way to another continues—and accelerates—with Federal Express, the fax, and e-mail. The pace quickens, but no matter how fast change comes it will never outrun the mystique of those black specks, racing toward us from the horizon.

the populists

"caught in the tentacles of circumstance"

by Kevin Baker

AFTER THE CIVIL WAR, thousands of farmers found themselves sinking into a European-style serfdom. By 1883, they were at their wits' end, boxed into peonage by nearly every other element of society.

The monopolistic pricing practices of merchants and railroads ate up their profits. They were hamstrung by the federal government's decision to return to the gold standard after the Civil War; the capricious demands of Wall Street drained money not only out of rural banks but entire regions. They were bedeviled by the conundrum that the harder they worked, the more they produced, the less they had to show for it.

An early attempt to band together, called "The Farmer's Alliance," to do something for themselves began in Lampasas County, Texas in 1877. The Alliance spread quickly to Kansas, but by 1883 it seemed to be running out of steam.

Enter the first Populist, a thirty-six-year old, former tenant farmer from Mississippi, S.O. Daws. It was Daws's brainstorm to make the Alliance an overtly political organization, with its own "People's" or "Populist" platform, candidates, and party structure; but his real genius lay in his dazzling oratory and his grasp of tactics.

Daws got the Alliance to appoint him "Traveling Lecturer," and he spread the word by mouth and by foot, moving about the country, telling his fellow farmers what they had to do. One of his converts, a thirty-four-year old Tennessean named William Lamb, had all of twenty-five days of formal education but an unsurpassed talent for organization.

Together, Daws and Lamb provided the spark the Alliance had been missing; they used the sweeping executive powers the farmers granted them to bring hundred of thousands of new recruits into the fold. All told, they enlisted some 2 million people in forty-three states—an accomplishment the leading Populist historian, Lawrence Goodwyn, characterized as the most massive organizing drive of any citizen institution in nineteenth-century America.

Yet the Populists were never about their leaders. They were about an idea—or rather, many ideas, anything that might enable men to make a living off the land without losing every shred of human dignity. Over the years, they have been derided as nativist boobs, and worse, in part because of latter-day imitators. But at their best, at the beginning, they were staunchly antiracist, and brought a firestorm of new ideas into what had become a moribund American political system.

The Populists' political program included a graduated income tax, the eight-hour work day, direct election of U.S. senators, the use of citizen referendums, the secret ballot, laws to protect union organizing—and, above all, some kind of regulation of the agricultural markets, to ensure farmers received a decent return on their labors. Many of these ideas, of course, were taken up by subsequent, progressive movements and eventually adopted. Former President Lyndon B. Johnson's father, Sam Ealy Johnson, a rural legislator who served in the Texas House of Representatives from 1905–1924, believed "the job of government is to help people who are caught in the tentacles of circumstance." His belief was undoubtedly Populist inspired.

Time and fate worked against the Populists. They were undermined by an increasingly industrialized America. But what ultimately derailed the Populists was the lure of the city—not just in America, but all over the Western world. After running their candidate for president in 1892, and winning numerous state, local, and even congressional elections, they folded themselves into William Jennings Bryan's silver wing of the Democratic Party.

Their real legacy lived on in a thousand other ways, both more and less tangible. Here were men and women capable of standing in the hot sun for hours, listening to speeches about obscure and esoteric subjects like the ever-normal granary and the sub-treasury system. Here were people willing to form collectives, cooperative stores, credit unions, and whatever other innovations it took to stand up to the faceless, money men who used them all until they were all used up.

"How is a democratic culture created?" asked Goodwyn, surveying the Populists's massive rallies out on the lonely plains of Kansas and Texas.

"Apparently in such prosaic, powerful ways. When a farm family's wagon crested a hill en route to a Fourth of July 'Alliance Day' encampment and the occupants looked back to see thousands of other families trailed out behind them in wagon trains, the thought that 'the Alliance is the people and the people are together' took on transforming possibilities. Such a moment—and the Alliance experience was to yield hundreds of them—instilled hope in hundreds of thousands of people who had been without it."

preceding page: This farming couple in Custer County, Nebraska, 1888, used every bit of their land for crops. **right:** Old Glory, Mr. and Mrs. James Pierce, Kearney, Nebraska, 1886.

WILLIAM FAULKNER didn't give a damn about self-promotion. In fact, you could spell his last name with or without the "u." "Either way suits me," he said. When he was a little boy, his parents took him to visit the great Confederate general, James Longstreet. Little William asked the general, who had lost the battle, "What was the matter with you at Gettysburg?" He was prickly his whole life. Asked about grants, Faulkner said: "I've never known anything good in writing to come from having accepted any free gift of money. The good writer never applies to a foundation. He's too busy writing something." But as much as his work was admired by other writers, by 1945 all of his books, except for two, were out of print.

Yet just four years later, the colossally myopic Nobel Prize committee made an unusually clear-sighted decision to award its prize for literature to Faulkner. A major reason for the award, and for Faulkner's revival, was the critic Malcolm Cowley, about whom Faulkner would say, "I owe him a debt no man could ever repay." Cowley's rescue of Faulkner reminds us that greatness, in its own time—and even for all time—can be overlooked and that we owe a considerable debt to those who recognize, or rediscover, greatness on our behalf.

In June of 1943, Faulkner found an unopened letter in his desk, where it had lain for three months, ignored because he didn't recognize the return address. The letter was from Malcolm Cowley, seeking permission to visit Faulkner for the purpose of a long essay the critic intended to write to "redress the balance between Faulkner's worth and his reputation." With Faulkner's blessing, Cowley completed the essay the next year. Although the piece encountered some resistance, it was finally accepted by *The New York Times Book Review*. An excerpt was published in the October 29, 1944 issue, and with that Faulkner's rediscovery had begun.

In August of the next year, Faulkner heard from Cowley that Viking Press would publish *The Portable Faulkner*, as part of its Portable Library Series. It was to be a collection of excerpts from Faulkner's works, edited and introduced by Cowley. Still, the corner had been turned. Cowley was subsequently able to interest Random House in printing new editions of *The Sound and the Fury* and *As I Lay Dying*. Faulkner was pleased but still abided by his own code. When, for instance, Cowley suggested to Faulkner that he ask Hemingway to write a preface, Faulkner refused, saying, "It's like asking one race horse in the middle of the race to broadcast a blurb on another horse in the same running field."

Malcolm Cowley believed in Faulkner's work and used his own reputation and talent to stay the course. Recognition for Faulkner's work was resurrected in his lifetime and, even more importantly, in the lifetimes of readers who may otherwise have missed altogether the road to Yoknapatawpha County.

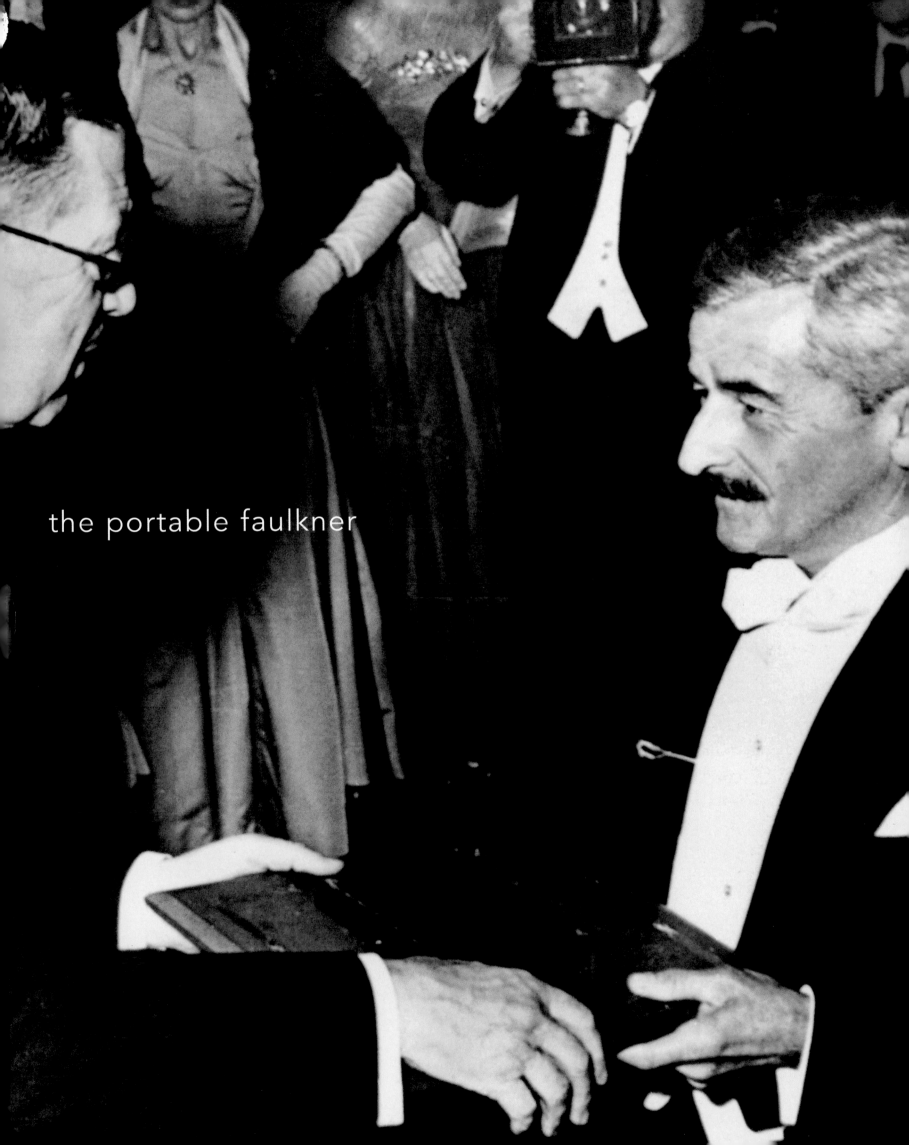

the portable faulkner

the transfer of presidential power

by Michael Beschloss

IN THE SUMMER OF 1933 a group of financiers dabbled at a plot to overthrow the President of the United States. Irate at Franklin Roosevelt's efforts to redistribute American wealth, they secretly asked a popular, newly-retired two-time Medal of Honor winner, General Smedley Butler, to issue the president an ultimatum: FDR must plead incapacitation caused by polio and allow a substitute, chosen by them, to run the country on their behalf. If Roosevelt balked, General Butler would march with a half million war veterans against the White House and force him out of power. Butler refused to play ball. Years later, House Speaker John McCormack said he could not "emphasize too strongly" Butler's role "in exposing the fascist plot . . . by persons possessing tremendous wealth."

John F. Kennedy was not convinced that a coup d'etat against a president could never happen here. With his trenchant imagination and his James Bond-like affinity for danger, JFK privately mused that a military plot like the one in *Seven Days in May* (1962) might succeed if a president thwarted the generals too many times, as he had done during the Bay of Pigs crisis.

In August 1974, when President Richard Nixon was about to be impeached, some worried that he might use extra-constitutional means to keep himself in power. Defense Secretary James Schlesinger told the Joint Chiefs that any military command from Nixon should first be referred to him. Nixon's Chief of Staff, General Alexander Haig, discussed surrounding the White House with the 82nd Airborne Division.

Dramatic stories, but if you look at American history, what strikes you is not how fragile but how resilient is the process by which we transfer power from one president to another. For this we can thank not only the framers of the Constitution, who worked hard to prevent the rise of an American dictator, but also the human beings who have carried out the sometimes ambiguous strictures of the document.

When the newly-inaugurated President William Henry Harrison died in 1841, his Vice President, John Tyler, established a precedent by insisting that he and others who succeeded to the office by death, resignation, or removal be 100 percent authentic president, not some "acting" chief executive.

During World War II, there were rumors that President Roosevelt might suspend the presidential election of 1944, but the thought never crossed FDR's mind. He thought that to hold the national plebiscite while Americans were fighting would be a magnificent demonstration to the world of what democracy was all about.

After the hairbreadth election of 1960, Richard Nixon toyed with demanding an investigation of vote fraud in Illinois and Texas. If he prevailed, he would defeat John F. Kennedy after all. The Senate Republican leader, Everett Dirksen, told Nixon to insist on a recount. Worried that Nixon might contest the outcome, the nervous JFK asked to see him privately in Florida and conceded that "we still don't know who really won the election."

Nixon was convinced—and remained so until his death—that Kennedy's allies had stolen victory. Unwilling to look like a sore loser, he also believed that throwing the people's choice into the courts for months, until well after Inauguration Day, was too great a price to pay for the presidency. In an act of statesmanship for which he never got sufficient credit, Nixon gave up his claim.

Aboard Air Force One at Love Field in Dallas, on November 22, 1963, an hour after John F. Kennedy's murder, Lyndon Johnson wanted to be sworn in as president as fast as possible. Disturbed that the assassination might be the spearhead of some Soviet surprise attack, LBJ wished to ensure that he could respond with full presidential power, if necessary. He called the thunderstruck Attorney General, Robert F. Kennedy, who felt the oath was a formality: the Constitution had already made Johnson president. Sentimentally, he wished that LBJ would wait until he landed in Washington so that his brother could return to the Capitol one final time as president.

preceding page: President Lyndon Johnson meeting to brief President-elect Richard Nixon. above (left to right): President Herbert Hoover joins President-elect Franklin Roosevelt for the ride to Roosevelt's inauguration on March 4, 1933. Harry S. Truman takes the oath of office in the Cabinet Room of the White House following the death of President Roosevelt on April 12, 1945. John F. Kennedy being sworn in by Chief Justice Earl Warren, on January 20, 1961. Lyndon Johnson, with his wife Lady Bird at his right and Jacqueline Kennedy at his left, being sworn in on Air Force One in Dallas following the assassination of John Kennedy on November 22, 1963.

Johnson disagreed. He felt the nation needed reassurance that someone was fully in charge. A Dallas judge and political friend, Sarah Hughes, was called to the plane to swear him in—the first time a woman had served that function and the first time a president had been sworn in on an airplane. RFK later said that LBJ's refusal to wait was one of the first things that made him "bitter" toward Lyndon B. Johnson.

The Kennedy assassination threw light on another chink in the Constitution—the line of succession. With Johnson as president, the Oval Office was occupied by a man who had eight years earlier suffered a near-fatal heart attack. If he died, he would be succeeded by the aged Speaker McCormack, who had collapsed with vertigo when he heard the news about JFK from Dallas—and the rumor that Johnson might also have been wounded. In 1967, came the 25th Amendment, with procedures for a president by succession to choose a vice president and for an incapacitated president like Woodrow Wilson to be temporarily removed.

Even then, the process was not foolproof. On the eve of the presidential election of 1968, it looked as if candidates Richard Nixon, Hubert Humphrey, and George Wallace might so divide the electoral vote that the outcome would be thrown into the House of Representatives. *Newsweek* prepared a post-election cover emblazoned "CLIFFHANGER." There was the specter of a Constitutional crisis like in 1876, when Republicans in the House gave the presidency to the popular vote loser, Rutherford Hayes.

Facing an almost-certain Democratic House, terrified to have another victory slip from his fingers, Nixon publicly called on Humphrey to agree that whoever won the popular vote should be president. With only the hint of a sense of humor, Humphrey rebuffed him. He said he was sure that members of Congress would vote not as partisans but as "freethinking citizens selecting the man they regarded as the best President."

After two centuries, presidential power has been transferred over and over, through crisis after crisis, with few defects. The government of law works, but as always, only thanks to a government of men and women who respect the sanctity of the system.

President Gerald Ford and Mrs. Ford, David Eisenhower and Julie Nixon Eisenhower, wave as the helicopter with former President Richard Nixon and Mrs. Nixon leaves the White House grounds following his resignation from office on August 9, 1974.

# the pursuit of happiness

THE MOST INSCRUTABLE PHRASE in the otherwise quite declarative Declaration of Independence is the phrase that at cursory glance seems deceptively clear: the pursuit of happiness. It's an active, good-sounding phrase, providing the verbal flourish to propel the document's most famous sentence toward a lofting conclusion: "We hold these truths to be self-evident; that all men are created equal; that they are endowed by their Creator with certain inalienable rights; that among these are life, liberty, and the pursuit of happiness."

But what, really, does it mean—the pursuit of happiness? The author, Thomas Jefferson, failed to adequately explain himself in his private papers. And today, the act of "pursuing happiness" seems hedonistic. Granted, a great deal of the context in which Jefferson wrote has become dry history. There was a familiar ring to the phrase, relating to "life, liberty, and property." Many would even have known that it came from John Locke's *Second Treatise on Government*, written in 1690, in the philosopher's famous attempt to explain the moral necessity of the Glorious Revolution against England's King James II.

Educated colonists knew that Locke was the world's leading thinker on the emerging and radical theory of "natural rights," (i.e., that certain rights were natural, belonging to each person, and could never be infringed on by any government that presumed to claim legitimacy). America's founding generation elaborated at length on Locke's philosophy, in the Declaration and Constitution. Natural rights were themselves a part of the rationalization for the century-long shift in power in England from an absolute monarch to a powerful aristocracy, a movement that dates back to the Magna Carta. The most powerful weapon used to restrain the encroachment of regal, autocratic rule, was property. Disposition of property had been the king's greatest tool in controlling the lives of his people. As the emerging aristocracy took power and transferred a great deal of that power to Parliament, property became its greatest ally.

Locke had envisioned property as the most important bulwark in the protection of the free individual. Throughout his work, one comes on variations of that thought: "life, liberty, and estate," for example.

by Jack Hitt

The Statue of Liberty was a gift to the United States from the people of France. Built between 1875 and 1884 by sculptor Auguste Bartholdi, it was shipped to the United States in 214 crates. Dedicated by President Grover Cleveland on October 28, 1886, the statue measures 151' 1" from base to torch. Its construction required 100 tons of copper and 125 tons of steel. The tablet, which the statue holds in her left hand reads, in Roman numerals, "July 4, 1776." In-scribed on its base is the Emma Lazarus poem "The New Colossus." Its final stanza is one of the nation's most memorized: "Give me your tired, your poor, / Your huddled masses yearning to breathe free, / The wretched refuse of your teeming shore. / Send these, the homeless, the tempest-tossed to me, / I lift up my lamp beside the golden door."

Kings of Hollywood: Clark Gable, Van Heflin, Gary Cooper, and James Stewart, New Year's Eve, 1957, at Romanoff's in Beverly Hills.

To a colonist's ear that final phrase in the Declaration has the satisfying effect of raising even the lowliest farmer, at least grammatically—and more importantly, potentially—to the status of an aristocrat. All men, not just nobles, were now avowed to have been created equal; and all men, not just aristocrats, would be "free."

Yet it's puzzling why Jefferson didn't simply lift Locke's familiar and felicitous phrase and drop it into place. Some people believe that is more or less what he did. Newspaper columnist William Safire dismisses the phrase as nothing more than an "inspirational lift," adding, then, that a "euphemism started the trouble."

Euphemism? Was Jefferson really just trying to find some prettier synonym for "property"? Those who knew, and agreed with, Jefferson's own ideal of limited government would argue that any government's sole job is merely to protect our ability to accumulate property. The marketplace will resolve all other matters of conflict. The framers of the Constitution believed, like Locke, that governments are instituted to protect the good and productive citizen—his life, liberty, and property. Nothing more.

However, there are others who feel that Jefferson intended to focus the American ideal on something bigger than the economic simplicity of seventeenth-century aristocratic Britons. Jefferson married Lockean defense of property to the ancient Greek ideal of individual fulfillment. For the classical authors, "happiness" was the philosophical, even aesthetic satisfaction that individuals attained when they were left to freely explore the range of their natural gifts, and then develop those gifts and deploy them to great effect and achievement. Such happiness was only available to those who had the freedom to make such personal discoveries.

Elsewhere in Jefferson's papers, it is curious that he also tosses around the phrase, "life, liberty and the pursuit of fame." There again, the curious word does not mean "celebrity," as we might mistakenly believe today. But rather, fame was the high regard rewarded to one who had developed a natural gift to an extraordinary level and was honored and envied for it.

If we Americans, so comfortable with inherited benefits whose meaning or worth we rarely consider, find Jefferson's phrase vague, others do not. The Czechoslovakian film director Milos Foreman said that when he read the words "in the pursuit of happiness" in the Declaration of Independence, "I knew exactly what the men who wrote it meant. Not the right to happiness, which doesn't exist, but the right to pursue it." It is, Foreman added, "people like us, the ones who were not born here, who really appreciate this country."

193

a romance with the road

"light out for the territory"

by Mike Ritchey

"HUNGER FOR MOVEMENT," James Agee wrote, in of all places, *Fortune Magazine* in 1934, is "probably the profoundest and most compelling of American racial hungers." The road can satisfy that hunger. Just put the hood ornament on the center line, the speedometer on 80 and let 'er rip. The urge was there before the car, long before. That urge headed the country west. As Huck Finn said, "But I reckon I got to light out for the territory ahead of the rest, because Aunt Sally she's going to adopt me and civilize me, and I can't stand it. I been there before."

The road is our nation's ticket to ride and, more precisely, ride away. Maybe it's away from who we are but it's for sure from where we are. To? Who knows? How about just a fresh start. We can put it all behind us as fast as the car will go. William Saroyan, who liked getting behind the wheel of his Buick, said about his desire to hit the road, "It isn't simply driving at night—it's going on to find out what's out there, not so much along the highway, in the terrain, under the sky, but in the interior of the driver himself."

The true north of the road is west. The West owns those lonesome, inexhaustible roads with few and far between motels designed so the car can be parked about twenty feet from the bed. There's a lot of nowhere for the roads of the West to cover. Distance measured by hours (eighteen hours from Amarillo to Santa Monica, ignoring speed limits) provides time to think. The playwright, Sam Shepherd, uses the road for writing and that explains, maybe, why he gets the West down so well.

Our "Mother Road," John Steinbeck said, was Route 66; the Okies called it their Highway to Heaven because it could get them to California. Highway 61 connected the North and South, running from New Orleans's Jackson Square, an old slave market, all the way to Canada; it took Elvis to Memphis and Muddy Waters to Chicago. Bluesman Robert Johnson asked in his song "Crossroads Blues" to be buried by its side so his "old evil spirit can take a Greyhound bus and ride."

Romance with the road is all about get up and go. Wherever you want to go, go. Whenever you want to go, go. There's no schedule to follow, no reservations to make. Time of arrival? It's open-ended. "I'll get there when I get there" has a lot of appeal. And that appeal is not restricted to Americans.

*Lolita*'s Humbert Humbert knew very well what he would find should he examine his own interior, and he chose instead to hit the road with the cause of his affliction riding shotgun. Humbert's creator, the Russian lepidopterist, Vladmir Nabokov, spent two summers on America's highways, chasing butterflies. As the landscapes and roadsides flashed by like movies viewed through a windshield, Nabokov took copious, careful notes of all he saw. Those journals, covering thousands of miles, were com-

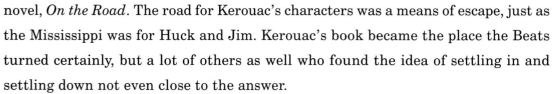

pressed into the middle-aged Humbert Humbert's year-long automobile journey across the country, showing his sights to his teenaged Lolita as he raced to escape the claustrophobia of convention. The author succeeded in his detailed descriptions, but he might not have done so well, if he had had to keep his eyes on the road. But he wasn't driving; he never learned how. His wife was behind the wheel every mile of the way.

A great year for the road was 1957. It was the year the painter, Edward Hopper, gave us his *Western Motel*; the year that Jack Kerouac, out of the grim, mill town of Lowell, Massachusetts, weighed in with the novel, *On the Road*. The road for Kerouac's characters was a means of escape, just as the Mississippi was for Huck and Jim. Kerouac's book became the place the Beats turned certainly, but a lot of others as well who found the idea of settling in and settling down not even close to the answer.

*On the Road* captured, as no other book had, that haul-assing energy of trying to satisfy the hunger for movement: "Dean hopped in his chair conclusively. 'Well yes, well yes, and now I think we'd better be cutting along because we gotta be in Chicago by tomorrow night and we've already wasted several hours.' The college boys thanked (rancher)Wall graciously and we were off again. I turned to watch the kitchen light recede in the sea of night. Then I leaned ahead."

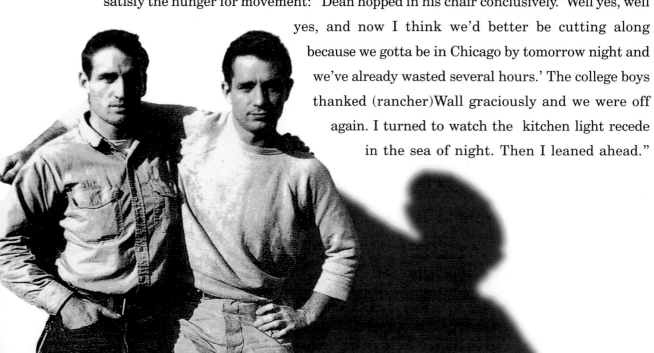

preceding page: Weathered Route 66 sign. **above:** Edward Hopper's *Western Motel*, painted in 1957. **facing page top right:** Steve McQueen on Mulholland Drive. **facing page middle right:** Martin Milner and George Maharis of the 1960s television show *Route 66*. **facing page bottom right:** Peter Fonda and Dennis Hopper in *Easy Rider* (1969). **facing page bottom left:** Neal Cassady and Jack Kerouac, taken with a Brownie camera by Carolyn Cassady in San Francisco, 1952.

can you tell me how to get to sesame street?

THIS IS A QUESTION millions of children have been asking every day for the last thirty years. So how did we get there in the first place?

In one television season, 1968, *Sesame Street* became the most famous street in America. Yet none of us had any idea when we started, that *Sesame Street* and the Children's Television Workshop would grow into the international institutions they are today, that *Sesame Street*, winner of more Emmys than any other single show, would also become the longest street in the world, benefiting more children in more countries than any program in history. None of us had any idea that the characters we were creating—wonderful, zany, vulnerable "Muppets" to teach children about letters, numbers, and getting along—would become so much a part of our culture, or that we were creating a family that every child watching would feel part of.

We only knew that we wanted to make a difference in the lives of children and families, particularly children in low-income families. In the late 1960s when we began our work, this seemed imminently possible. It was a time when many of us believed we had the responsibility and the power to make the world a better place, even if only just a little better.

Our original goal was simple, and only in retrospect, revolutionary: to use television to help children learn. We knew young children watched a great deal of television in the

by Joan Ganz Cooney

years before they went to school. We also knew they liked cartoons, game shows, and situation comedies; that they responded to slapstick humor, music with a beat, and above all—sadly—fast-paced, oft-repeated commercials.

If we created an educational show that capitalized on some of commercial television's most engaging traits—its high production value, its sophisticated writing, its quality film and animation—we believed we could attract a sizable audience that included, most importantly, low-income children. There was a lot of betting against us because of the number of UHF stations in the public television system, especially in the precable era, but our own instincts proved right. The wasteland was too vast and the yearning for something better too great: *Sesame Street* was an instant hit.

199

From the beginning we—the planners of the project—designed *Sesame Street* as an experimental research project with educational advisors, researchers, and television producers collaborating as equal partners.

That partnership is what has made *Sesame Street* work. Writers, producers, directors, researchers, and performers all strive together with clear goals in mind to find the best path to these goals.

Without the research and curriculum base, *Sesame Street* would never have had the impact or lasted as long. But the same can be said of any of the significant components of the show's success. What if Jim Henson and his team hadn't created such wonderful characters? What if Joe Raposo and Jeff Moss hadn't written *Sesame Street's* memorable, timeless music? What if the show's wonderful writers, researchers, educators, directors, and producers hadn't devoted themselves to making *Sesame Street* exceptional?

Thank heavens, we'll never know, because they all *did* contribute, joining forces to make a show that has changed—and continues to change—children's television, and manages to do some good along the way.

As *Sesame Street* enters its third decade, something quite extraordinary is happening: those of us present at its inception are now watching the show with our grandchildren. For me this has special meaning, because while many people have said that it must be wonderful to have affected the lives of so many, it always felt a bit like a statistic—gratifying certainly, but nonetheless somewhat remote—until seeing up-close how *Sesame Street* has helped my own granddaughter learn. Every day as she clicks on *Sesame Street,* two-year old Chloe belts out the "Sunny Days" theme song like Ethel Merman, with arms (and mouth) wide open. And the other night at dinner with my husband and me and another couple, this very bright (I am, after all, her grandmother) little girl so eager to be a part of the conversation, suddenly contributed a solo rendition of the ABC song—a skill mastered from her many mornings of watching *Sesame Street.*

I hope that thirty or so years from now, Chloe will be watching *Sesame Street* with her children, and that they will be singing the ABC song, counting and humming "People in Your Neighborhood" and "Rubber Duckie" learned from shows brought to them by the letter *S* and the number *two*, and that millions of other children throughout the world will be reciting the letters, learning the numbers, and humming along with them.

Muppets Bert, Ernie, Big Bird, and Oscar the Grouch, seen here with early cast members, have lived at their fabled address for more than three decades.

the skyscraper

FROM THE RUINS, lonely and inexplicable as the sphinx, rose the Empire State Building," F. Scott Fitzgerald wrote; the "ruins" referring to The Crash in 1929. Completed on May 1, 1931, no building ever reached so high, so fast: 102 stories tall with a 200-foot mast on top to hitch your dirigible to. Built in just over a year. During the nation's worst depression.

Just two years before, May 1, 1929, the architect, William Van Alen, had broken ground on the Chrysler Building; he had been commissioned by Chrysler to design and construct the tallest building in the world. He built it and at 925 feet, the Chrysler Building was, when it opened in April, 1930, the tallest—for twenty-eight days. Then the Manhattan Bank Tower completed its construction and opened at a height of 927 feet; by two feet it claimed the World's Tallest title.

But wait. The race wasn't over. In the history of high wire, no net architecture where one-ups-manship is an architect's oxygen, the Chrysler Building's William Van Alen wasn't about to give up the celebrity status the World's Tallest title would convey. Van Alen had designed a stainless spire of five sections, which was lowered in through the top of the building. At the appropriate time, before an appreciative audience, Van Alen delivered the coup de grace to the Manhattan Bank. A huge derrick, its gears slowly turning, raised the spire from the innards of the Chrysler Building. It "gradually emerged," Van Alen wrote, "from the top of the dome like a butterfly from its cocoon." At 1,046 feet the Chrysler Building was suddenly "The World's Tallest Building," and remained so—for less than a year— until the Empire State Building, topped out at 1,250 feet, grabbing the title for itself and holding it until 1971 when the World Trade Center towers opened. Fittingly, the group behind the Empire State Building was led by the Happy Warrior himself, former governor of the Empire State, Al Smith. Remember this. The World's Tallest Building Contest, in which the title changed four times in just over a year, an extravagance of energy and money, imagination and courage, took place during the nation's worst of times.

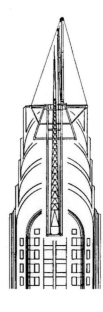

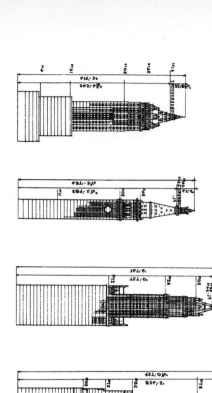

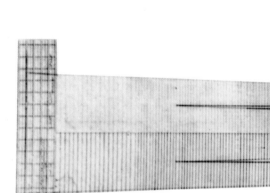

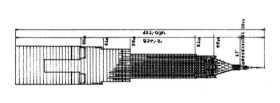

Frank Lloyd Wright pro-
posed the ultimate in 1956:
a mile-high skyscraper for
Chicago to be known as the
Mile High Illinois, but it was
never built. Other sky-
scrapers (left to right): New
York Life Insurance Building,
completed 1929, 619 feet;
Metropolitan Tower,
completed 1909, 700 feet;
Woolworth Tower, com-
pleted 1913, 792 feet; The
Manhattan Co. Tower,
completed 1930, 927 feet;
Chrysler Building, com-
pleted 1930, 1046 feet;
Empire State Building,
completed 1930, 1250 feet.

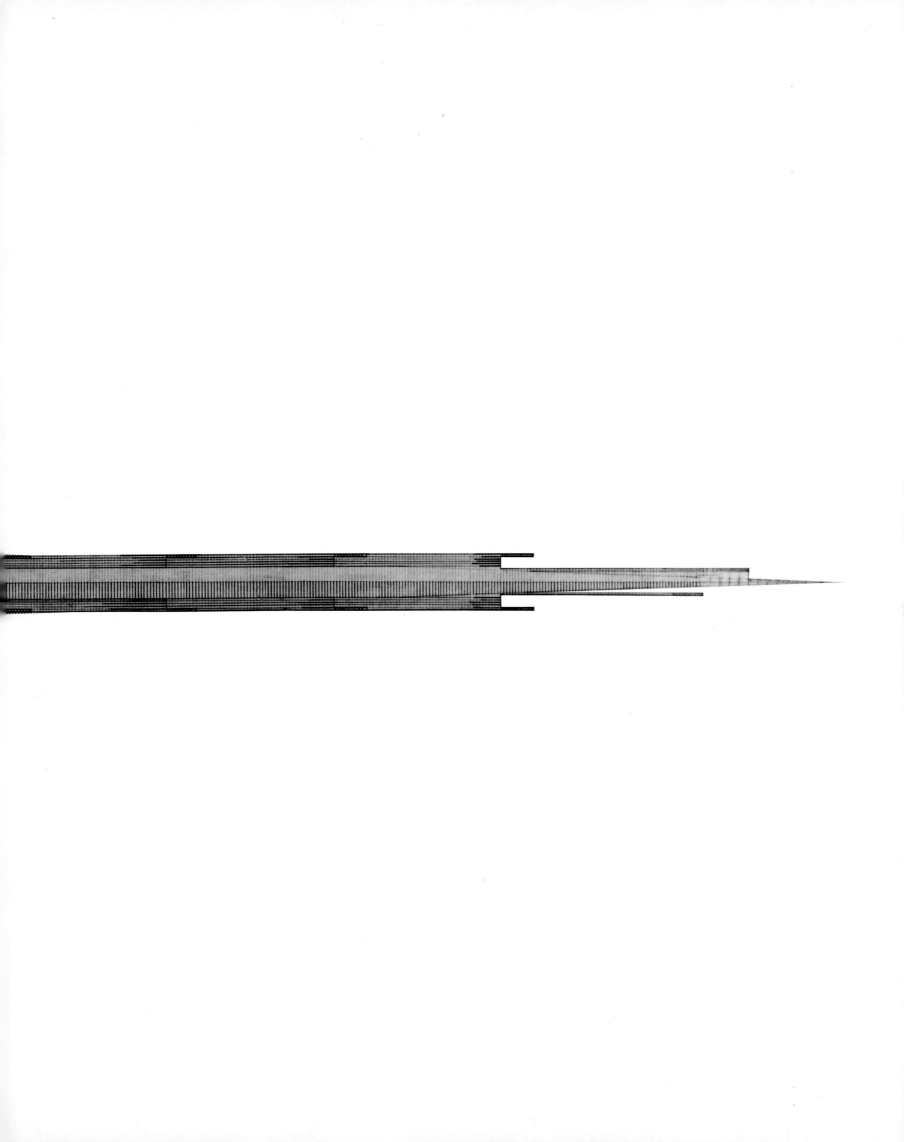

THERE WERE CERTAINLY those in 1835, including the President of the United States, Andrew Jackson, who wanted to kick the gift horse in the mouth. This particular gift horse was an Englishman, James Smithson, who had never set foot in America. His gift was 105 gold sovereigns valued at $500,000 (nearly $7 million today). Only a single, vague condition accompanied the bequest: it was to be used to "found at Washington, under the name . . . the Smithsonian Institution, an establishment for the increase and diffusion of knowledge among men."

So who was Smithson? And why did the United States nearly refuse a gift that eventually helped establish the world's largest museum system?

Born in Paris in 1765, Smithson was the illegitimate son of a direct descendent of King Henry VII. His parents were the first Duke of Northumberland, Hugh Smithson, and Elizabeth Hungerford Keate Macie, a widow who shared the King's bloodline. At nine, he was naturalized in England, and later attended Oxford. After inheriting his mother's wealth in 1800, Smithson dedicated himself to the pursuit of science. In recognition of discovering the carbon make-up in *calamine*, the mineral was posthumously renamed *Smithsonite*. He was an avid gambler and a nationalist who opposed unjust authority, most notably Napoleon's; he even spent five years in a Danish prison on suspicion of spying against France.

Smithson died in 1829, leaving his estate to a nephew, Henry James Hungerford. A clause stipulated that should Hungerford die childless, the fortune would go toward the Smithsonian's founding. In 1835 Hungerford died without heirs and the United States was suddenly first in line to inherit his wealth. For almost a year, politicians debated America's right to the gift. Nationalists, anglophobes, and states' rights advocates decried Smithson's bequest; all had their reasons, some just didn't believe the nation should accept the largesse of a man whose half-brother fought for England during the Revolutionary War. Finally, in 1836, the reasoned judgment of former President John Quincy Adams, by

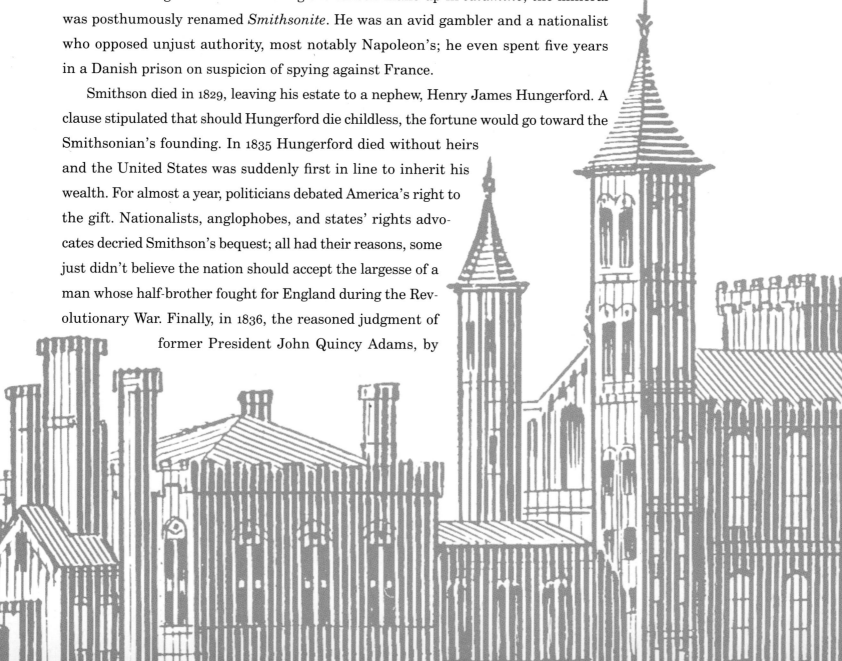

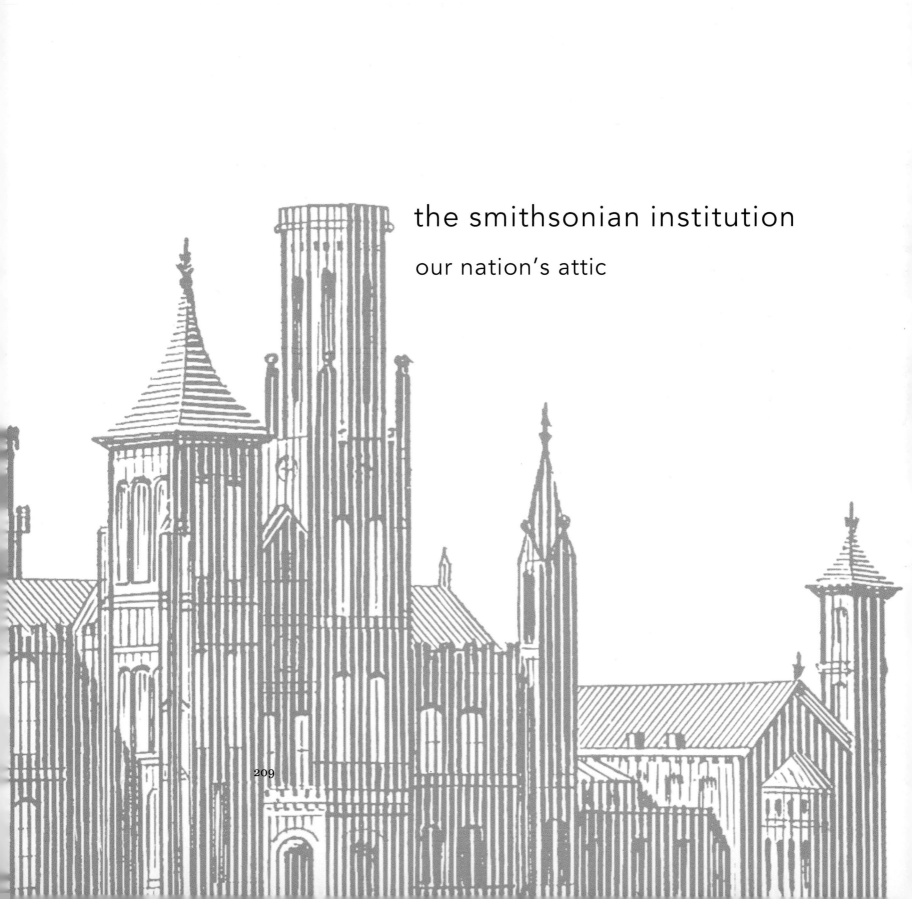

# the smithsonian institution

our nation's attic

209

preceding page: Nineteenth century engraving of the original Smithsonian building known as the "Castle." above: A ninety-two foot replica of the blue whale; the largest animal species on earth today. right: One of the original teddy bears, named in honor of Theodore Roosevelt. left: A sketch for an airmail stamp made by President Franklin Roosevelt, a stamp collector, and an actual stamp based on his design.

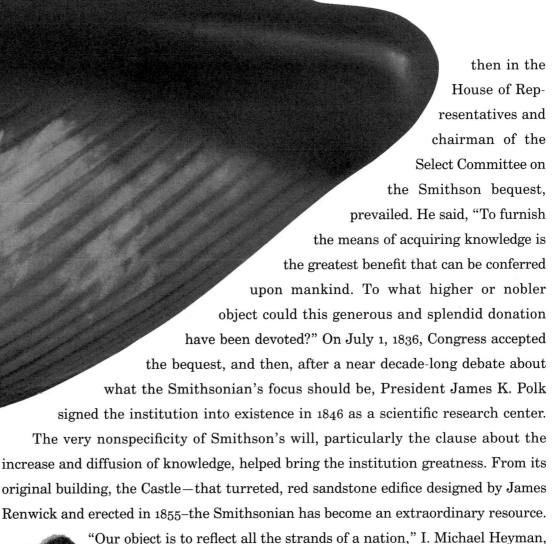

then in the House of Representatives and chairman of the Select Committee on the Smithson bequest, prevailed. He said, "To furnish the means of acquiring knowledge is the greatest benefit that can be conferred upon mankind. To what higher or nobler object could this generous and splendid donation have been devoted?" On July 1, 1836, Congress accepted the bequest, and then, after a near decade-long debate about what the Smithsonian's focus should be, President James K. Polk signed the institution into existence in 1846 as a scientific research center. The very nonspecificity of Smithson's will, particularly the clause about the increase and diffusion of knowledge, helped bring the institution greatness. From its original building, the Castle—that turreted, red sandstone edifice designed by James Renwick and erected in 1855–the Smithsonian has become an extraordinary resource. "Our object is to reflect all the strands of a nation," I. Michael Heyman, Smithsonian secretary from 1994 to 1999, said. "We do this to educate all Americans about our origins in a way that fosters pride and makes more attainable mutual respect and the recognition of our common aspirations." The institution's scope has branched from the sciences into art, popular culture, ethnic studies, and even postal history. Each year, nearly 30 million people visit the Smithsonian's sixteen museums, ten research centers and libraries, and the National Zoological Park. Its 140 million holdings range from a meteorite 4.5 billion

years old to the first spacecraft to take an American, Alan Shephard, into space, the *Freedom 7*; from daggers of the twelfth-century B.C. Shang Dynasty in China to Muhammad Ali's boxing gloves; from William Clark's compass to the fedora worn by Harrison Ford in *Raiders of the Lost Ark*.

James Smithson never visited the country that eventually gave him a measure of immortality. Since 1904, however, the Smithsonian Castle has housed his crypt. It was Alexander Graham Bell who brought his remains to one of Washington's best addresses.

We have no explanation as to why Smithson left his fortune to America. One theory has to do with the words on which this nation was founded: "All men are created equal." Despite his royal lineage, Smithson's illegitimacy closed him off from the highest ranks of English society. He once wrote, "The best blood of England flows in my veins . . . but this avails me not. My name shall live in the memory of a man when the titles of the Northumberlands . . . are long forgotten." Perhaps he had prescience for what a nation so conceived as ours could become and wanted to be a part of it. If that's so, he got his wish.

facing page top: Compass and case carried by William Clark during the 1804 Lewis and Clark expedition to the Pacific coast. facing page bottom: Space suit worn by Commander David Scott during the July 1971 Apollo lunar mission. above: The Bell X-I became the first American aircraft to break the sound barrier on October 14, 1947. right: Pilot's license Number One issued to Glen H. Curtiss by the Aero Club of America on June 8, 1911.

213

# the snapshot

THE PRICE WAS RIGHT and we joined the Brownie Camera Club by the thousands, when the ads ran in 1900. We'd been joining since 1888, the year the name "Kodak" was born and the Kodak Camera was placed on the market with the slogan "You push the button—we do the rest"; the advertising-conscious company owner, George Eastman himself, had dreamed it up. It was the birth of the snapshot, and the idea that every family, not just the rich, could record its own visual history. The snapshots were small but hugely democratic.

Those first Brownies, introduced in 1900, used film that sold for 15 cents a roll, making photography a financially feasible hobby for virtually everyone. More than a quarter of a million Brownies were sold the first year they were offered; over 50 million had been sold by the mid-1940s. Eastman, its creator, had unshakable faith in the effect of advertising on his company's sales and, even more significantly, on the education of the public. He wrote all the ads himself, and in 1897, as an indication of the camera's international appeal, the word "Kodak" sparkled from an electric sign on London's Trafalgar Square. It was one of the first such signs to be used in advertising. And Kodak's distinctive yellow, which Eastman also personally selected, now says "Kodak" in every language.

Where did the word "Kodak" come from? George Eastman explains it, "The letter 'K' had been a favorite with me. It seems a strong, incisive sort of letter. It became a question of trying out a great number of combinations of letters that made words starting and ending with 'K'." As simple as that.

But the word "hobby" hardly signifies the effect of Eastman's invention. Eastman's Brownie meant that fledgling photographers no longer bothered with camera settings, focus, or development. After exposing the film, the entire camera was shipped back to Eastman's factory. The film was developed, camera reloaded, and mailed back to the customer with mounted prints. In 1896, the 100,000th Kodak camera was manufactured; 400 miles of film and photographic paper were being made each month.

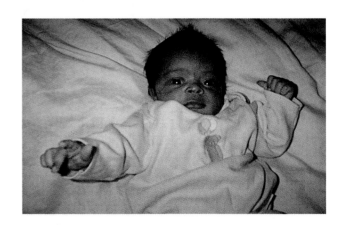

George Eastman had powerful ideas that created and defined an industry. What separated him from so many inventors, however, was that he understood if an idea was to really take off, it had to meet a need—or create one—and then fulfill it better than anyone else. Over time Kodak came to mean affordable cameras and film just as Gillette would mean razors and razor blades, just as Sony's Walkman would mean a private, convenient concert in your ear. Yet, even as successful as Kodak became, it was someone else, a Harvard dropout, who tied into our desire for greater speed and instant gratification. And his photography breakthrough was triggered by a simple complex question from his three-year-old daughter.

In December 1943, on a rare vacation with his family to Santa Fe, New Mexico, Edwin Land and his family walked around taking pictures. When they got back to the hotel, his daughter, Jennifer, asked, "Why can't I see them now?" Instead of the answer most of us would have given, "Because you just can't, that's why," Land began thinking. He recalled, "I undertook the task of solving the puzzle Jennifer had set me. Within the hour, the camera, the film, and the physical chemistry became so clear to me that with a great sense of excitement I hurried over to the place where Donald Brown, my patent attorney, was staying, and described to him in great detail a dry camera which would give a picture immediately after exposure." Polaroid created instant photography and owned the category for decades.

Their SX-70 camera, the first color "instant" camera, became an overnight sensation. As we had done half-a-century before, we responded to advertising, this time to television commercials, in which Sir Laurence Olivier sold us on Land's revolutionary idea. . . even though Sir Laurence had pronunciation difficulties with "SX," until he settled on a more familiar association—"Essex."

The power of snapshots still derives from the version of the amazing truths they record. That we were children once as our parents were before us. That we grew up. That we moved away. That we were once the youngest generation in a snapshot and overnight, it seemed like we became the oldest. Snapshots record the best times before time took us up the dark alley. The rare ones can even give us some hint of what we would become. Snapshots, too, are an uneven record of the homes we tried to create. They furnish final evidence that certain places exist because we were there. Sometimes, though, because of their power, it's best to look at snapshots, especially those you haven't seen in years, in the company of others; it's too unsettling by yourself.

Hold it, Right there! That's it.

# sousa's band
## "the music men"

He was known as the March King. And that was fine with him. Because, as John Phillip Sousa wrote in 1910, "I would rather be the composer of an inspired march than of a manufactured symphony." The music created by his band was of, by, and for the people at a time when the nation was feeling good about itself. And confident, too, about its place in the world. He wrote, "I wanted to make a music for the people, a music to be grasped at once."

The die was cast in 1860 when, as a thirteen-year-old boy, he tried to join a traveling circus band. But on the morning of his scheduled departure, his father intervened and led him to the Marine Corps headquarters, where the young Sousa enlisted as an apprentice in the U.S. Marine Band and began his march to greatness.

He learned his craft over the next two decades and in 1880 he was appointed the first American-born conductor of the U.S. Marine Band. Under Sousa's direction the band was transformed into a national treasure. He had the gift of knowing how to get the best from his musicians and it was during this period Sousa composed what he considered his finest march, "Semper Fidelis." Under Sousa, the Marine Band made more than two hundred recordings for a new invention called the phonograph.

After twelve years with the Marines, in 1892 he formed his own band. They became the world's most sought after musical attraction. There were European tours, four between 1900 and 1905. The band went on a World Tour in 1910–1911. They traveled over a million miles playing for the people, from kings and queens to working stiffs. He recruited the nation's foremost musicians, among them Meredith Willson who would go on to write *The Music Man*.

Because Sousa had the knack of making his bandmembers think they were better than they were, they often were. "He was a small man, not a dashing-dapper-dan who could tower over us. And he had a kind, little old pipsqueaky voice," Edmund Wall, a clarinetist recalled. "But when he stepped up on that podium, something happened. It can't be explained; it just happened. We knew we were playing with the immortals and no one could touch us."

During his career, Sousa composed 136 marches, 70 songs, 15 operettas, 11 suites, and 4 overtures. Despite his enduring canon, Sousa's immortality was secured with a single composition, the last piece he conducted during a rehearsal in Pennsylvania on the day he died, March 6, 1932: "The Stars and Stripes Forever."

John Phillip Sousa and his band leading a parade, May 22, 1914.

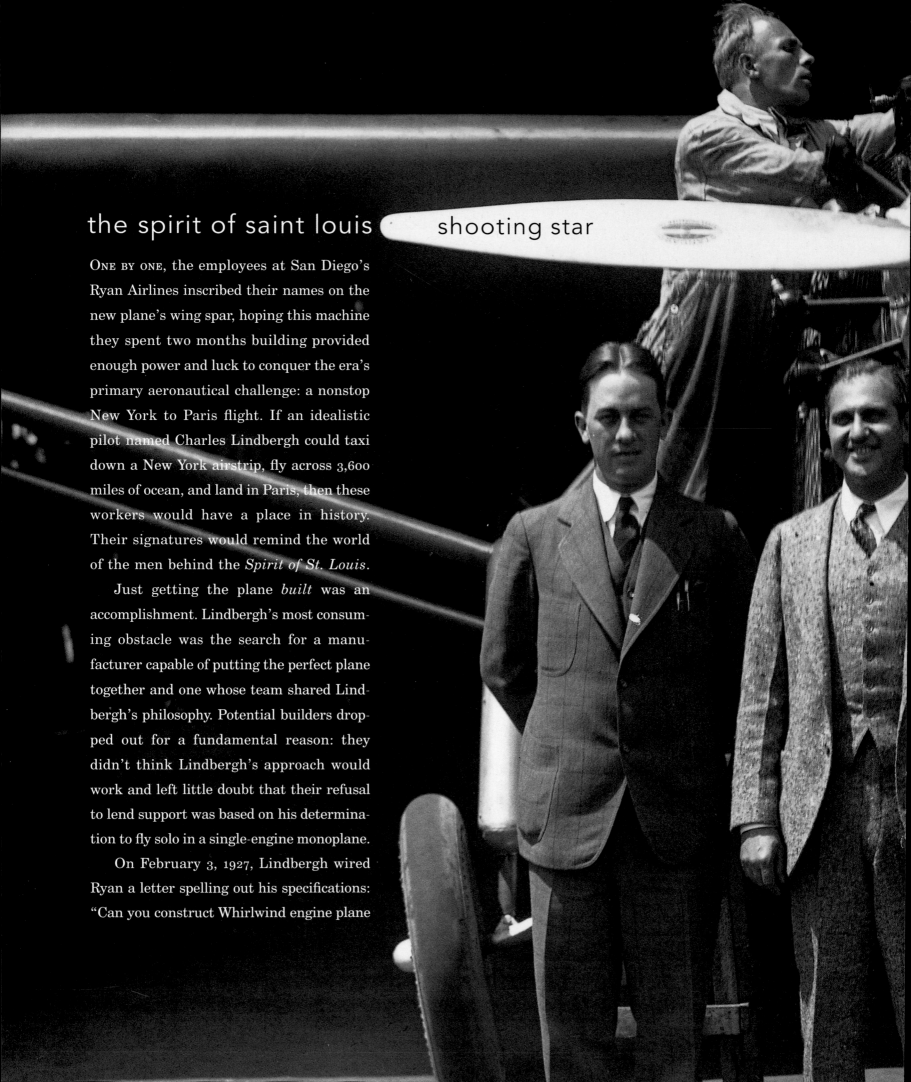

# the spirit of saint louis

ONE BY ONE, the employees at San Diego's Ryan Airlines inscribed their names on the new plane's wing spar, hoping this machine they spent two months building provided enough power and luck to conquer the era's primary aeronautical challenge: a nonstop New York to Paris flight. If an idealistic pilot named Charles Lindbergh could taxi down a New York airstrip, fly across 3,600 miles of ocean, and land in Paris, then these workers would have a place in history. Their signatures would remind the world of the men behind the *Spirit of St. Louis*.

Just getting the plane *built* was an accomplishment. Lindbergh's most consuming obstacle was the search for a manufacturer capable of putting the perfect plane together and one whose team shared Lindbergh's philosophy. Potential builders dropped out for a fundamental reason: they didn't think Lindbergh's approach would work and left little doubt that their refusal to lend support was based on his determination to fly solo in a single-engine monoplane.

On February 3, 1927, Lindbergh wired Ryan a letter spelling out his specifications: "Can you construct Whirlwind engine plane

capable of flying nonstop between New York and Paris. If so, please state cost and delivery date." Ryan responded the next day, saying they could satisfy his requirements of constructing a fuselage, minus engine, for $6,000 and deliver in three months. The price was right. (With engine, the *Spirit* ultimately cost $10,580.)

The Ryan deal was nearly sealed when Lindbergh received a wire on February 6 from Columbia Airlines and Giuseppe Bellanca, a man Lindbergh had approached earlier. Columbia was interested in selling him the ideal plane, the Wright-Bellanca. Dropping Ryan, Lindbergh began negotiations with Columbia. As the terms were being finalized, Columbia stipulated they would pick the flight crew; Lindbergh's only involvement would be as an investor. In his own word, "dumbfounded," Lindbergh walked away. He hoped the Ryan offer still stood.

After his first visit, Lindbergh described Ryan Airlines as "a small aviation company," one that probably "must live hand to mouth," but he was impressed. "I believe in Donald Hall's [Ryan's chief engineer] ability; I like B.F. Mahoney's [Ryan's president] enthusiasm. I have confidence in the character of the workmen I've met."

Throughout his search for a builder, Lindbergh maintained that a single-engine plane would be lighter, therefore allowing it to carry additional fuel, and decrease the chances of engine failure. No one else agreed. No one until Donald Hall. Not only did Hall *not* dismiss the single-engine theory, he embraced the idea of a single pilot. Though concerned with Lindbergh's ability to remain alert for the flight's duration, he understood that less weight meant more fuel.

Four other teams were well ahead of "Lindy" in planning the nonstop crossing. The $25,000 Orteig Prize awaited the first person to make a nonstop New York to Paris connection. Lindbergh considered scrapping the flight, certain that at least one rival would claim the reward before he got off the ground; a transpacific crossing was his contingency plan. But Lindbergh's luck held: The other planes, three of which had multiple engines, crashed.

The staff at Ryan pushed to complete the project in sixty days. Hawley Bowlus, Ryan's factory manager, and Bert Tindale, the shop superintendent, took a fanatical interest in the plane's assembly. On receiving orders from Hall to hold the fuselage fairings (which reduce the surface drag) to an accuracy of one thirty-second of an inch, Tindale made a scale with inches divided into those exact divisions. Hall, after fretting over Lindbergh's stamina, worked a sleepless thirty-six-hour shift.

Two months after its first screws were fastened, the *Spirit of St. Louis* was completed. Its only means of forward visibility was a periscope. There was no radio, no parachute, and other than a compass and eight-day clock, few navigation devices. The plane had a wing-span of forty-six-feet to accommodate the 425 gallon gas tank.

Hall estimated that with that much fuel, Lindbergh could fly 4,100 miles—giving him a 500-mile comfort zone if the plane went off course.

On May 10, the Ryan Airlines staff watched Lindbergh take-off from San Diego's North Island Naval Station, on the way to New York's Curtiss Field. Ten days later, their plane began its flight toward Paris, from the adjacent Roosevelt Field.

With the *Spirit of St. Louis*'s journey complete, Ryan became a leading commercial airplane manufacturer. Only two months after Lindbergh's flight, Mahoney changed the company's name to B.F. Mahoney Aircraft, then, on New Year's Eve, 1927, he sold it to a St. Louis investment group for $1 million dollars. The new owners closed the San Diego factory and moved to St. Louis.

preceding page: Photographed in front of the Spirit of St. Louis just before take off for Paris are Charles Lindbergh with B. F. Mahoney, president of Ryan Airlines, Harry Guggenheim, and S. L. Lawrence, President of the Wright Motor Company. facing page top: Donald Hall, Ryan Airlines's chief engineer, working in his bare drafting room at the Ryan factory in San Diego. His design had to meet Lindbergh's overriding concern: range above everything else. facing page bottom: Starting the Whirlwind engine on the Spirit of St. Louis for the first time. Lindbergh watches next to the cockpit window, while Ryan Airlines factory manager Hawley Bowlus sits at the controls. right: Lindbergh, having arrived in Paris, poses with French engineer and inventor, Louis Bleriot, who, in 1909, was the first aviator to fly across the English Channel, and American Ambassador to France, Myron T. Herrick.

sportswriting  the golden age

by Allen Barra

Notre Dame's attack is more like a modern war offensive than anything we have seen. The infantry is there to strike through the line, with the air fleet above busy bombing holes in the rival defense.

—Grantland Rice on the 1922 Notre Dame–Army game

Brazil can cheer about its coffee as Ceylon raves about its tea. Let Florida and California speak with passion of their orange groves as Kentucky points with a finger of pride to the thoroughbred. But out in Notre Dame, South Bend, Indiana, football grows on trees and bushes . . .

—Grantland Rice on the 1923 Notre Dame–Army game

Outlined against a blue, gray October sky, the Four Horsemen rode again. In dramatic lore, they were known as Famine, Pestilence, Destruction, and Death. These are only aliases. Their real names are Stuhldreher, Miller, Crowley, and Layden. They formed the crest of the South Bend cyclone before which another fighting Army team was swept over the precipice of the Polo Grounds this afternoon before 55,000 spectators peering down upon the bewildering panorama spread out upon the green plain below.

—Grantland Rice on the 1924 Notre Dame–Army game

It took Grantland Rice three tries to get it right. When he finally found his rhythm and the right imagery, he changed his own life, his profession, and the course of college football.

The 1920s, as has often been remarked, was the Golden Age of Sportswriting. By the middle part of the decade a handful of talented and ambitious journalists who found other paths to literary fame blocked, began to notice, as indeed their editors had already noticed, that an increasingly affluent middle class was responding more to the exploits of Jack Dempsey, Babe Ruth, and Bobby Jones than to what would later be known as "hard" news stories. Paul Gallico, of the *New York Daily News*, who later went on to better things, admitted to being one of the hipsters. He labeled the sportswriters who wrote in "the most florid and exciting prose" they could invent "Gee-Whizzers."

Grantland Rice was the crown prince of the Gee-Whizzers. As Murray Sperber wrote in his history of Notre Dame football, *Shake Down the Thunder*, "Each day he flung out metaphors about athletes and sports events and, indeed, some of his words stick to the American psyche."

His lines that stick with us today were a happy combination of skill and circumstance. To begin with, Rice had picked the right sport, college football, and the right team, Notre Dame. The rise of football, particularly college football, coincided precisely with the rise of the sports pages and the Gee-Whizzers. Their near-hysterical coverage made it a national game in the rank of, if not actually on a par with, major league baseball.

College football and sports pages combined to make each other and both helped to create Grantland Rice. Rice got a big boost, for example, when the night editor of the *New York Herald-Tribune* put the lead for Rice's 1924 Notre Dame–Army story on the front page. An odd point of fact, the game wasn't even college football's biggest story that day: the "Galloping Ghost," Red Grange, had scored five touchdowns for Illinois against Michigan, and most papers, including Rice's own, considered it the bigger event. Rice, a close friend of Knute Rockne, correctly perceived that Notre Dame would be the college football team with national appeal, and for thousands and thousands of fans that Sunday, and for millions more who would read the story in weeks and months and, as it appeared in anthologies of sportswriting, years to come, that fall Saturday would forever be the day the Four Horsemen rode, thanks to a lead that would never die.

George Strickler, a Notre Dame press assistant, gave Rice his immediate inspiration when he likened the Irish backfield to the stars of the Rudolph Valentino film, *The Four Horsemen of the Apocalypse*. Further, Strickland telephoned back to South Bend for a photographer to shoot the four backs on horses. It was a cute shot, but for many it only seemed to diminish the myth—in truth, the four heroes looked a little uneasy on horses.

preceding page: From 1922 to 1924, the vaunted backfield of (from left) Don Miller, Elmer Layden, Jim Crowley, and Harry Stuhldreher led Notre Dame to a combined record of 27–2–1. During their final season together, after defeating Army 13–7, *New York Herald-Tribune* writer Grantland Rice immortalized them as the Four Horsemen. left: Aside from coining many of the most memorable phrases in American sports history, Rice also wrote the famed quatrain: when the one great scorer comes / to write against your name / he marks not that you won or lost / but how you played the game.

# sun records

## "when all hell broke loose"

MEMPHIS DISC JOCKEY Sam Phillips wanted his own studio, a place where Southern rhythm and blues artists could record their music, the kind, as Phillips said, "where the soul of man never dies." In 1949, Phillips bought a radiator shop at 706 Union Avenue and converted it into the place that would become rock and roll's Plymouth Rock. With the motto "We record anything—any-where–anytime," the Memphis Recording Service and its label, Sun records, were open for business.

Elvis Presley caught his ring here. You know the story: Poor boy born in Tupelo, Mississippi, grows up listening to black Delta and Chicago bluesmen. Moves to Memphis in 1948, graduates from Humes High. In 1953, on his day off from M. B. Parker Machinists' Shop, goes to Sun's Memphis Recording Service, where anyone willing to spend $3.98 could cut an acetate disc and record the Ink Spots's "My Happiness" as a present for his mother. Returns a few months later and records "Careless Love" and "I'll Never Stand in Your Way." Phillips hears songs, is underwhelmed but asks the young singer to rehearse with a local act, the Starlite Wranglers. On July 5, 1954, with Scotty Moore playing guitar and Bill Black slapping bass, Presley records "That's All Right, (Mama)." Two days later the song debuts on Memphis radio and Sun's rise began.

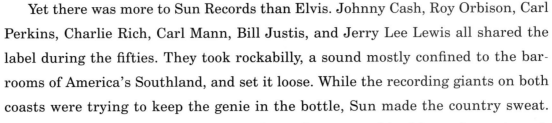

Yet there was more to Sun Records than Elvis. Johnny Cash, Roy Orbison, Carl Perkins, Charlie Rich, Carl Mann, Bill Justis, and Jerry Lee Lewis all shared the label during the fifties. They took rockabilly, a sound mostly confined to the barrooms of America's Southland, and set it loose. While the recording giants on both coasts were trying to keep the genie in the bottle, Sun made the country sweat.

Before Presley walked through the doors, Sun was making history but not much money. Ike Turner, a deejay from Clarksville, Mississippi, arranged a session with teenaged Jackie Brenston. Their version of "Rocket 88," recorded by Sam Phillips in 1951, is considered by many to be the first rock record. Yet Phillips knew the key to financial success was "a white man who had the Negro sound and the Negro feel." So when WHBQ disc jockey Dewey Phillips (no relation to Sam) spun "That's All Right" for the first time, as Sam put it, "all hell broke loose." Sam had his man.

Rockabilly's momentum was propelled by Sun's subsequent discoveries of Jerry Lee Lewis, Carl Perkins, and Johnny Cash. Perkins sold 2 million copies of "Blue Suede Shoes," making it the first rockabilly song to reach number one on the pop, country, and rhythm and blues charts. Lewis recorded Sun's most successful hits with "Great Balls of Fire" and "Whole Lotta Shakin Going On," while Johnny Cash became the label's most consistent act, with twenty releases on the original Sun label, selling over 10 million records.

The good times didn't roll forever. A lack of capital kept Sun from reaping the financial rewards of its success. Strapped to meet consumer demands, Phillips sold Elvis's contract to RCA in 1955. Of that infamous decision, Phillips said, "I looked at everything for how I could take a little extra money and get myself out of a real bind. I wasn't broke, but man, it was hand to mouth." For $40,000 ($5,000 of which went to Elvis) Phillips released Presley from his Sun obligations.

After RCA's coup, for two years, 1956–1957, it prospered during the golden age of rockabilly, but by 1958, the pendulum was swinging the other way.

Johnny Cash's skyrocketing fame pulled him to Nashville and California.

Alcoholism and an automobile accident all but finished the rise of Carl Perkins. "Blue Suede Shoes" in fact, the number Perkins wrote and first made famous, was a huge hit for Elvis as well. Finally, in 1969, Phillips sold Sun to Mercury Records producer Shelby Singleton. Within months, there were more Sun LPs on the market than Sam Phillips had ever issued.

Recording just ten of Elvis's tracks, though, fixed Phillips's place in history; he was an original inductee to the Rock and Roll Hall of Fame in 1989.

229

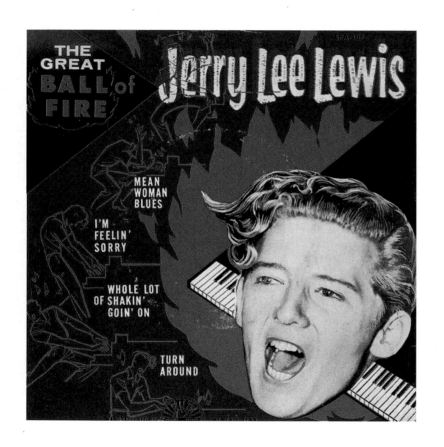

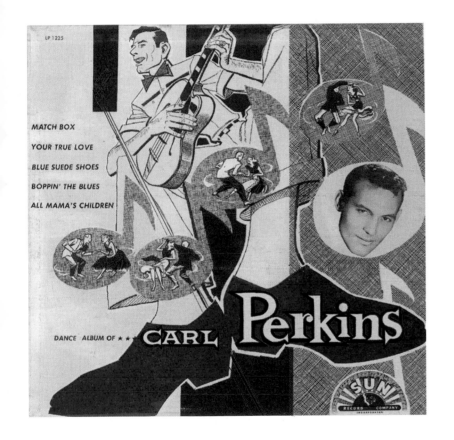

above (left to right): First album recorded by Jerry Lee Lewis for Sun records in 1958. Scotty Moore and Bill Black played with Elvis Presley on his first recording made for Sun records in 1954. They appeared together as Elvis Presley and the Blue Moon Boys for a short time afterwards. Carl Perkins's first album for Sun records. While recording for Sun records, Johnny Cash's back up was the Tennessee Two, Luther Perkins on electric guitar and Marshall Grant on bass.

# surfing oahu's north shore

## "eddie would go"

"[SUNSET'S] the worst punishment. It don't let go," Derrick Doerner says. "It sucks you back into the whitewater, throws you through Boneyards [a razor-like coral reef], you hit bottom, jump back up, it throws you right back down. There's five or six waves coming. Scariest thing in the world." This from a legend—a man who surfs the North Shore almost daily.

No place exemplifies Hawaii's pastime like Oahu's North Shore, where the world's best surfers gather every October through January when the winds shift and shape the waves to their menacing apex. Eleven spots comprise the Shore: there's Doerner's favorite, of course, Sunset; there's also Waimea Bay, Banzai Pipeline, and Off-the-Wall. As well as Backyard, Backdoor, and Jocko's. There's also Velzyland, Ehukai Beach, Rocky Point, and Haleiwa. Each is renowned for its own particular menace: thirty-foot waves at Waimea; Ehukai's massive walls; tuberiding at Off-the-Wall; racing curls at Pipeline. The North Shore is a comprehensive examination of will and ability, with death never out of the question.

Ancient Polynesians arrived in Hawaii around 400 A.D. and happened on the recreation of surfing soon after. The first published account of surfing came from Lt. James King, Captain Cook's second-in-command. While sailing through Kealakekua Bay in 1779, King noted the Islanders' unusual form of amusement: "Twenty or thirty of the natives, taking a long narrow board, set together from the shore. They lay themselves at length on the board and prepare for their return. Their first object is to place themselves on the summit of the largest surge. The boldness and address with which I saw them perform these difficult maneuvers was altogether astonishing and is scarcely to be believed."

It wasn't until Hawaiian swimmer Duke Paoa Kahanamoku competed in the 1932 Summer Olympics at Los Angeles that surfing became a nationwide fixation. Duke won a bronze medal, but his exploits in the surf grabbed all the attention. The surfing lifestyle soon became commonplace, from California's coastline to the Texas Gulf, even along New England's beaches. Still, no locale ever replaced the challenge of North Shore.

Each year, the North Shore hosts professional surfing's most-coveted contest: the Triple Crown of Surfing. The sport's elite compete for cash and the opportunity to conquer Haleiwa, Sunset, and Ehukai. There is also the Eddie Aikau Memorial Contest at Waimea, an event honoring surfing's guiding spirit. Aikau was the consummate "waterman." He tamed Waimea's massive swells, pulling off startling rides with ease, and even became the beach's first lifeguard. It's the story of his end, though, that resonates across the North Shore. On March 16, 1978, Aikau joined a crew aboard the *Hokule'a* and set out to sail around the Islands. The ocean overwhelmed the *Hokule'a* during the first night at sea, forcing it perilously far off course. Miles from land, surrounded by night's blackness and massive swells, Aikau volunteered to seek help. He left the boat on his surfboard and began paddling, away into the night and toward shore. Rescuers saved the *Hokule'a* crew the following morning. Eddie was never seen again.

From Aikau's disappearance came a rallying call, a credo, really, for the true surfer spirit. It's seen on bumper stickers, printed on T-shirts, heard on the street. But it sounds loudest to the North Shore surfer, standing alone on a beach, staring out past the breakers and wondering whether to answer the challenge set forth by the waves: "Eddie would go."

above: Duke Paoa Kahanamoku, 1915. right: Eddie Aikau, shown at Waimea Bay, was already a North Shore legend when, on March 16, 1978, he disappeared after a failed attempt to paddle his surfboard to shore to bring help for a lost boat.

TABASCO SAUCE has gone into combat with the U.S. military and into space with the astronauts. The bottles of red pepper sauce sit on the tables of presidents and royalty. It is sprinkled on eggs, on meat loaf, on vegetables, even added to liquid libations. But sprinkle gently—it doesn't take much. Those little bottles of red can be found around the world, yet it is produced in just one place: on top of a salt dome called Avery Island in rural Iberia Parish, 140 miles west of New Orleans, Louisiana. Its creator, Edmund McIlhenny, came up with the recipe between 1866 and 1868 and reportedly first sold it in small cologne bottles, sealed with green wax. He obtained a patent for his formula for making peppers into hot sauce in 1870. Tabasco sauce, as McIlhenny called it, was a hit with Americans and by the end of the decade was being exported to Europe.

For more than a hundred years, McIlhenny's descendants have supervised the planting and harvesting of the capsicum peppers used to make the fiery potion. Workers mash the ripe peppers with salt and let them ferment for three years in oak barrels. The process has changed little. When a family member determines that the mash has reached the right color, texture, and aroma, vinegar is added. The solution is stirred with wooden paddles for a month, then strained, bottled, and shipped to more than one hundred countries. Its distinctive label is printed in twenty languages. No matter the language, Tabasco means hot.

Pepper pickers harvest the *Capsicum frutescens* peppers used in Tabasco sauce when they are at their peak of ripeness. They match the peppers on the bushes to the color on a painted stick or "baton rouge" which is the shade of a perfectly ripe pepper. This system means each plant is picked several times during the harvest, as each pepper changes from green to yellow to orange then bright red.

television situation comedy: a great job

by James L. Brooks

MY INSIDE TRUTHS about television will not take long. I can let you have it with two short quotes: "Do you realize you could fly across the country on a Saturday Night, jump out of the plane and very likely land on someone watching your show?"

Grant Tinker, founding head of MTM, former chairman of NBC, and last of the good guys said that in wonder to me once. The fact that I actually once had a boss capable of wonder shows how long I have been involved with television.

"There is no better job in the world than running a successful series." That quote is from me. I bring it to you now—when I am not actively running a show on a day-to-day basis—in an attempt to share a religious truth. As if having been to the Grand Canyon without a camera, I stagger to your side, feeling that the privilege of having seen it requires me to describe it to you orally, in nuanced detail, out of a sense of responsibility and passion.

This sense of responsibility is a part of my personality that fair-minded people frequently find obnoxious. They have a point. My enthusiasm can redline to a point where the unbridled gives way to the slightly deranged. But damn it, a truly great job is an awesome freak of existence.

Case in point: A group of us is standing on the set of a half-hour comedy show. It is minutes before the start and a new joke is needed for the end of a scene. Little did I know that instead of a joke we would get wisdom for the ages. But before getting to one of the three smartest things I have ever heard about television comedy, let me go into why this little cluster of young men and women proves the central point of "no greater job."

For starters, we ran the stage we were clustered on. Director, crew, young assistants, terrific and sexy actors. All of them worked for us. Yet, because we were outsiders most of our lives, the fact that we were in charge was only remotely perceived by us, so that it became a nonfact, demanding no sense of mission or adult responsibility. The artichoke of life had blown up and been stupidly put back together; so here we were— the pointy things at the edges of the vegetable's hardest leaf—now serving as its heart.

We the boys and girls who mocked the system, *were* the system and mocked it still. And all of us were wildly well paid. And all of us were friends. And any of us who had a fight at home, a crazy date, a physical scare, a current passion could turn it into an episode and three weeks later, on a Saturday Night, jump out of that plane, and very likely land on someone laughing at our lives. All the hazards of social interactions— rejection, humiliation, inadequacy—were grist for the mint. And, for as long as people watched our television show, the constant struggles of the other more highly regarded creative worlds need not concern us. For the years ahead, there would be no need to raise production money, nor a need for anyone's approval but our own. There was also no danger of hubris. We lived in the trenches and died by the ratings, and we fought each year for the right time slot.

Our fame was friendly fame. None of this isolating crap of literature, or movies, or theatre. No one ever whispered, "look who that is," as we entered a restaurant. I used to repeat this joke when I went to a fancy restaurant and was blocked by the maître d', who had an eagle eye for movie people. "I'm in television. Here are my credits, and could you figure out whether they get me a table or not. Either way I'll understand." Then I'd stand very close to him and softly go over my career up to that moment. "I've written for such and such a show, and I created the such and such show, and right now I'm working on a pilot that's about such and such." Sometimes they'd get mad, and sometimes they'd smile, but I always had to wait for the table.

Television fame is more like someone asking what you do for a living and then feeling *more* comfortable when you tell them. That thing about going into people's homes is real and wonderful. Some great job, huh? Oh, and we would get two-months vacation every year. That was the length of time we had before having to get ready for the next season. And we'd travel in groups of friends who worked together and meet each day at some hotel bar in Europe and write funny postcards to people we knew in common. We almost always talked in jokes to each other, even in times of great spirit-bending stress.

One of my friends was talking about that sort of thing the other day. (Is there anything better than being reminded of something really funny you said that you'd totally forgotten?) The friend was Danny DeVito, whom I did the television series *Taxi* with, and who is more noteworthy for his brio for living than anyone else of life or legend. Yet he lives much of his vivacious life palling around with guys like me who frequently find themselves sweatily holding onto a gyrating mood swing.

He was recalling a time of foreboding in my life, when I was about to take a plane trip just before we were scheduled to work together. I was sure the plane was going to crash. Really sure. But I never considered the option of canceling my ticket. To do so would fatten up my fear. No, the plane crash was clearly preferable. (I've since conquered all such chubby demons and am a model of personal evolvement but that's a far less interesting story.) So here I was, my anxiety over the flight spilling all over Danny, my fears at the time very real. Danny responded, "Look there's no way you're going to crash because I am the LUCKIEST MAN ALIVE, and since I need you to do this work with me when you come back, there is no way you don't make it back."

"Great," I said, "I can just picture it; the plane is on fire, and, as we crash, I'm screaming, 'Ha, ha Danny. Your luck has run out.'" Somehow that joke made the flight bearable.

There was another vacation from television where I convinced myself I had cancer just before the flight. I was in New York and called the doctor back home for the results of the test. He put me on hold. Can you imagine what it was like waiting for the click of his return and then the word? The television writer friend I was traveling with got out his camera and pointed it at me. "Either way," he said, "it's an interesting picture." So right there—on life and death hold—I laughed. That's what we did for each other, in television land.

These moments took place at a time in television when, if there was a college graduate in the show's rewrite room, we chided him. If anyone came from a functional family, he had to serve as a target for our thoroughly traumatized group. Given the power of our numbers we could make someone feel deep guilt over a normal life.

All that has changed. Sitting in *The Simpsons* writers' room, I am the only one not to have graduated from college, or Harvard for that matter. In a concurrent revolution, the barricades movies erected to bar those of us from television have been blown away. The fundamentals have changed. It is my deep conviction that here, as everywhere, though having already mutated as a society, we refuse to step in front of the mirror. The fear of our new reflection is too great. Yet clues nag at us like a clever hag. Could it be any clearer, for example, that our once honorable professions are being seriously degraded; being a doctor, or politician, or journalist, or cop (and maybe a hundred other things) have lost the central dignity and simple purpose at their center. These jobs are no longer about fundamentals like healing, serving, informing, or preserving peace. It is with this in mind that I note television comedy is maintaining its center. There is a purity about trying to be funny.

Back to that group of young men and women clustered in the middle of the set looking for a joke to end their scene. One of our number pitches a not very funny joke. Nobody says anything. Meanwhile the pressure is building. There is an audience waiting, and the director wants the writers off the set so he can start the show. But the writers, who run the show, these inmates in total control of their asylum, know that five minutes in, there will be their new line that either gets a laugh or bombs. The one writer pitches the same frail joke, and after half-a-beat of the ensuing silence says, "That will work. What's wrong with that line? That's funny."

And now someone else speaks words that instantly tattooed themselves on my psyche. "You know when it's funny," he said, "'cause everyone laughs and walks away and the show starts."

God, let more things be that simple.

above: Writers and cast of the *Mary Tyler Moore Show*. Top row (left to right): Unknown, Lynn Ephraim, Valerie Harper, Mary Tyler Moore, Grant Tinker. Front row (left to right): David Lloyd, Joel Israel, and Albert Brooks. right: Creators of *Taxi* (left to right): Ed Weinberger, Jim Brooks, and Stan Daniels.

ticker-tape parades

IN THE CITY WHERE, as someone said, everybody rebels, but nobody mutinies, the ultimate symbol of making it big is the ticker-tape parade. And because it's New York, they recognize whomever they damn well please. Heroes, of course. Lindbergh. Howard Hughes for setting the round-the-world flying time (with his crew of three) in 1939: 3 days, 19 hours, and 17 minutes. John Glenn and other astronauts. Bobby Jones. Winston Churchill. Charles de Gaulle. But they also turned out, more than 7 million strong, for a general, Douglas MacArthur fired by his commander in chief, Harry S. Truman.

Perhaps, the most whimsical of all the ticker-tape parades was the one on August 5, 1938, given in honor of yet another pilot; it was estimated that more confetti and ticker tape fell on this parade than on Lindbergh's. The pilot being honored, first name Douglas, was better known as Wrongway Corrigan, who in a directional mix up because of an alleged broken compass, took a left instead of a right and landed in Ireland instead of Los Angeles. Corrigan's mistake and then his good humor appealed to the ticker-tape decisionmakers, who, by the way, can make their decision fast. Corrigan got his ticker-tape parade just three weeks after his Ireland flight.

The intensity of these blizzards of acclaim is measured just like a natural blizzard. But instead of snowfall, the city's sanitation department measures and records the tons of ticker tape, confetti, etc. that they pick up. The ticker-tape parade two days after V-J Day in 1945 is still the record: 5,438 tons.

The tradition began October 28, 1866, with a parade honoring the dedication of the Statue of Liberty. At least 175 ticker-tape parades later there's still nothing like it; so get out there and win a war, play for the Yankees, or as the lyricist Bart Howard wrote, "let us know what spring is like on Jupiter and Mars."

previous page: August 13, 1969, Apollo 11 astronauts Buzz Aldrin, Michael Collins, and Neil Armstrong receive a New York City salute after their historic moon flight and walk on July 20, 1969. above: On June 14, 1927, Charles Lindbergh's first successful solo flight from the United States to Paris is celebrated. left: Veterans of Desert Storm are saluted upon their return.

above: After a ticker-tape parade, crews from the Sanitation Department of the
City of New York remove tons of paper in a matter of hours. The granddaddy
of all clean-ups came after V-J Day August 14, 1945, when 5,438 tons of paper
were removed. left: Bird's-eye view of 1927 Lindbergh parade up Broadway.

# travis's letter from the alamo

## "victory or death!"

WHEN WILLIAM BARRETT TRAVIS and twenty-nine other men joined the "Texian" freedom fighters at the Alamo on February 2, 1836, they brought the total number of volunteers inside the tiny mission to 130. The arrival of Antonio Lopez de Santa Anna, president of Mexico and general of its Centralist Army, was only three weeks away. Accompanying him north into San Antonio de Bexar and the Mexican controlled state of Coahulia y Texas were, depending on the account, anywhere from 3,500 to 5,000 soldiers. Santa Anna could have never foreseen how this small force inside the Alamo would help bring an end to his country's rule over Texas.

The Texas Revolution began October 2, 1835, with the Battle of Gonzales—actually more of a skirmish—called by some the "Lexington of Texas." It exploded on December 10, 1835, when one hundred Texian colonists drove a Centralist division from its Alamo garrison. Instead of following orders from their superiors to blow up the Alamo and retreat, the colonists stayed and waited for Santa Anna. When the uprising's original leader, Col. James C. Neill, left the Alamo, the twenty-six-year-old Travis, a poet and lawyer, took command. He had no formal military training.

On February 23, the Mexican Army finally reached San Antonio, and General Santa Anna wasted no time in declaring that if the colonists inside the Alamo did not surrender, they would be put to the sword. The Texians knew they were overwhelmed, yet even after Travis explained the odds, they remained. (The story of Travis drawing a line in the sand and asking those ready to face fate to cross it may be more folklore than fact.) The day after Santa Anna's warning, Travis sent a messenger with his reply. It read: "I am determined to sustain myself as long as possible and die like a soldier who never forgets what is due to his honor and that of his country: VICTORY OR DEATH!"

But neither Travis nor his men were suicidal. They were looking for help from any quarter as the wide net cast by Travis's salutation suggests: "To the people of Texas

by A. C. Greene

and All Americans in the World." The letter's overriding message was to send help fast: "I call on you in the name of Liberty, of patriotism and everything dear to the American character, to come to our aid, with all dispatch." But his appeal had only limited results. Travis's most revealing feeling, in fact, was reflected in a letter written to a friend: "If my countrymen do not rally to my relief, I am determined to perish in the defense of this place, and my bones shall reproach my country for her neglect."

The final thirty-two men to join the Texas rebels arrived a week later on March 2, the same day Texas officially seceded from Mexico. The volunteers facing Santa Anna's forces now totaled 187. Until the final hours of the thirteen-day siege, it would have been possible for the defenders to retreat with minimal losses; messengers, in fact, escaped even in the final forty-eight hours. But not one volunteer left, and then, just before dawn broke on March 6, the Alamo came under attack. Though the battle was intense, by sunrise, every Texian volunteer was dead or captured; according to some historical accounts, so too, were 600 Centralists. Two months later, an army of colonists, inspired by the courage of Travis and the Alamo defenders, defeated Santa Anna at the Battle of San Jacinto and won independence for Texas.

Why do we remember the Alamo and Travis's letter? Part of the reason has to do with the mystique associated with the long history of men who chose death over surrender or retreat. And the tradition that what we remember sometimes turns out to be not quite the way it was. The hopeless stand of the Alamo force, the reckless bravery, and defiance all come through in the letter of their inspired and inspiring commander who was one of the first to die that March 6 morning, William Barrett Travis. We choose to remember most that his warrior code recognized only two alternatives: "Victory or death!"

251

the tuskegee airmen

THE GERMANS called them "Schwartze Vogelmenshen," Black Birdmen. The all-white American bomber crews whom they escorted with courage and distinction during World War II referred to them as the Black Redtail Angels after their P-51's stabilizers, which were painted bright red. History has come to know these black pilots as the Tuskegee Airmen, 926 men who earned their wings at Tuskegee Army Airfield from March 1942 through June 1946. They flew more than two hundred bomber escort missions without losing a single bomber to the enemy. Sixty-six Tuskegee Airmen were killed in action, another thirty-two shot down.

Theirs is the story of black men fighting for the right to fly in a segregated military, for a country still reluctant to grant them certain freedoms, especially freedom of opportunity.

all blood runs red

"We were fighting two battles," Maj. Joseph P. Gomer, USAF (ret) and member of the Tuskegee Airmen, recalled. "I flew for my parents, for my race, for our battle, for first-class citizenship and for my country. We were fighting for the 14 million black Americans back home. We were there to break down barriers, open a few doors, and do a job."

African Americans had shown their ability to fly before World War II. During World War I, Georgia-born air ace Eugene Jacques Bullard flew for France. Known as the "Black Swallow of Death," his plane carried the slogan "All Blood Runs Red." He earned the highest French medals for valor. Following World War I, other black private citizens had earned pilots' licenses, owned planes, ran flying schools, and made record-breaking cross-country flights. Yet, in 1939, when President Franklin D. Roosevelt started the Civil Aviation Authority's Civilian Pilot Training Program (CPTP) to train 20,000 college students a year for private flight-level licenses, not a single black was allowed to participate.

It took the efforts of America's most prominent African-American leaders and a little-known senator from Missouri to persuade the CPTP to accept and train black pilots. The NAACP's Walter White joined Mary McLeod Bethune of the National Youth Administration, A. Phillip Randolph from the Brotherhood of Sleeping Car Porters—the nation's largest black union—and Senator Harry S. Truman. Together they successfully persuaded Congress to include blacks in the CPTP program. Tuskegee Institute in Alabama, a black vocational college founded by Booker T. Washington, was selected as one of the training sites. Hoping to upgrade their facilities, the school requested financial assistance from the Julius Rosenwald Fund of Chicago. First Lady Eleanor Roosevelt, a member of the Fund's board, visited the institute and flew with Tuskegee's black flying instructor Charles "Chief" Anderson. What she saw and that flight convinced her that the school deserved the Rosenwald Fund's support.

After the necessary improvements were completed, President Roosevelt declared Tuskegee an official training site for African-American pilots and the 99th Pursuit Squadron was established. Tuskegee was appropriated $4 million for a new airfield.

In March 1942, the Tuskegee Airmen began flying combat missions. Four hundred and fifty of the 926 pilots who earned wings at Tuskegee would participate in the battles to control the sky during World War II. On July 26, 1948, Truman, by then president, desegregated the military with executive order 89981. The Tuskegee Airmen's performance helped accelerate the decision. "It was a wondrous sight to see those escort fighter planes coming up to take care of us," said World War II veteran and former senator George McGovern. "They were flown by men with enormous skill and coordination and competence."

Aviation cadets training at Tuskegee Army Air Field in 1943, where the 99th Pursuit Squadron had been established by the War Department in January 1941. These men were among the 926 pilots who earned their wings at Tuskegee.

253

# the underground railroad

## following the north star

IN THE 1830s, word spread plantation-to-plantation, about a "railroad to freedom," an Underground Railroad with no tracks, no locomotives, no tickets, and no timetables.

This illegal network of good citizens was set clearly in the young nation's tradition of civil disobedience. Also known as the Gospel Train or Freedom Train, the string of individuals helped fugitive slaves elude slave-hunters hired by owners and find their way to freedom. Quakers, Roman Catholics, Jews, and Protestants, even American Indians were bound together by a determination to see slavery ended. They numbered several thousand and included black and white Abolitionists who lived in states bordering the South and in major cities of the North.

The very existence of the Underground Railroad was a bold challenge to the Fugitive Slave Law of 1850, which required the return of runaway slaves, even after they reached states that had abolished slavery. The secrecy of its hierarchy created a mythic and mysterious history, related informally by the narratives of escaped slaves, those who led them out, and others who made the case for the breaking of the Fugitive Slave Law.

Many slaves who made the decision to seek freedom simply walked away from their masters with no plan other than to travel only at night, always following the North Star. Success depended on finding strangers willing to risk their own lives, by offering help along the way.

Other slaves plotted their escapes carefully, bolstering their chances with food and money taken surreptitiously from their plantation masters. They followed the lead of a "conductor" who knew where to go and who would help them. Slaves along the route who chose not to go, offered what assistance they could.

Once the slaves crossed the border into the North, members of the Underground Railroad would hide them, feed and nurse them, even provide papers identifying them as freedmen—then send them on to the next station. Churches, stables, basements, and attics became hiding places. For many, Canada represented the safest destination, while others settled in Northern states where public opinion was favorable to their cause.

Among the Underground Railroad's more heroic engineers was Harriet Tubman, born a slave on Maryland's Eastern Shore about 1820, she escaped to Philadelphia in 1849. Once free, Tubman wrote, "I looked at my hands to see if I was the same person now I was free. There was such a glory over everything I felt like I was in heaven." Her own escape made Tubman determined to rescue as many slaves from bondage as she could.

Her trips were made in the winter months when nights were long. Escapes began on Saturday nights; the slaves would not be missed till Monday. When "wanted" posters went up, Tubman paid black men to tear them down. She kept a supply of paregoric to put babies to sleep, so their cries would not arouse suspicion. She carried a gun, not simply for self-defense, but as inspiration—to threaten anyone in her group professing fatigue. For her, it was the welfare of the group that counted. If pursuers got too close, Tubman would hustle her people onto a *southbound* train, knowing that authorities would not expect fugitives to flee in that direction.

After making nineteen trips into slave states, and leading more than three hundred men, women, and children to freedom, Harriet Tubman became known as "Moses." And to those who wondered why she was not afraid, she answered: "I can't die but once."

left: Former slave Harriet Tubman, on the left holding a pan, was one of the most active members of the Underground Railroad. Slave owners reportedly offered $40,000 for her capture.

volkswagen's campaign in america

## by Roy Grace

ONCE UPON A TIME, advertising was very different. People lived happily ever after in a world of pure fantasy, where all life's problems were solved. Cars were glamorous objects, retouched and airbrushed to a fare-thee-well, often accessorized with mansions and sold by beautiful women wearing little more than diaphanous gowns and dazzling smiles.

And then onto the scene came an ugly, little car called Volkswagen. Nothing else was ever quite the same.

It didn't look like any other car, and its advertising didn't look or speak like anything that had gone before.

First off, the car didn't have a fancy name. People dubbed it "the Bug" or "the Beetle." And the name stuck.

It was shown in simple photos, often plain black-and-white, without flattering airbrushing. No mansions hovered in the background; no one gamboled in the foreground. There was no suave, debonair driver. And no gorgeous female. There the Bug sat in all its dumb flat-footed homeliness.

Sometimes it was shown upside down, or in pieces, or floating in water, or mired in mud. It was dented, it was battered. It appeared as a lump of clay, as a hunk of meat. It was shown without wheels, without a body, even crushed out of shape. It was seen as a police car, as a taxicab, and not quite seen under snow. It was shown wearing giant sunglasses or covered with psychedelic designs, or with a huge windup key. It was shown as a single simple line. Sometimes it wasn't even shown at all.

Volkswagen ads sold the steak instead of the sizzle. They talked about air-cooled engines that never needed antifreeze or water, about how the engine was mounted over the drive wheels to give better traction, how the car was inspected thousands of times, how easy it was to replace parts, how economical it was, and how it sustained its value.

Just as unusual as the way the ads looked was their tone of voice. Early on, the decision was made that this was an honest product, honestly made, and could be sold no other way but honestly. So these ads would go where advertising had seldom gone before—right to people's intelligence. They would appeal to commonsense and logic and would never resort to fluff or hype.

The copy spoke to readers as though they were bright, quick-witted friends. The tone was self-deprecating rather than self-congratulatory. It was irreverent. The car was never treated as an object of quasi-religious idolatry. Instead it was . . . well, human, with all of humanity's oddities and quirks. The overall impression was friendly, straightforward, and plain spoken. A German car with all-American attributes.

For the first time, advertising talked *to* people and not *at* them. The ads were designed to make people think, to appeal to their intelligence. (And indeed, research throughout the years showed that VW buyers were better educated than other car buyers.) People were respected, flattered; their sense of humor tickled as they read the ads. They felt smart driving the little Bugs: they had made a thoughtful choice. The advertising became part of the car—they "drove" the advertising.

The copy in the ads was crafted to leave the reader with a little smile at the end, a smile relevant to the selling message. (Almost fifty years later, this continues to be the style of copy in "creative" advertising.) The campaign spoke to Americans' traditional desire to root for the underdog.

And Americans responded. They were entertained by the ads. They found them fresh, endearing, and fun. They talked about them at cocktail parties. Hundreds wrote their own ads and sent them in. It may have been the first advertising people looked forward to. In one of those wonderful marriages of cause and effect, extraordinary sales resulted. In 1968, VW's best year, 423,000 of the little Bugs were sold.

In 1978, twenty years after the campaign began, it ended. The Beetle was killed, a victim of the falling dollar, the surging Deutsche Mark, tough new EPA standards, and newly savvy competition. As someone once said, the car ran out of gas before the advertising did. Those of us who were in on the creation of the campaign ads will never forget the experience.

It was a great ride.

right: Examples of Doyle Dane Bernbach's advertisements for Volkswagen circa mid 1960s. These ads appeared in magazines, newspapers, on billboards, and television beginning in the late 1950s throughout the period of time the "Beetle," as it became known, was in production.

# Joint savings account.

## Lemon.

This Volkswagen missed the boat.

The chrome strip on the glove compartment is blemished and must be replaced. Chances are you wouldn't have noticed it; Inspector Kurt Kroner did.

There are 3,389 men at our Wolfsburg factory with only one job: to inspect Volkswagens at each stage of production. (3000 Volkswagens are produced daily; there are more inspectors than cars.)

Every shock absorber is tested (spot checking won't do), every windshield is scanned. VWs have been rejected for surface scratches barely visible to the eye.

Final inspection is really something! VW inspectors run each car off the line onto the Funktionsprüfstand (car test stand), tote up 189 check points, gun ahead to the automatic brake stand, and say "no" to one VW out of fifty.

This preoccupation with detail means the VW lasts longer and requires less maintenance, by and large, than other cars. (It also means a used VW depreciates less than any other car.)

We pluck the lemons; you get the plums.

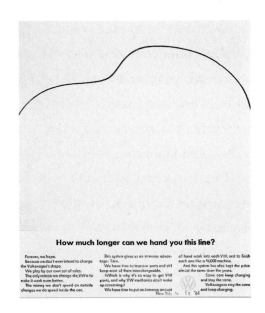

# It makes your house
# look bigger.

## Think small.

Our little car isn't so much of a novelty any more.

A couple of dozen college kids don't try to squeeze inside it.

The guy at the gas station doesn't ask where the gas goes.

Nobody even stares at our shape.

In fact, some people who drive our little flivver don't even think 32 miles to the gallon is going any great guns.

Or using five pints of oil instead of five quarts.

Or never needing anti-freeze.

Or racking up 40,000 miles on a set of tires.

That's because once you get used to some of our economies, you don't even think about them any more.

Except when you squeeze into a small parking spot. Or renew your small insurance. Or pay a small repair bill. Or trade in your old VW for a new one.

Think it over.

### How much longer can we hand you this line?

Forever, we hope.

Because we don't ever intend to change the Volkswagen's shape.

We play by our own set of rules.

The only reason we change the VW is to make it work even better.

The money we don't spend on outside changes we do spend inside the car.

This system gives us an immense advantage: Time.

We have time to improve parts and still keep most of them interchangeable.

(Which is why it's so easy to get VW parts, and why VW mechanics don't wake up screaming.)

We have time to put an immense amount of hand work into each VW, and to finish each one like a $6,000 machine.

And this system has also kept the price almost the same over the years.

Some cars keep changing and stay the same.

Volkswagens stay the same and keep changing.

259

# webster's american dictionary

## "the final volley of independence"

IT TOOK one good man a good part of twenty years to create. To prepare himself, wrote his biographer, "he restudied his college Greek, Latin, and Hebrew; perfected his French and German; and then studied Danish, Anglo-Saxon, Welsh, Old Irish, Persian and seven Asiatic and Assyrian-based languages." Noah Webster meant business. His dictionary, and "his" is the right word since he did it himself, was compiled from his 70,000 hand-written entries. His *American Dictionary of the English Language*, comprising two volumes, each about 800 pages, sold for $20 in 1828, the year it was published.

When he began, thinking the dictionary would require three to five years, Webster said, "I ask no favors: the undertaking is Herculean but is of far less consequence to *me* than to my *country*. . . . I shall pursue [the task] with zeal and undoubtedly with success." That sentiment could have been expressed by so many of those remarkable men and women who brought this nation into being. Nothing seemed too big for them, no sacrifice too great for the sake of their own particular American dream.

Webster believed we needed our own dictionary, not Dr. Johnson's, which he attacked and scorned, going overboard in his criticism: "Not a single page of Johnson's dictionary is correct." We needed a dictionary, Webster was convinced, that was clearly ours, containing words unique to the young nation's growing vernacular.

Webster had his own agenda to advance in this regard. For instance, in the case of the word "equal," he believed the Declaration of Independence was wrong in stating "all men are created equal." Webster believed in equality of opportunity, but not equality of condition. He also disagreed with the prevailing understanding of the meaning of the word "free," that all men were free to act according to their will. That sense threatened government, giving people the sense they were above authority. The tension associated with the meaning of "free" carries on; neither Webster's dictionary nor any other can remove it.

AN

# AMERICAN DICTIONARY

OF THE

# ENGLISH LANGUAGE:

### INTENDED TO EXHIBIT,

I. THE ORIGIN, AFFINITIES AND PRIMARY SIGNIFICATION OF ENGLISH WORDS, AS FAR AS THEY HAVE BEEN ASCERTAINED.
II. THE GENUINE ORTHOGRAPHY AND PRONUNCIATION OF WORDS, ACCORDING TO GENERAL USAGE, OR TO JUST PRINCIPLES OF ANALOGY.
III. ACCURATE AND DISCRIMINATING DEFINITIONS, WITH NUMEROUS AUTHORITIES AND ILLUSTRATIONS.

### TO WHICH ARE PREFIXED,

### AN INTRODUCTORY DISSERTATION

ON THE

### ORIGIN, HISTORY AND CONNECTION OF THE
### LANGUAGES OF WESTERN ASIA AND OF EUROPE,

### AND A CONCISE GRAMMAR

OF THE

# ENGLISH LANGUAGE.

### BY NOAH WEBSTER, LL. D.

### IN TWO VOLUMES.
### VOL. I.

He that wishes to be counted among the benefactors of posterity, must add, by his own toil, to the acquisitions of his ancestors.—*Rambler.*

### NEW YORK:
### PUBLISHED BY S. CONVERSE.
PRINTED BY HEZEKIAH HOWE—NEW HAVEN.
### 1828.

TITLE PAGE OF WEBSTER'S AMERICAN DICTIONARY, VOLUME 1, PUBLISHED IN 1828

Who could have been better for the job? Webster, as a young teacher just out of Yale, was sharply critical of education. Without a common language, common pronunciation, and a shared understanding of America's history, he envisioned chaos that could hobble any shared sense of unity on which, he believed, America's survival depended. In "one of the most audacious and fateful decisions in America's cultural history," he set out to ensure that America would have all three.

For Noah Webster, spelling was the first battle to be fought because "the spelling book does more to form the language of a nation than all other books." By trying different teaching methods, with his own classes in the small community of Goshen, New York, he designed a new spelling book. The simple approach he created "unified the language and speech of the children he taught and made it remarkably easier for them to learn reading, writing and spelling than ever before." And in a few years the methods and spelling Webster advocated would do the same "for the entire American people and their children both foreign and native born."

Protector of copyrights. Editor of Governor Winthrop's Journal. A founder of Amherst College. Active in the initiative to plant elms along New Haven's streets. Noah Webster's lasting place in the nation's memory, however, derives from his conviction in the power of language and the necessity of fully understanding the language to exercise its power. That conviction produced *The American Spelling Book* and then, over four decades later, *An American Dictionary of the English Language*, the final volley of independence from England.

Webster took twenty years (fifteen years longer than he had planned), to compile his dictionary, including one year abroad in Paris, London, and Cambridge, where he studied books not available in America. The finished work, nearly 1,600 pages in length, sold as a two-volume set for $20.

# the western

LACONIC MEN, with a code to steer by: stand up, don't run, count on no one but yourself. Men who never learned to deceive themselves. Men who liked simple stories that seemed almost incidental. In 1966, Howard Hawks, one of the best Western directors, called Robert Mitchum for a role in *El Dorado*:

> "You available, Bob?"
>
> "Sure, Howard. Uh, what's the story?"
>
> "Oh you know, Bob. There's no story."

The director and writer, Peter Bogdanovich, has six personal favorites, all directed by either John Ford or Howard Hawks. In order of release, they are: *My Darling Clementine* (Ford), *Red River* (Hawks), *She Wore A Yellow Ribbon* (Ford), *The Searchers* (Ford), *Rio Bravo* (Hawks), and *The Man Who Shot Liberty Valence* (Ford). That nucleus of favorites underscores the Western's focus: the clarity between right and wrong.

"Certainly," Bogdanovich wrote, "the western is one of the most pervasive icons of Americana: a symbol of frontiers challenged and tamed; a series of morality tales of good and evil that contain within them the essential history of the United States."

Symbols. Legends. Ford, the director, was prickly and unafraid. He walked the walk. From his first efforts, made before 1920, to his last western, *The Man Who Shot Liberty Valence*, in 1962, his films helped fashion the myth of the West and of the men and women who belonged there. "When the legend becomes fact, Sir, print the legend," the young reporter told Jimmy Stewart, playing a United States Senator in *Liberty Valence*. That is advice John Ford both gave and followed.

The mythic western theme is pervasive, thanks in large part to the movies. It was, for a long time, how the rest of the world saw us: We're all cowboys, gunslingers operating according to some unwritten rules way out in the wide open spaces. In truth, our filmmakers have often taken their leads from colleagues working in other countries. Akira Kurosawa's classic Samurai pictures became box office and critical successes in America, remade as westerns. *The Seven Samurai* (1954), was moved to indigenous screens as *The Magnificent Seven*, and *Yojimbo* (1961), catapulted Clint Eastwood to fame as the "Man with No Name," in *A Fistful of Dollars*, in 1964. And even *Yojimbo cum A Fistful of Dollars* was the beneficiary of further foreign aid: Its director was Sergio Leone, the Italian responsible for Eastwood's "spaghetti western" phenomenon.

While moviegoers the world over recognize the western as our defining movie genre (at least, until the ongoing saga of *Star Wars*), American film audiences have lost interest; people being killed slowly, just one at a time, is a plot line that won't hold our attention. Only two westerns have been Academy Award recipients: *Cimarron* (1931), then six decades later, Eastwood's *Unforgiven* (1992). In *Unfor-*

*given*, Eastwood, who also directed, makes use of another western movie theme: The lone man, isolated, trying to scratch a living from the characteristically unyielding soil. A former gunfighter, he is unfit for farming. When the opportunity presents itself, to pick up his gun again and make some money the only way he knows how, money he wouldn't care about if he didn't need it to take care of his two motherless children, he moves comfortably on to another western movie tradition, and takes a sidekick, Morgan Freeman. The bonds that tie men together in the West are inviolable. Death is the only severance.

John Ford's stories, at bottom, are simply about the individual as the last line of defense; a man takes a stand, no matter how high the price, refusing to ask for help. (Ford, in fact, had low regard for *High Noon*, because, he said, "No real western sheriff would ever ask for help.") It is widely considered, even by his friendly competitor, Howard Hawks, that Ford, beginning with *Stagecoach* (1939), directed the best Westerns. When Bogdanovich once asked Hawks about a particularly evocative shot in *Red River*, Hawks responded: "Once in a while you get lucky—you get one of those Ford shots." Asked, too, if that thought, that humbling yardstick of comparison, was ever *really* in his mind, Hawks said, "Hard to do a western *without* thinking of Jack Ford."

Watch *The Searchers*. John Ford, the director, and the star, John Wayne (that brilliant, unselfconscious, perfectly nondescript name for the Iowan who, until Hollywood decided otherwise, was called Marion Morrison). The unambivalent technicolor and the vastness of Monument Valley. A spare story: embittered loner Ethan Edwards, played by Wayne, the Duke, goes alone to search for and bring home Natalie Wood, kidnapped as a little girl by the Indians (and in this early role just beginning to smolder). The big man brings her back. Stands watching, one arm across his body, gripping

his other elbow, as the family folds the daughter back into itself. Door closes. John Wayne, alone, turns and walks away. You know that walk. The Sons of the Pioneers sing, "What makes a man to wander? What makes a man to roam? Ride away. Ride away."

John Wayne *was* the Western. But why? People who call movies "films" try to explain it. Maybe no one summed it up better than the director, Raoul Walsh, when he said, "Dammit, the son of a bitch looked like a man." Perhaps that's it: he did look and act like a man, and we never read or heard anything to make us doubt it. Joan Didion, in a profile of the Duke in his last years, spoke for a lot of us: "When John Wayne rode through my childhood and perhaps through yours, he determined forever the shape of certain of our dreams."

265

# the woman suffrage movement

Neisa McMein leads a parade
of women seeking the right to
vote prior to the passage of
the Nineteenth Amendment.

# "failure is impossible"

On November 5, 1872, Susan B. Anthony wrote to Elizabeth Cady Stanton: "Well I have been & gone & done it!!—positively voted the Republican ticket—strait—this a.m. at 7 o'clock." Anthony cast her ballot at a barber shop in Rochester, New York. She was one of 6,431,149 citizens who voted in the election between Ulysses S. Grant and Horace Greeley, an election Grant won decisively by 762,991 votes. Three weeks later, on Thanksgiving Day, Anthony and the handful of other women who voted with her were arrested and indicted for having "knowingly voted without having a lawful right to vote."

The verdict at her trial was foreordained: The judge refused to let her take the witness stand and then instructed the all-male jury to find her guilty without deliberation. Anthony succeeded in being heard, however, when the judge asked if she had "anything to say why sentence shall not be pronounced?" She replied: "Yes, your honor, I have many things to say, for in your ordered verdict of guilty, you have trampled underfoot every vital principle of our government. My natural rights, my civil rights, my political rights, are all alike ignored. Robbed of the fundamental privilege of citizenship, I am degraded from the status of a citizen to that of a subject; and not only myself individually, but all of my sex, are, by your honor's verdict, doomed to political subjection." She refused to pay the $100 fine the judge ordered, but he refused

267

to imprison her, thereby preventing her from appealing to a higher court. Undeterred, Anthony took her case to the public and had thousands of copies of the trial proceedings printed and distributed.

Anthony would find other ways to press the cause of woman suffrage. Brought up as a Quaker and active as an early temperance supporter, she soon realized that until women could vote, politicians would not listen to them. For more than fifty years she urged lawmakers to enfranchise the other half of America's population. She attended her first women's rights convention in Syracuse, in 1852, and with Elizabeth Cady Stanton founded the American Equal Rights Association in 1866. The two women published a feisty newspaper *The Revolution* whose masthead proclaimed "Men their rights, and nothing more; women, their rights, and nothing less."

She appeared before every U.S. Congress between 1869 and 1906 to ask them to pass a suffrage amendment. She was prepared as any modern-day lobbyist—her copy of the seating chart of all the members of Congress has survived. Her speech to a Senate committee in 1904 reflected her frustration: "I never come here, and this is the seventeenth Congress that I have attended, but with a feeling of injustice which ought not to be borne, because the women, one-half the people are not able to get a hearing from the Representatives and Senators of the United States." Her combative tone did not mellow with age. When President Theodore Roosevelt sent congratulations in 1906 to her eighty-sixth birthday celebration, her response was indignant: "I wish the men would do something besides extend congratulations. . . . I would rather have him say a word to Congress for the cause than to praise me endlessly." She ended that evening's gathering, her final public appearance, with a ringing prophecy: "There have been others also just as true and devoted to the cause . . . with such women consecrating their lives, failure is impossible!"

Less than a month later, March 13, 1906, she died at her home in Rochester, New York. The rights for which she had worked so tirelessly were finally won when the Nineteenth Amendment, the Susan B. Anthony amendment, passed on June 4, 1919, as women gathered on the steps of the Capitol to cheer. The vote was close, only one more than the required two-thirds. To achieve the win, two Congressmen had come from hospitals to vote aye; a third left his suffragist wife's death bed to cast a vote, then returned to her funeral. When the state of Tennessee became the thirty-sixth state to ratify, the amendment was officially adopted August 18, 1920—nearly a half century after Susan B. Anthony had illegally voted for Ulysses S. Grant.

Suffrage opponents formed the National Anti-Suffrage Association to rally support for denying women the right to vote.

the wright brothers

concept of genius

by John Keegan

MEN HAD DREAMED of flying since the dawn of history. The first to fulfill the dream were American nobodies of the sort who have so often surprised humanity, Orville and Wilbur Wright. What made their achievement on December 17, 1903, so distinctive was that they flew "like birds." Before the Wright Brothers everyone, in one way or another, had been fettered by the belief that an aeroplane—the word had not yet been coined—must, like a ship, be inherently stable. A ship, if rudder and sails were set right, would point itself into the seas, righting itself whatever the force of wind and water playing on its surfaces, and so sail as long as it retained it buoyancy. The Wrights hit on an alternative concept, that of an inherently unstable craft which, by the pilot's constant correction or application of pitch, yaw, and roll, could be made either to maintain level flight or to dive, climb, bank, and turn.

The Wrights set out to construct a machine that would do all those things. This was their concept of genius. Unlike other experimenters, moreover, they adopted from the outset a method that was strictly scientific. Rather than guess how a collection of bird-like components—wing, tails—might work if assembled into a flying machine, they designed each separately and tested it exhaustively until satisfied that it would perform as needed. Only then did they proceed to the next stage of experimentation.

What made the brothers' successful early experiments so remarkable is that neither had any academic education in physics. They were entirely self-taught. The sons of a bishop of the Church of the United Brethren in Christ, neither had progressed beyond high school; they had begun life as bicycle manufacturers in a small workshop they had

preceding page: On December 17, 1903, Orville makes his first flight at Kitty Hawk, North Carolina, while Wilbur watches. above: Wilbur gliding, Kitty Hawk, 1901.

273

**RECEIVED** at                                                                                             176

176 C KA 33 33 Paid.        Via Norfolk  Va

Kitty  Hawk N C Dec 17

Bishop M Wright

        7 Hawthorne St

Success four flights thursday  morning  all against twenty one mile

wind started from Level with engine power alone  average speed

through air thirty one miles longest 57 seconds inform  Press

home ~~above~~ Christmas .                          Orevelle Wright      525P

set up themselves in Dayton, Ohio, where their father's bishopric was then located. Like so many pioneers of America's nineteenth-century industrial revolution, they were hard-working practical engineers, craftsmen rather than technologists, who learned as they went. The difference between them and other small town entrepreneurs was that they had a genius for learning and for identifying new problems to solve.

By September 1900, when Wilbur wrote to Bishop Wright that he was to start for the Outer Banks of North Carolina "for the purpose of making some experiments with a flying machine," most of their theoretical problems had been solved. It remained to design an internal combustion engine light enough to lift itself, an airframe, and a pilot from the ground. From 1900-1903, the brothers continued to perfect their gliding technique and means of glider control at Kitty Hawk, North Carolina; then, on trips home to Dayton, they designed and built a motor to meet the requirements of autonomous flight.

The final program of tests began on the Outer Banks in September 1903. There were setbacks—cracks in the motor block—and frequent crashes caused by the high Atlantic winds. They had chosen Kitty Hawk on the Outer Banks because it was so windy—the sixth windiest place in the nation. On December 3, they were ready.

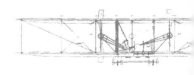

Instead of starting from one of the sandhills, which would have given an unfair advantage, invalidating their ambition to show that the Flyer, as they called their aeroplane, could rise higher than its starting point, they placed it on a wooden rail on level ground. Wilbur began first but stalled. Then Orville took the controls and, setting off into the strong wind with Wilbur steadying the wingtip at a run, rose into the air, held the Flyer straight and level and descended safely 120 feet further at a height equal to that of take-off. Man had finally flown like a bird.

The Wrights made three more flights that morning, the last covering 852 feet, when a windgust broke the airframe. The pieces were packed up and sent to Dayton. Orville telegraphed ahead to the bishop, "Success four flight Thursday morning . . . started from level with engine power alone . . . home Christmas."

It would be several years before the Wright revolution was recognized for what it was. Some deny it to this day, claiming "first flight" for other Americans and many Europeans. It was not until 1908, when Orville and Wilbur brought a successor of the Flyer to Europe and flew it at the Le Mans aeronautical meeting in France that one of their European competitors uttered the plain truth. After watching them fly round a closed one-mile circuit, turn, climb, dive, and bank, Leon Delagrance, a French flyer, exclaimed, "We are beaten. We don't exist."

Today the Flyer hangs above the entrance to the Smithsonian Aviation Museum in Washington, D.C. Under it an inscription proclaims, "By Original Research the Wright Brothers Discovered the Principles of Human Flight. As Inventors, Builders and Flyers They Further Developed the Aeroplane, Taught Men to Fly and Opened the Era of Aviation."

No objective aviation historian today disagrees. Their concept of genius ensures their reputation not only as great technologists but also, through their modest practicality and self-taught achievements, as great men of a distinctively American type.

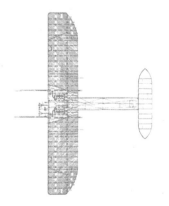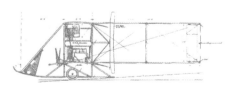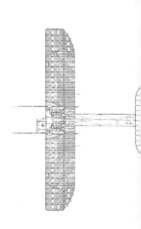

yellow fever

# "a common cause for a disease all too common"

THE FRENCH were no strangers to the *Stegomyia fasciata*. It was, after all, that tiny mosquito that wiped out 90 percent of Napoleon's expeditionary teams in the South-ern United States in 1802, influencing him to sell the Louisiana Territory. Then, in 1889, Ferdinand de Lesseps's near-decade long and terminally troubled attempt to build a canal across the Isthmus of Panama crumbled after 20,000 workers—one-third of his force—died from yellow fever, the highly contagious, usually fatal, disease con-tracted from a single mosquito bite.

In America, the fever reached epidemic proportions as well. More than three-hundred-thousand cases were reported in the United States between 1793 and 1900; at times, mortality rates soared to 85 percent. The disease attacks the liver, turns the skin yellow, raises body temperature, and causes internal bleeding before the victim lapses into a coma; more U.S. troops were killed during the Spanish-American War by yellow fever than by the enemy.

Yellow fever, nicknamed "yellow jack" after the pennants that flew to signal a quarantine, arrived in Central America in the mid-sixteenth century aboard slave ships traveling from Africa. Despite countless hypotheses, the cause of the disease and its rapid spread remained a mystery.

Dr. Carlos Finlay, of Havana, Cuba, had long-theorized that mosquitoes carried and spread yellow fever. The conventional medical establishment criticized Finlay, calling him "mosquito man." But no one had a better idea. Finally, in desperation, U.S. Army Major Walter Reed, his fellow doctors, and a detachment of soldiers traveled to Havana in June of 1900 and tested Finlay's theory by volunteering to let the indigenous mosquitoes bite them.

On August 27, Dr. James Carroll, one of the volunteers, allowed himself to be bitten; he fell ill with the disease, but survived. Reed survived his bout as well. Their colleague, however, Dr. Jesse William Lazear, died of the disease on September 25. Reed and Carroll sustained lasting damage to their health from the tests. The soldiers who volunteered to be bitten were just as valiant. To a man, they refused a $250 reimbursement, believing money would cheapen the courage of their sacrifice.

Public opinion was cynical and negative. American newspapers generally mocked the experiment, if they covered it at all. Congress denied a pension to the volunteer who developed the first controlled yellow-fever case, Pvt. John R. Kissinger, even though the experiments left him paralyzed. (By 1925, the combined monthly payment to Kissinger and the widows of Reed, Lazear, and Carroll, totaled only $475.)

Yet the team prevailed. In October 1900, Major Reed declared before the American Public Health Association that "the mosquito serves as the intermediate host for the parasite of yellow fever." The disease's cycle was unraveled soon after: Female mosquitoes picked up yellow fever in the first three days of a patient's infection, and after a twelve-day incubation period, they became contagious with the pandemic disease.

After the discovery of yellow fever's host, Maj. William Crawford Gorgas drew an assignment to eradicate the disease by means of installing wire window screens, fumigating, and disposing of all standing freshwater near human dwellings in Havana (the *Stegomyia fasciata* bred in freshwater and needed human blood nearby to thrive). By 1901, he had eliminated mosquito breeding grounds and subsequently, yellow fever, from the city.

Then, an appeal to President Theodore Roosevelt by chief engineer John Stevens brought Major Gorgas to Panama in 1905. Gorgas not only eradicated the insect in the Canal Zone, but also wiped out another mosquito that spread malaria and rats carrying bubonic plague. Gorgas's triumph allowed the United States to begin their canal dig; by 1914, it was open, and Panama's death rate from yellow jack had dropped to only half that of the United States.

...tions of Temperature beginning *January 21st 1901.* 189 , at *Post Hosp. Col. Bks. Cuba.*

| NAME. | COMPANY. | REGIMENT. | NATIVITY. | | AGE. | DIAGNOSIS. |
|---|---|---|---|---|---|---|
| ...insler | "a" | 2d Art | N.Y. | | 30 | Yellow Fever: |
| 22 | 23 | 24 | 25 | 26 | 27 | |

above: A temperature chart for thirty-year-old Pvt. Frank Heinsler, who contracted typhoid fever as part of the yellow fever experiment. He died at 4:10 P.M., January 27, 1901. right: Maj. Walter Reed as a young man.

yellowstone, our first national park

An Act to set apart a certain tract of Land lying near the headwaters of the Yellowstone River as a Public Park" passed the U.S. Congress in March 1872, thanks in part to the work of two nineteenth-century artists. Thomas Moran's color sketches and paintings and William Henry Jackson's photographs had helped convince the members of Congress in 1872 to set aside 2.2 million acres of Wyoming and Montana wilderness as the nation's first national park. Because Congress got the pictures, America got Yellowstone. Before their work was made public, little reliable proof had been offered to support the fanciful reports about the land that began to filter back East shortly after Lewis and Clark's Corps of Discovery returned from their three-year epic journey in 1806.

The eye-witness reports of trappers and mountain men described a strange landscape filled with foul-smelling vapors, boiling springs, and towering water geysers. Fur trader Warren Angus Ferris wrote "the largest of these wonderful fountains, projects a column of boiling water several feet in diameter to the height of more than one hundred and fifty feet."

However, without images to back their claims, those who heard the early descriptions considered them exaggerated and farfetched. Finally, in 1870, *Scribner's* magazine published a credible account based on Nathaniel P. Langford's journal from the privately financed Washburn-Doane expedition. Thomas Moran, then the magazine's illustrator, had reworked Langford's amateur sketches for the article. Moran was so intrigued by the sketches that he decided to go West and see for himself.

Borrowing money—using one of his paintings as collateral—to pay his own expenses, Moran joined Ferdinand Hayden of the U.S. Geological Survey. The Hayden Survey of 1871 had been organized to chart the lands around the Yellowstone river. Hayden also enlisted the services of photographer William Henry Jackson who had just completed work documenting construction along the Union Pacific railroad's Western route. The Moran color sketches, combined with the Jackson photographs, would give the public their first evidence of the spectacular drama of the landscape and vistas to be found in the nearly 3,500 square miles that became Yellowstone Park.

Moran's field sketches were done on site; he then added small amounts of color each day when he returned to camp. Jackson worked with two new large format cameras, a "6 [fr 1/2]-by-9" and an "8-by-10," purchased for the expedition. The two collaborated frequently on the "point of view" from which they would each capture an image. Moran's journal records the terrain, so difficult and dense, that one night they were "lost for several hours." After nearly a month in the wilderness, a hungry Moran wrote "as the Wonders of the Yellowstone had been seen, I concluded to return. Four biscuits a day for last 5 days." Jackson later wrote of Moran, "it was my good fortune to have him at my side during all that season to help me solve many problems of composition."

The press fed the anticipation for Moran's rapidly executed sketches and Jackson's photographs. In September 1871, *The New York Times* asserted that the images "will be trustworthy, exact, and comprehensive, and will thus supply much needed information as one of the most wonderful tracts of the American continent." The newspaper was correct. Jackson credited Moran whose "wonderful coloring, in pictures of canyons and hot springs . . . made the convincing argument for their preservation for the benefit of all posterity."

The bill to designate Yellowstone as our first national park was helped by the Northern Pacific railroad, seeking a new destination to generate tourism, and local inhabitants who saw a park as an economic booster for the region. But nothing was more convincing or influential than the Moran and Jackson images that laid to rest forever the idea that early accounts had been overblown exaggerations. Seeing was believing.

Yellowstone was America's first national park. As the twentieth century concludes, the democratic impulse that set aside land for public use has converted nearly 81 million acres into more than 375 national parks, battlefields, lakeshores, preserves, rivers, seashores, and memorials. Yellowstone National Park was the beginning of a worldwide movement to create national parks; since Yellowstone, more than 100 nations have set aside some 1,200 parks or preserves.

preceding spread: During the 1871 Hayden Expedition, Thomas Moran often sketched on horseback. His watercolor titled "In the Cañon" shows his pencil notations for further colors to be added when he returned to the campsite. **above, clockwise from the top:** Thomas Moran sketched Yellowstone Canyon, while the Hayden Expedition camped in the canyon during the last week of July 1871. Moran sketched "In the Grand Canyon of the Yellowstone" the same week. Willliam Henry Jackson photographed the Hayden Expedition's fully equipped pack train; the expedition's odometer was carried in the cart seen near the front of the line. **following pages:** Crystal Falls, Cascade Creek as photographed by Jackson and rendered in watercolor by Moran. The two often worked side by side, exchanging advice as to choice of subjects and which location offered the best perspective from which to work.

# your show of shows

## "a legacy of laughter"

left: Four of the best:
(from left) Sid Caesar,
Nanette Fabray, Howard
Morris, and Carl
Reiner. above: Caesar
with Imogene Coca

FALL 1949. Inside a twenty-third floor room at NBC's midtown Manhattan headquarters, an ensemble of comedy writers were preparing to give Americans a reason to sit in front of their ten-inch television sets on Saturday nights; before long, their efforts would also spread fear down Broadway. This sophisticated, rowdy and mainly twenty-something staff, which at various times included Mel Brooks, Lucille Kallen, Woody Allen, Larry Gelbart, Neil and Danny Simon, Mel Tolkin, Joe Stein, Carl Reiner, and Sid Caesar, used the new medium of television to make the nation laugh as hard as it ever has.

From its premiere on February 25, 1950, until June 5, 1954, the manic energy of *Your Show of Shows*, starring Caesar, Reiner, Imogene Coca, and Howard Morris, turned Saturday nights into a showcase for comedic genius. Aside from launching several legendary careers, the live, ninety-minute revue provided hope and direction to a medium that needed both.

NBC's programming chief Pat Weaver pitched *Your Show of Shows* in 1949 to Al Leibman, a veteran revue producer. Since television's 1946 debut, networks attracted advertising revenue by allowing companies to buy entire time slots and produce their own shows, *The Texaco Star Theater*, for example. Weaver had a different idea. His network would air its *own* shows and, much like magazines, sell small "spots" of airtime to multiple companies. Liebman, who was the first to pair Caesar and Coca when he directed another popular, sponsor-driven program, the *Admiral Broadway Review*, agreed to produce this new, NBC-owned show. He quickly reunited Caesar and Coca, and formed the writing team around them.

A dream team as it turned out.

"This writing staff was a dream," Caesar said. "[We] were all crazy." All that talent converged in one smoke-filled office called the Writers' Room. It was where the twenty-one-year-old Brooks would punctuate his chronic tardiness by screaming "Lindy has landed," and where he once found himself in Caesar's clutches, dangling upside down out a window after riling the comedian's considerable temper. Lucille Kallen, the lone woman writer, said the team "lived" *Your Show of Shows*, working seven days a week, thirty-nine weeks a year from that office.

In this, television's Golden Age as it came to be known, the unparalleled staff created a gallery of memorable sketches, brought to life by Caesar, Coca, Reiner, and Morris. There were movie parodies like "From Here to Obscurity"; a "This is Your Life" satire that featured Caesar as an aggressive, unwilling guest; Brooks's "2,000 Year Old Man" routine; the extraordinary chemistry between Coca and Caesar, displayed best during the continuing saga of Doris and Charlie Hickenlooper's floundering marriage; and of course, Caesar's portrayal of the "Professor." The show was so popular that Broadway movie-theater owners, after experiencing a dramatic decline at the box office, pleaded with NBC executives to move *Your Show of Shows* to a weeknight.

Even the new medium's critics loved it. "Sid Caesar doesn't steal jokes; he doesn't borrow ideas or material," wrote the notoriously harsh *Chicago Tribune* columnist Larry Wolters. "A gag is as useless as a fresh situation is to Milton Berle." Alfred Hitchcock said, "the young Mr. Caesar best approaches the great Chaplin of the early 1920s."

After the program's run, many from the *Your Show of Shows* stable went on to greater fame. Carl Reiner, with Jim Brooks, created *The Mary Tyler Moore Show* and won seven Emmys; Mel Brooks and Woody Allen won Oscars for films they wrote and directed; Neil Simon became one of America's most notable playwrights, and brought his Writers' Room days to Broadway in the play *Laughter on the 23rd Floor*; Larry Gelbart not only launched the *M\*A\*S\*H* television series, but wrote the movie *Tootsie* (when asked what it was like working with Dustin Hoffman, *Tootsie's* star, Gelbart said the experience was terrible, but it taught him to never work with an actor who's shorter than an Oscar). That high-caliber wit typified *Your Show of Shows*, live for ninety minutes, thirty-nine Saturday nights a year, 160 shows in all.

What did *Your Show of Shows* mean to television? Consider this: When the show debuted in 1950, television sets were in less than 4 million American households; four years later, when the final curtain fell on the Hickenloopers and company, over half the nation's 48 million homes had a television. The credit for television's rise didn't belong entirely to Sid Caesar and the *Your Show of Shows* cast and writers, but it's a good part of the reason. It's also a reminder of what television at its best could be, before the "wasteland" encroached.

*Douglas McArthur, 1903*

*George Patton, 1909*

*Robert York, 1938*

west point

*Dwight Eisenhower, 1915*

*Omar Bradley, 1915*

*James Torrence, 1954*

*Kenneth Good, 1952*

*Harold G. Moore, 1945*

*Donald York, 1954.*

*Matthew Ridgeway, 1917*

# by David Halberstam

I AM ALWAYS MOVED when I go there. Part of it is the sheer beauty of the site, located on a cliff above the Hudson, the view absolutely magnificent, or more accurately perhaps, majestic. But more importantly, it is the sense of the past that is so palpable there. The idea that this is where so many great, American military figures arrived from their small towns, eighteen years old, completely raw and unfinished, filled with the notion of serving their country, and many went on to do precisely that. When I am at West Point my imagination runs free, and I can see the young Ulysses Grant arriving here in another century. Then earlier in this century, that remarkable crew of young men who would bring such honor to America during World War II; Eisenhower, Bradley, and Bedell Smith, and in time, my special favorite and hero, Matt Ridgway. They were small-town boys most of them, more often than not from very humble backgrounds, and they brought only their hopes and their ambitions; their notion of duty was formed here. The MacArthurs and the Pattons with their talents and their greater vainglory tend to be the exception: The quintessential West Point graduate is more likely to be like an Eisenhower or a Bradley.

I am impressed by this place because it is so uniquely American, small town, godfearing America at that. It may have on occasion in the past have helped create an elite within the military itself, and certainly in an earlier era if not in this one. For the graduate, there was a distinct career advantage in having the West Point ring, but it was not as occasionally happens in other countries, part of a self-perpetuating elite, an elite that on occasion tends to look down on the ordinary citizenry around it. Sometimes there is a sense of obligation that extends generation after generation in a particular family like the Truscotts. Going to West Point seems to be in the Truscott DNA. Still, however, America's military academy is not part of a self-perpetuating (and self-isolating) class.

For one thing the place itself is simply far too demanding, and the rewards, particularly in an America that now offers talented people a chance at a very fast track, are on the surface at least, too small. By its very nature, West Point is self selective of a certain kind of young American: the admissions system tends to find good, committed kids from all over the country; the combination of the demanding curriculum and the harsh daily regimen suffices to warn off most of the more privileged children of the upper, middle class. The people who come here tend to bring a certain hunger with them; it is one of the principal attractions that the education is both good and free. As such, it is more meritocratic than France's St. Cyr, which has tended to reflect a certain kind of French elite (and, in the past, a somewhat ideological one at that) and Britain's Sandhurst, which has traditionally reflected more of England's upper class.

I think we are lucky in this country. Unlike the military in other countries, the American military has rarely been politicized; it tends to be more conservative than the general societal norm, but that is a most natural and normal phenomenon. Over the years those generals with serious political ambitions, like Douglas MacArthur, have tended to give off the wrong scent to their fellow Americans, and their political ambitions inevitably crash; it is those more modest officers, who tend to reflect the culture of this special place, like Eisenhower, men who do not even want to run for office that badly, whom their countrymen tend to trust. And to no small degree, I credit West Point with its unique selection process and its codes for that. Over the years, I have come to know a number of distinguished generals who went here—Matt Ridgway and Hal Moore, who so brilliantly commanded the American soldiers at the Ia Drang in Vietnam in November 1965, and Bob York— as good and honorable a man as I have ever met—and I was always moved by the combination of strength, honor, and humanity in all of them.

For West Point has always seemed to me to be unusually close to Main Street in middle America; it is a place without glitz that without consciously trying to do so, reflects the norm, the center, and the diversity of America. Again and again it turns out good people of significant personal modesty and a powerful sense of obligation. One of my favorite West Point stories is of the gifted, talented, but relatively poor Dwight Eisenhower leaving his Mennonite home in Abilene, Kansas, his mother, Ida Stover Eisenhower, who hated the very idea of war, virtually unable to watch his departure, returning from the train station and bursting into tears.

When I was a reporter in Vietnam in the early sixties, the young American advisers there were almost exactly my age, and a significant number of them were from the Point. We talked easily and naturally, because we were all the same age and we were, I as a reporter, they as officers, all volunteers for this assignment. A number of them were good to me, young and green and scared as I was at twenty-eight; on my first operation in the field, I was escorted by Capt. Ken Good, West Point class of 1952, and then the next time by Capt. Jim Torrence, class of 1954. And I was impressed, as much as anything else, by their sense of decency and obligation; they reminded me very much of the young Americans I had already met in Africa who were serving in the Peace Corps, in their sense of duty, their modesty, and, for this is an old fashioned word, their innate goodness.

top: Ulysses S. Grant, 1843  bottom: Robert E. Lee, 1829  right: Main Chapel, completed in 1911

Ken Good was killed early in the war, during his first tour in January 1963, and Jim Torrence, who I thought was surely going to be a general, went back for a second tour and advised a Vietnamese regiment in 1970. His story seems to me to embody everything that is special about this place; he was the West Point son of a West Point graduate, born at West Point during a time when his father, the senior Jim Torrence, taught math at the academy. He had never considered going anywhere else, and he had never considered any other career. Because the family moved around so much when he was young, he always thought of West Point as his one real home. He had gone to Vietnam, as I had, in 1962, full of enthusiasm for the cause, but by the time he was ordered back for his second tour as the senior adviser to a Vietnamese regiment, he was deeply skeptical and full of misgivings; he was disillusioned with the war, but he had accepted his assignment, and was killed there in May 1971 in the crash of a command helicopter—it was said that the chopper on takeoff was taking fire, dipped too low to avoid the fire, and its propellers hit some nearby water, causing the crash. I

think often of him and Ken Good and another young officer I knew, Don York, class of 1954, who was killed there in those early days. Don was my friend, Bob York's nephew, and one reason why Bob York took the war more seriously and earlier than other American generals there and treated the enemy with more respect. Now, on occasion when I go back to the Point to teach a class, it is their names on the list of men who died serving their country that I seek out.

Class of 1915, known as the "Class the Stars Fell On" because fifty-nine of its 164 graduates reached the rank of brigadier general or above. Class members included Dwight Eisenhower, Omar Bradley, and James A. Van Fleet.

295

# bibliography

COMMON SENSE: 'TIS TIME TO PART

Fruchtman, Jr., Jack. *Thomas Paine: Apostle of Freedom.* New York: Four Walls Eight Windows, 1994.
Paine, Thomas. *Common Sense.* Mineola, NY: Dover, 1997.

THE AUTOMOBILE SELF-STARTER:
KETTERING'S PRACTICAL SOLUTION

Boyd, T.A. *Professional Amateur: The Biography of Charles Franklin Kettering.* New York: E.P. Dutton, 1957.
———, ed. *Prophet of Progress: Selections from the Speeches of Charles F. Kettering.* New York: E.P. Dutton, 1961.
Leslie, Stuart W. *Boss Kettering.* New York: Columbia University Press, 1983.

BARBED WIRE: THE DEVIL'S HATBAND

Clifton, Robert. *Barbs, Prongs, Points, Prickers & Stickers.* Norman: University of Oklahoma, 1979.
Glover, Jack. *The "Bobbed Wire" Bible,* 7th ed. Sunset, TX: Cow Puddle Press, 1991.
McCallum, Henry D. and Frances T. *The Wire That Fenced the West.* Norman: U. of Oklahoma, 1965.
Barbed Wire Museum, La Crosse, KS. Tel: 913-222-9900.

THE BASEBALL DIAMOND

Ahuja, Jay. *Fields of Dreams: A Guide to Visiting and Enjoying All 30 Major League Ballparks.* Secaucus, New Jersey: Carol Publishing Group, 1998.
Gershman, Michael. *Diamonds: The Evolution of the Ballpark from Elysian Fields to Camden Yards.* Boston: Houghton Mifflin, 1993.
Ritter, Lawrence S. *Lost Ballparks: A Celebration of Baseball's Legendary Fields.* New York: Viking Studio Books, 1992.
Video: "The Story of America's Classic Ballparks." Tel: 1-800-544-8422.

THE BERLIN AIRLIFT:
"WE STAY IN BERLIN. PERIOD."

Bohlen, Charles E. *Witness to History, 1929-1969.* New York: W. W. Norton, 1973.
Bowles, Chester. *Promises to Keep: My Years in Public Life, 1941-1969.* New York: Harper, 1971.
Fromkin, David. *In the Time of Americans: The Generation That Changed America's Role in the World.* New York: Alfred A. Knopf, 1995.
Hamby, Alonzo. *Man of the People: A Life of Harry S. Truman.* New York: Oxford University Press, 1995.
Isaacson, Walter and Evan Thomas. *The Wise Men: Six Friends and the World They Made.* New York: Simon & Schuster, 1986.

Jackson, Robert. *The Berlin Airlift.* Wellinborough, England: Patrick Stephens, 1988.
Kennan, George. *Sketches from a Life.* New York: Pantheon, 1989.
LaFeber, Walter. *America, Russia, and the Cold War, 1945-1990.* New York: McGraw-Hill, 1991.
McCullough, David. *Truman.* New York: Simon & Schuster, 1984.
Wilcox, Francis O. *Arthur H. Vandenberg, His Career and Legacy.* Ann Arbor: University of Michigan Press, 1975.

THE BIRDS OF AMERICA:
AUDUBON'S GREAT IDEA

Ford, Alice, ed. *Audubon, By Himself.* New York: Natural History Press, 1969.
Herrick, Hobart. *Audubon the Naturalist: A History of His Life and Times.* New York: Dover, 1968.
McDermott, John Francis, ed. *Audubon in the West.* Norman: University of Oklahoma Press, 1965.
National Audubon Society. Tel: 212-979-3000.

BLACK BASEBALL:
THE BUMPY, BEGRUDGING ROAD

Holtzman, Jerome. *Commissioners: Baseball's Midlife Crisis.* New York: Total Press, 1998.
Rampersad, Arnold. *Jackie Robinson: A Biography,* New York: Random House, 1998.
Tygiel, Jules. *Baseball's Great Experiment: Jackie Robinson and His Legacy.* New York: Vintage Books, 1984.
Voight, David. *American Baseball, Volume I: From the Gentlemen's Agreement to the Commissioner's System.* Norman: Oklahoma University Press, 1966.

THE BROOKLYN BRIDGE

Brooklyn Museum. *The Greatest River Bridge, 1883-1983.* New York: Harry N. Abrams, 1983.
McCullough, David. *The Great Bridge.* New York: Simon & Schuster, 1982.
Lattimer, Margaret, Brooke Hindle, Melvin Kranzberg, eds. *Bridge to the Future, Centennial Celebration of the Brooklyn Bridge.* New York: New York Academy of Sciences, 1984.
Website to download 3D images of bridge: www.greatbuildings.com/models/Brooklyn_Bridge_mod.html.
Video: Modern Marvels (A & E). Tel: 1-800-597-6774.

BURROUGHS-WELLCOME AND GERTRUDE ELION:
THE PERFECT CHEMISTRY

Altman, Lawrence K. "Gertrude Elion, Drug Developer, Dies at 81." *The New York Times,* 23 February 1999.

Elion, Gertrude B. "The Importance of Patents to Medical Research." Bicentennial Proceedings, Events, and Addresses. Washington, D.C.: Foundation for a Creative America, 1991.

Lienhard, John H. "Engines of Our Ingenuity." University of Houston, www.uh.edu/engines.

Porter, Roy. ed. *Cambridge Illustrated History of Medicine*. Cambridge: Cambridge University Press, 1996.

Dr. Marti St. Claire (close friend of Gertrude Elion) interview by Robert A. Wilson, 21 May 1999.

Gertrude B. Elion interview, 6 March 1991, "The Hall of Science and Exploration," http://www.achievement.org/autodoc.

Website: www.bwfund.org.

## C-SPAN: Where Content is the Star

Charen, Mona. "Channel of the Patriots," *The Washington Times*, 23 April 1998.

Goodman, Tim. "C-SPAN's Nerdy Look Hides Raw, Journalistic Horsepower," *The Detroit Free Press*, 9 March 1996.

Grimes, William. "Putting the Fun Back in British Politics," *The New York Times*, 13 July 1998.

Frantzich, Stephen and John Sullivan. *The C-Span Revolution*. Norman: University of Oklahoma Press, 1996.

"America's Town Hall Turns Twenty," supplement to *Multichannel News and Cablevision Magazine*, 22 March 1998.

Brian Lamb interview by Robert A. Wilson and Mike McFarland, 5 May 1999.

## Calder Mobiles

Hayes, Margaret Calder. *Three Alexander Calders: A Family Memoir*. New York: Universe Publishing, 1987.

Lipman, Jean. *Alexander Calder and his Magic Mobiles*. New York: Hudson Hills, 1981.

Prather, Marla. *Alexander Calder 1898-1976*. Washington, D.C.: National Gallery of Art, 1998.

Rower, Alexander S.C. *Calder Sculpture*. New York: Universe Publishing, 1998.

Video: *Alexander Calder-Calder's Universe*.

Video: *Alexander Calder: An American Masters Special*. WNET.

Video: *Mobile by Alexander Calder*, National Gallery of Art.

## Carnegie Libraries

Bobinski, George S. *Carnegie Libraries: Their History and Impact on American Public Library Development*. Chicago: American Library Association, 1969.

Carnegie Corporation of New York. *Carnegie Corporation Library Program, 1911-1961.*

Jones, Theodore. *Carnegie Libraries Across America*. New York: John Wiley, 1997.

Van Slyck, Abigail A. *Free to All: Carnegie Libraries & American Culture, 1890-1920*. Chicago: University of Chicago Press, 1995.

Wall, Joseph F. *Andrew Carnegie*. New York: Oxford University Press, 1970.

Swetnam, George. *Andrew Carnegie*. Boston: Twayne Publisher, G.K. Hall & Co., 1980.

Website: www.carnegie.org/philanth.htm.

Video: WGBH: *American Experience: The Richest Man in the World*. Tel: 1–800–255–9424.

Video: A & E Biography: *Andrew Carnegie Prince of Steel*. Tel: 1–800–469–7977.

## There is Only One Chez Panisse

Waters, Alice. *The Chez Panisse Menu Cookbook*. New York: Random House, 1995.

## The Chicago Defender: Aiding and Abetting the Great Migration

Suggs, Henry Lewis. *The Black Press in the Middle West, 1865-1985*. Westport, CT: Greenwood, 1996.

Video: *The Black Press: Soldiers without Swords*, produced and directed by Stanley Nelson, Half Nelson Productions, 1998.

Website: www.chicagohistory.org (The Chicago Historical Society).

*The Chicago Defender,* 2400 South Michigan Avenue, Chicago, IL 60616.

## Coca-Cola's Recipe: The Greatest Secret Ever Kept, Told by the Man Who Keeps It

Allen, Frederick. *Secret Formula: How Brilliant Marketing and Relentless Salesmanship Made Coca-Cola the Best-Known Product in the World*. New York: HarperBusiness, 1995.

Applegate, Howard L. *Coca-Cola: A History in Photographs 1930-1969*. Osceola, WI: Iconographfix, 1996.

Website: www.cocacola.com.

To view more of Michael Witte's work, visit his online portfolio at www.theispot.com/artist/witte.

## Coney Island

Kasson, John F. *Amusing the Million: Coney Island at the Turn of the Century*. New York: Hill & Wang, 1978.

Nasaw, David. *Going Out: The Rise and Fall of Public Amusements*. New York: Basic Books, 1993.

Peiss, Kathy. *Cheap Amusements: Working Women and Leisure in Turn-of-the-Century New York*. Philadelphia: Temple University Press, 1986.

Snow, Richard. *Coney Island: A Postcard Journey to the City of Fire*. New York: Brightwaters Press, 1984.

## The Corvette: Like A Bat Out of Hell

Adler, Dennis. *Corvettes: The Cars That Created the Legend*. Iola, WI: N.P. Krause Publications, 1996.

Antonick, Michael. *Illustrated Corvette Buyer's Guide*. 4th edition. Osceola, WI: Motorbooks International, 1997.

_____. *The Corvette Black Book, 1953-1999*. Osceola, WI: Motorbooks International, 1998.

Leffingwell, Randy. *Corvette: America's Sports Car*. Osceola, WI: Motorbooks International, 1997.

Miller, Ray. *The Real Corvette: An Illustrated History of Chevrolet's Sports Car*. Oceanside, CA: Evergreen Press, 1975.

Schefter, James. *All Corvettes are Red: Inside the Rebirth of an American Legend*. New York: Pocket Books, 1998.

National Corvette Museum, Bowling Green, KY. Tel: 502–781–7973.

For Corvette development chronology see Website: web.islandnet.com/~kpolsson/vettehis.htm.

## Country Music: The Bristol Sessions

Dawidoff, Nicholas. *In The Country of Country: People and Places in American Music*. New York: Pantheon Books, 1997.

Bristol Sessions historic recording can be purchased from Country Music Hall of Fame. Tel: 615–256–1639.

Video: *America's Music: Roots of Country*, 1996.

Websites: www.countrymusic.org.
www.nashville-collection.com.

## The Duke Ellington Orchestra

Giddins, Gary. *Visions of Jazz*. New York: Oxford University Press, 1998.

Hasse, John Edward and Wynton Marsalis. *Beyond Category: The Life and Genius of Duke Ellington*. New York: Da Capo Press, 1995.

Nicholson, Stuart. *Reminiscing in Tempo: A Portrait of Duke Ellington*. Boston: Northeastern University Press, 1999.

Recordings: Complete Capitol Recordings by Duke Ellington. Cemac Enterprises Ltd, CD Audio edition, March 1999.
Centenial Collection by Duke Ellington (5 CD's). Delta, CD Audio edition, April 1999.

## Edison's Invention Factories: "Stick-To-Itiveness"

Baldwin, Neil. *Edison: Inventing the Century*. New York: Hyperion, 1995

Friedel, Robert and Paul Israel with Bernard S. Finn. *Edison's Electric Light: Biography of an Invention*. New Brunswick, NJ: Rutgers University Press. 1986.

Millard, Andre. *Edison & the Business of Innovation*. Baltimore: Johns Hopkins University Press, 1990.

Wachhorst, Wyn. *Thomas Alva Edison: An American Myth*. Cambridge: MIT Press, 1981.

"The Lesser Known Edison," *Scientific American*. February 1997.

"The Undiscovered World of Thomas Edison," *Atlantic Monthly*. December 1995.

Videos (available from Edison Birthplace Museum Shop. Tel: 419–499–2135): *Friends of Edison National Historic Site: The Invention Factory: The Story of Thomas Edison and his West Orange Lab.*
*The American Experience: Edison's Miracle of Light.*
*Questar Home Video: The Story of Thomas A. Edison.*

Websites: www.thomasedison.com ("Thomas Edison's Home Page").
www.invent.org (Inventure Place, National Inventors Hall of Fame).
www.nps.gov/edis (National Park Service. Edison related sites).

## *The Elements of Style*: Parvum Opus

Strunk, William B., Jr. and E. B. White. *Elements of Style*. New York: Macmillan, 1959. The latest edition of *The Elements of Style* may be ordered from Allyn & Bacon. Tel: 1–800–278–3525.

## Farm Security Administration Photographers

Fleischlauer, Carl and Beverly W. Brannan, eds. *Documenting America: 1935-1943*. Berkeley: University of California Press, 1988.

Hurley, F. Jack. *Portrait of a Decade: Roy Stryker and the Development of Documentary Photography in the Thirties*. Baton Rouge: Louisiana State University Press, 1972.

Lange, Dorothea and Paul S. Taylor. *An American Exodus*. New Haven, CT: Yale University Press, 1969.

O'Neal, Hank. *A Vision Shared: A Classic Portrait of American and its People, 1935-1943*. New York: St. Martin's, 1976.

Scott, William. *Documentary Expression and Thirties America*. New York: Oxford University Press, 1973.

Stryker, Roy and Nancy Wood. *In This Proud Land: America 1935-1943 as seen in FSA Photographs*. Greenwich, CT: New York Graphic Society, 1973.

## FDR's Fireside Chats: Holding Us Together

Adams, Henry H. *Harry Hopkins: A Biography*. New York: Putnam, 1977.

Brown, Robert J. *Manipulating the Ether: The Power of Broadcast Radio in Thirties America*. Jefferson, NC: McFarland, 1997.

Buhite, Russell D., and David W. Levy, eds. *FDR's Fireside Chats*. Norman: University of Oklahoma Press, 1992.

Burns, Kanes MacGregor. *Roosevelt: The Lion and the Fox*. New York: Harcourt Brace Jovanovich, 1984.

Dallek, Robert. *Franklin Roosevelt and American Foreign Policy, 1932-1945*. New York: Oxford University Press, 1979.

Davis, Kenneth S. *FDR: The New Deal Years, 1933-1937*. New York: Random House, 1993.

Miller, Nathan. *F.D.R.: An Intimate History*. New York: Doubleday, 1983.

Neal, Steve. *Dark Horse: A Biography of Wendell Wilkie*. Garden City, NY: Doubleday, 1984.

Schlesinger, Arthur M., Jr. *The Age of Roosevelt: The Coming of the New Deal*. Boston: Houghton Mifflin, 1959.

Ward, Geoffrey C. *A First-Class Temperament: The Emergence of Franklin Roosevelt, 1905-1928*. New York: Harper & Row, 1989.

## Freedom Riders: "We Are Prepared To Die"

Branch, Taylor. *Parting the Waters: America in the King Years 1954-63*. New York: Simon & Schuster, 1988.

Cagin, Seth, and Philip Dray. *We Are Not Afraid: The Story of Goodman, Schwerner, and Chaney and the Civil Rights Campaign for Mississippi*. New York: Macmillan, 1988.

Farmer, James. *Lay Bare the Heart: The Autobiography of the Civil Rights Movement*. New York: Arbor House, 1985.

Grant, Joanie. *Ella Baker: Freedom Bound*. New York: John Wiley, 1998.

Halberstam, David. *The Children*. New York: Random House, 1998.

Oates, Stephen B. *Let the Trumpet Sound: The Life of Martin Luther King, Jr.* New York: Harper & Row, 1982.

Payne, Charles M. *I've Got the Light of Freedom: The Organizing Tradition and the Mississippi Freedom Struggle*. Berkeley: University of California Press, 1995.

Raines, Howell. *My Soul is Rested: Movement Days*

*in the Deep South Remembered.* New York: Putnam, 1977.

Williams, Juan. *Eyes on the Prize: America's Civil Rights Years, 1954-1965.* New York: Viking Press, 1987.

## THE G.I. BILL: HELPING CREATE THE MIDDLE CLASS

Bennett, Michael J., *When Dreams Came True: The GI Bill and the Making of Modern America.* Washington, DC: Brasseys, 1996.

Evans, Harold, Gail Buckland and Kevin Baker. *The American Century.* New York: Alfred A. Knopf, 1998.

Goulden, Joseph C. *The Best Years 1945-1950.* New York: Atheneum, 1976.

Greenberg, Milton. *The G.I. Bill: The Law That Changed America.* New York: Lickly Publishing, 1997.

Jones, Landon Y. *Great Expectations: America and the Baby Boom Generation.* New York: Ballantine, 1980.

Manchester, William. *The Glory and the Dream: A Narrative History of America 1932-1972.* Boston: Little, Brown, 1974.

O'Neill, William L. *American High: The Years of Confidence, 1945-1960.* New York: The Free Press, 1986.

Olson, Keith W. *The G.I. Bill. The Veterans and the College.* Lexington: University of Kentucky Press, 1974.

Perrett, Geoffrey. *Days of Sadness, Years of Triumph: The American People 1945-1963.* New York: Coward, McCann & Geoghegan, 1973.

_____. *A Dream of Greatness: The American People 1945-1963.* New York: Coward, McCann & Geoghegan, 1979

Video:

*The G.I. Bill.* PBS-WNET. Tel: 212–560–2000.

## THE GETTYSBURG ADDRESS

Wills, Gary. *Lincoln at Gettysburg: The Words that Remade America.* New York: Simon & Schuster, 1992.

For complete multivolume "Collected Works of Abraham Lincoln" see website: www.alincolnassoc.com.

## A GREAT DAY IN HARLEM

Graham, Charles and Dan Morgenstern. *Great Jazz Day in Harlem: Rare Photographs by Dizzy Gillespie, Milt Hintin and Art Kane.* San Francisco: Woodford Publishing, 1998.

## *HUCKLEBERRY FINN*

Cooley, Thomas, ed. *Adventures of Huckleberry Finn: An Authoritative Text Contexts and Sources Criticism.* Norton Critical Edition. New York: W. W. Norton, 1998.

## THE IDITAROD: THE LAST GREAT RACE

Paulsen, Gary. *Winterdance: The Fine Madness of Running the Iditarod.* San Diego: Harcourt Brace, 1997.

Dougherty, Patrick, ed. "Iditarod 25: Tales of the Last Great Race." *Anchorage Daily News Special Section.* March, 1997.

Websites: www.iditarod.com. www.starfishsoftware.com/idog97.

## INDUSTRIAL DESIGN: A SUPERIOR SENSE OF THE PRACTICAL

Albrecht, Donald, ed. *The Work of Charles and Ray Eames: A Legacy of Invention.* New York: Harry N. Abrams, 1997.

Bel Geddes, Norman. *Horizons.* Boston: Little, Brown & Company, 1932.

Dreyfuss, Henry. *Designing for People.* New York: Simon & Schuster, 1955

Eames Offiice Gallery, Santa Monica, CA. Tel: 310–396–5991. Web site: www.eamesoffice.com or www.powersof10.com.

Flinchum, Russell. *Henry Dreyfuss Industrial Designer: The Man in the Brown Suit.* New York: Rizzoli International, 1997.

Kirkham, Pat. *Charles and Ray Eames: Designers of the Twentieth Century.* Cambridge: MIT Press, 1995.

Loewy, Raymond F. *Industrial Design.* Woodstock, New York: The Overlook Press, 1979.

Industrial Designers Society of America. Tel: 703–559–0100. Websites: www.idsa.org. www.si.edu/ndm.

Visuals available from these websites: Powers of Ten^a interactive CD-ROM exploring the notion of scale and the Eames Design Process; Films of Charles and Ray Eames Volumes 1–5 and 901: after 45 years of working.

## INDUSTRIAL LIGHT & MAGIC: "TO LEAP WITHOUT LOOKING"

Smith, Thomas G. *Industrial Light & Magic: The Art of Special Effects.* New York: Del Rey, 1986.

Vaz, Mark Cotta and Patricia Rose Duigan. *Industrial Light & Magic: Into the Digital Age.* New York: Ballantine Books, 1996.

Duncan, Jody. "A Twentieth Century Salute to Industrial Light & Magic." *Cinefex Magazine.* March 1996.

Website: www.ilmfan.com.

## OUT IN THE GARAGE: WHERE INVENTIONS BEGIN

Carlton, Jim. *Apple: The Inside Story of Intrigue, Egomania and Business Blunders.* New York: HarperCollins, 1998.

Lager, Fred. *Ben & Jerry's, The Inside Scoop: How Two Real Guys Built a Business With a Social Conscience and a Sense of Humor.* New York: Crown Publishers, 1994.

Video: "Big Dream, Small Screen," The American Experience. Tel.: 1.800.828.4PBS.

Websites: www.cinemedia.net. www.songs.com/philo.

## KEENELAND: RACING AS IT WAS MEANT TO BE

Strode, William. *Keeneland: A Half-Century of Racing.* Louisville, KY: Harmony House, 1986.

Website: www.keeneland.com.

### THE KIMBELL MUSEUM: "THE CLIENT IS HUMAN NATURE"

Brownlee, David and David G. De Long. *Louis I. Kahn: In the Realm of Architecture*. New York: Rizzoli International, 1991.

Hochstim, Jan. *The Paintings and Sketches of Louis I. Kahn*. New York: Rizzoli International, 1991.

Johnson, Nell E., comp. *Light is the Theme: Louis I. Kahn and The Kimbell Art Museum*. Fort Worth, TX: Kimbell Art Foundation, 1975.

Loud, Patricia Cummings. *The Art Museums of Louis I. Kahn*. Durham, NC: Duke University Press/Duke University Museum of Art, 1989.

Ngo, Dung, ed. *Louis I. Kahn: Conversations with Students*. 2nd edition. Houston, TX: Rice University School of Architecture, 1998.

### LEND LEASE: "THE MOST UNSORDID ACT"

Adams, Henry H. *Harry Hopkins: A Biography*. New York: Putnam, 1977.

Burns, Kanes MacGregor. *Roosevelt: The Lion and the Fox*. New York: Harcourt Brace Jovanovich, 1984.

Cole, Wayne S. *Roosevelt and the Isolationists, 1932-1945*. Lincoln: University of Nebraska Press, 1983.

Dallek, Robert. *Franklin Roosevelt and American Foreign Policy, 1932-1945*. New York: Oxford University Press, 1979.

Davis, Kenneth S. *FDR, Into the Storm, 1937-1940*. New York: Random House. 1993.

Dobson, Alan P. *U.S. Wartime Aid to Britain, 1940-1946*. Dover, NH: Croom Helm, 1980.

Fehrenbach, T.R. *F.D.R.'s Undeclared War, 1939-1941*. New York: David McKay, 1967.

Freidel, Frank. *Franklin D. Roosevelt: A Rendezvous with Destiny*. Boston: Little, Brown, 1990.

Kimball, Warren F. *The Most Unsordid Act: Lend Lease. 1939-1941*. Baltimore: Johns Hopkins Press, 1969.

Kinsella, William E., Jr. *Leadership in Isolation: FDR and the Origins of the Second World War*. Boston: G. K. Hall, 1978.

Marks, Frederick W. *Wind Over Sand: The Diplomacy of Franklin Roosevelt*. Athens: University of Georgia Press, 1988.

McJimsey, George. *Harry Hopkins: Ally of the Poor and Defender of Democracy*. Cambridge: Harvard University Press.

Miller, Nathan. *F.D.R.: An Intimate History*. New York: Doubleday, 1983.

Neal, Steve. *Dark Horse: A Biography of Wendell Wilkie*. Garden City, New York: Doubleday, 1984.

### THE LIBRARY OF AMERICA

Ordering information. Tel: 212–308–3360.

### M*A*S*H: THE FINAL EPISODE

Clauss, J. *M*A*S*H*: The First Five Years*. Aeonian Press.

Gelbart, Larry. *Laughing Matters*. New York: Random House, 1998.

Hooker, Richard. *MASH*. New York: William Morrow & Co., 1997.

Kalter, Suzy. The *Complete Book of M*A*S*H*. New York: Abradale Press/Abrams, 1988.

Reiss, David S. *M*A*S*H*: The Exclusive Inside Story of TV's Most Popular Show*. Indianapolis: Bobbs-Merrill Co., 1983.

Wittebols, James H. *Watching M*A*S*H, Watching America: A Social History of the 1972-1983 Television Series*. Jefferson, NC: McFarland & Co., 1998.

Websites: M*A*S*H Archives: www.ildo.com/tv/mash. M*A*S*H: http://www.user.shentel.net/lem3u. Best Care Anywhere: www.geocities.com/TelevisionCity/5575/Index.html. The *M*A*S*H* 4077 Home Page: www.netlink.co.uk/users/mash/index.html.

### THE MARSHALL PLAN: ESSENTIALS FOR EUROPEAN RECOVERY

Bohlen, Charles E. *Witness to History, 1929-1969*. New York: Norton, 1973.

Bowles, Chester. *Promises to Keep: My Years in Public Life, 1941-1969*. New York: Harper, 1971.

Fossedal, Gregory A. *Our Finest Hour: Will Clayton, the Marshall Plan, and the Triumph of Democracy*. Stanford, CA: Hoover Institution Press, 1993.

Fromkin, David. *In the Time of Americans: The Generation That Changed America's Role in the World*. New York: Alfred A. Knopf, 1995.

Hamby, Alonzo. *Man of the People: A Life of Harry S. Truman*. New York: Oxford University Press, 1995.

Hoffman, Stanley and Charles Maier, eds. *The Marshall Plan: A Retrospective*. Boulder, CO: Westview Press, 1984.

Isaacson, Walter and Evan Thomas. *The Wise Men: Six Friends and the World They Made*. Boston: Faber & Faber, 1986.

Kennan, George. *Sketches from a Life*. New York: Pantheon, 1989.

Kindleberger, *Charles P. Marshall Plan Days*. Boston: Allen & Unwin, 1987.

LaFeber, Walter. *America, Russia, and the Cold War, 1945-1990*. New York: McGraw-Hill, 1991.

McCullough, David. *Truman*. New York: Simon & Schuster, 1984.

Mee, Charles L. Jr. *The Marshall Plan: The Launching of the Pax Americana*. New York: Simon & Schuster, 1984.

Pogue, Forrest C. *George C. Marshall: Statesman*. New York: Viking Press, 1987.

Wilcox, Francis O. *Arthur H. Vandenberg, His Career and Legacy*. Ann Arbor: University of Michigan Press, 1975.

### MOHAWK STEEL WORKERS: DEALING WITH THE FEAR

Talese, Gay. *The Bridge*. New York: Harper & Row, 1964.

Wilson, Edmund. *Apologies to the Iroquois, With a Study of The Mohawks in High Steel, by Joseph Mitchell*. New York: Vintage Books, 1964.

Kennedy, Randy. "Mohawk Memories: An Indian Community Flourished and Faded in a Section of Brooklyn." *The New York Times*, 28 December 1996.

Kanatakta, Executive Director of the Kahnawake Community Cultural Centre in Quebec's Kahnawake reservation. Interview by Kevin Baker. 18 December 1998.

## Making Journalism History: "We Take You Now To London"

Bliss, Edward, ed. *In Search of Light*. New York: Da Capo, 1997.

Cloud, Stanley and Lynne Olson. *The Murrow Boys: Pioneers on the Front Lines of Broadcasting Journalism*. New York: Houghton Mifflin, 1996.

Persico, Joseph E. *Edward R. Murrow: An American Original*. New York: Da Capo, 1997.

Videos: A & E: Edward R. Murrow #SOE–14267 Tel: 877–998–4330
  CBS: Edward R. Murrow, Video #NLG15893; Fax: 212–975–9117.

## N.C. Wyeth's *Treasure Island* Illustrations: Scaring Us Stiff

Allen, Douglas and Douglas Allen, Jr. *N.C. Wyeth: The Collected Paintings, Illustrations, and Murals*. New York: Crown, 1972.

Michaelis, David. *N.C. Wyeth A Biography*. New York: Alfred A. Knopf, 1998.

Stevenson, Robert Louis. *Treasure Island illustrated by N.C. Wyeth*. New York: Charles Scribner's Sons, 1911.

## Navajo Code Talkers: The Century's Best Kept Secret

Bernstein, Alison R. *American Indians and World War II: Toward a New Era in Indian Affairs*. Norman: University of Oklahoma Press, 1991.

Bixler, Margaret T. *Winds of Freedom: The Story of Navajo Code Talkers of World War II*. Darien, CT: Two Bytes Publishing, 1992.

Donovan, Bill. "Navajo Code Talkers Made History Without Knowing It." *Arizona Republic*, 14 August 1992.

Jere, Franco. *Patriotism on Trial: Native Americans in World War II*. Ann Arbor, MI: University Microfilms International, 1990.

Kahn, David. *The Codebreakers*. New York: Macmillan, 1967.

Kawano, Kenji. *Warriors: Navajo Code Talkers*. Flagstaff, AZ: Northland, 1990.

McCoy, Ron. "Navajo Code Talkers of World War II: Indian Marines Befuddled the Enemy." *American West* 18, no. 6. (1981).

Paul, Doris Atkinson. *The Navajo Code Talkers*. Philadelphia: Dorance, 1973.

"Pentagon Ceremony Praises American Indians." *Crosswind*, November 1992.

## The New York Times

Diamond, Edwin. *Behind the Times: Inside the New York Times*. Chicago: University of Chicago Press, 1995.

Talese, Gay. *The Kingdom and The Power*. New York: World Publishing, 1969.

## The New Yorker

Brennan, Maeve. *The Long-Winded Lady: Notes from The New Yorker*. New York: Morrow, 1969.

Corey, Mary F. *The World Through a Monocle: The New Yorker at Midcentury*. Cambridge: Harvard University Press, 1999.

Gill, Brendan. *Here at the New Yorker*. New York: Da Capo, 1997.

Kunkel, Thomas, *Genius in Disguise: Harold Ross of the New Yorker*, New York: Random House, 1995.

## The Oklahoma Land Rush of 1889: "A Handful of White Dice Thrown Out Across the Prairie"

Hoig, Stanley. *The Oklahoma Land Rush of 1889*. Oklahoma City: Oklahoma Historical Society, 1984.

Baldwin, Kathlyn. *The 89ers*. Oklahoma City, OK: Western Heritage, 1981.

## The Outermost House

Beston, Henry. *The Outermost House: A Year of Life on the Great Beach of Cape Cod*. New York: Henry Holt, 1992.

## The Paris Review Interviews with Writers: Getting Black on White

Plimpton, George, ed. *The Paris Review Anthology*, New York: W. W. Norton, 1990.

## The Pony Express

Bloss, Roy S. *Pony Express-The Great Gamble*. Berkeley, CA: Howell-North, 1959.

Chapman, Arthur. *Pony Express*. New York: G. P. Putnam, 1932.

Settle, Raymond W. and Mary Lund Settle. *Saddles and Spurs: The Pony Express Saga*. Lincoln: University of Nebraska Press, 1972.

## The Populists: "Caught in the Tentacles of Circumstance"

Barnes, Donna A. *Farmers in Rebellion: The Rise and Fall of the Southern Farmers Alliance and People's Party in Texas*. Austin: University of Texas Press, 1984.

Clanton, Gene. *Populism: The Humane Preference in America, 1890-1900*. Boston: Teayne Publishers, 1991.

Goodwyn, Lawrence. *Democratic Promise: The Populist Moment in America*. New York: Oxford University Press, 1976.

Kazin, Michael. *The Populist Persuasion: An American History*. New York: Basic Books, 1995.

McMath, Robert C., Jr. *Populis Vanguard: A Social History, 1877-1989*. New York: Hill & Wang, 1993.

Painter, Nell Irvin. *Standing at Armageddon: The United States, 1877-1919*. New York: W. W. Norton, 1987.

Woodward, C. Vann. *Tom Watson: Agrarian Rebel*. New York: Oxford University Press, 1963.

## The Portable Faulkner

Faulkner, William. *The Portable Faulkner:* Revised and expanded edition. Malcolm Cowley, ed. New York: Viking Press, 1968.

## The Skyscraper

Cerver, Francesco Asensio. *The Architecture of Skyscrapers*. New York: Whitney Library of Design, 1997.

Dupré, Judith. *Skyscrapers: A History of the World's*

*Most Famous and Important Skyscrapers.* New York: Black Dog & Leventhal, 1996.

Landau, Sarah B. *Rise of the New York Skyscraper.* New Haven, CT: Yale University Press, 1991.

Scully, Vincent. *Architecture: The Natural and the Manmade.* New York: St. Martin's, 1991.

Van Leeuwen, Thomas A. P. *The Skyward Trend of Thought: The Metaphysics of the American Skyscraper.* Cambridge: MIT Press, 1988.

Walton, Thomas. "The Sky was No Limit." *Portfolio* (April/May 1979).

Whitehouse, Roger. *New York: Sunshine and Shadows.* New York: Harper & Row, 1974.

Wright, Frank Lloyd. *A Testament.* New York: Horizon, 1957.

## THE SMITHSONIAN INSTITUTION: THE NATION'S ATTIC

Goodwin, Daniel H., ed. *America's Smithsonian: Celebrating 150 Years.* Washington, DC: The Smithsonian Institution Press, 1996.

Website: www.si.edu.
    www.sil.si.edu.
    www.150.si.edu.

## THE SNAPSHOT

Brayer, Elizabeth. *George Eastman: A Biography.* Baltimore: Johns Hopkins University Press, 1996.

Klochko, Deborah, introduction. *Innovation/Imagination: 50 Years of Polaroid Photography.* New York: Harry N. Abrams, 1999.

McElheny, Victor K. *Insisting on the Impossible: The Life of Edwin Land.* Reading, MA: Perseus Books, 1998.

Nickel, Douglas R. *"Snapshots": The Photography of Everyday Life, 1888 to the Present.* San Francisco: San Francisco Museum, 1998.

Website: www.kodak.com.

## SOUSA'S BAND: "THE MUSIC MEN"

Berger, Kenneth. *The March King and His Band.* New York: Exposition, 1957.

Bierley, Paul E. *John Philip Sousa: American Phenomenon.* Englewood Cliffs, NJ: Prentice-Hall, 1973.

Newsom, Jon, ed. *Perspectives on John Philip Sousa.* Washington, DC: Library of Congress, Music Division, 1983.

## THE SPIRIT OF ST. LOUIS: SHOOTING STAR

Berg, A. Scott. *Lindbergh.* New York: G. P. Putnam, 1998.

Lindbergh, Charles A. ed. *An Autobiography of Values.* New York: Harcourt Brace Jovanovitch, 1978.
_____*Spirit of St. Louis.* New York: Charles Scribner's Sons, 1953.

Tekulsky, Joseph D. "B.F. Mahoney was the Mystery Man Behind the Spirit of St. Louis." *Aviation History,* March 1996.

## SPORTSWRITING: THE GOLDEN AGE

Heffelfinger, W. W. *Yes, This Was Football.* New York: Barnes, 1954.

Rice, Grantland. *The Tumult and the Shouting: My Life in Sports.* New York: Barnes, 1954.

Sperber, Murray. *Football.* New York: Henry Holt, 1993.

## SUN RECORDS: "WHEN ALL HELL BROKE LOOSE"

Guralnick, Peter. *Last Train to Memphis: The Rise of Elvis Presley.* New York: Little Brown, 1995.

Moore, Scotty and James Dickerson. *That's Alright, Elvis.* New York: Schirmer, 1997.

Nager, Larry. *Memphis Beat.* New York: St. Martin's, 1998.

Szatmary, David. *A Time to Rock: A Social History of Rock and Roll.* New York: Schirmer, 1996.

## SURFING OAHU'S NORTH SHORE: "EDDIE WOULD GO"

Ambrose, Greg. *Surfer's Guide to Hawaii.* Honolulu, HI: Bess Press, 1997.

Finney, Ben and James D. Houston. *Surfing: A History of the Ancient Hawaiian Sport.* San Francisco: Pomegranate, 1966, 1996.

Jenkins, Bruce. *North Shore Chronicles: Big Wave Surfing in Hawaii.* Berkeley, CA: North Atlantic Books, 1990.

"Sucker Punch." *Surfer Magazine 40,* no.4 (1991).

## TABASCO SAUCE

McIlhenny, Paul and Barbara Hunter. *The Tabasco Cookbook: 125 years of America's Favorite Pepper Sauce.* New York: Clarkson Potter, 1993.

Website: www.tabasco.com.

## TRAVIS'S LETTER FROM THE ALAMO: VICTORY OR DEATH

Hardin, Stephen L. *Texian Iliad: A Military History of the Texas Revolution, 1835-1836.* Austin: University of Texas Press, 1996.

Lord, Walter. *A Time to Stand.* Lincoln: University of Nebraska Press, 1978.

Nofi, Albert A. *The Alamo and the Texas War of Independence, September 30, 1835 to April 21, 1836: Heroes, Myths, and History.* New York: Da Capo, 1994.

Tinkle, Lon. *Thirteen Days to Glory.* New York: McGraw-Hill, 1958.

## THE TUSKEGEE AIRMEN: ALL BLOOD RUNS RED

Francis, Charles E. and Adolph Caso. *The Tuskegee Airmen: The Men Who Changed a Nation.* Boston: Branden, 1997.

Holway, John B. *Red Tails, Black Wings: The Men of America's Black Air Force.* Las Cruces, NM: Yucca Tree, 1997.

McKissack, Pat. *Red-Tail Angels: The Story of the Tuskegee Airmen of World War II.* New York: Walker & Co., 1995.

Websites:
    www.geocities.com/Pentagon/Quarters/1350 (Permission given to quote Douglass, Phyllis G. *The Tuskegee Airmen: A Tribute to my Father,* found at this website).
    www.afroam.org/history/tusk/tuskmain.htm.
    www.achiever.com/freehmpg/tai.
    www.blackaviation.com.

## THE UNDERGROUND RAILROAD: FOLLOWING THE NORTH STAR

Blockson, Charles L. *Hippocrene Guide to the Underground Railroad.* New York: Hippocrene, 1994.

Gara, Larry. *The Liberty Line: The Legend of the Underground Railroad*. 1961. Reprint, Lexington: University of Kentucky Press, 1996.

Siebert, Wilbur H. *The Underground Railroad from Slavery to Freedom*. New York: Macmillan, 1898.

Still, William. *The Underground Railroad*. Philadelphia, 1872. Reprint, Chicago: Johnson Publishing, 1970.

U.S. Department of the Interior. Division of Publications. *The Underground Railroad, Official National Park Handbook, No. 156*. Washington DC, 1998.

Video: *Harriet Tubman* (Black Americans of Achievement–Vol. 1). Tel: 1–800–469–7977.

Website: www.cr.nps.gov/nr/underground/states.htm (for historic sites in various states).

## WEBSTER'S AMERICAN DICTIONARY: "THE FINAL VOLLEY OF INDEPENDENCE"

Mencken, H.L. *The American Language*. New York: Alfred A. Knopf, 1923.

Rollins, Richard M. *The Long Journey of Noah Webster*. Philadelphia: University of Pennsylvania Press, 1980.

Shoemaker, Ervin C. *Noah Webster Pioneer of Learning*. New York: Columbia University Press, 1936.

Unger, Harlow Giles. *The Life and Times of Noah Webster: An American Patriot*. New York: John Wiley, 1998.

## THE WOMAN SUFFRAGE MOVEMENT: "FAILURE IS IMPOSSIBLE"

Barry, Kathleen. *Susan B. Anthony: A Biography*. New York: New York University Press, 1988.

Flexner, Eleanor. *Century of Struggle: The Woman's Rights Movement in the United States*. Rev. ed. Cambridge: Harvard University Press, Belknap Press, 1975.

Gage, Matilda. *Woman, Church & State*. Watertown, MA: Persephone Press, 1980.

Sherr, Lynn. *Failure Is Impossible*. New York: Times Books, Random House, 1995.

Stanton, Elizabeth Cody, Susan B. Anthony and Matilda Joslyn Gage. *History of Woman and Suffrage*, Vol.2, 1892. Reprint, Salem, NY: Ayer, 1985.

Video: *Susan B. Anthony* (American Women of Achievement Series. Tel: 1–800–469–8977). Susan B. Anthony (A & E.Tel: 1–800–597–6774).

## WRIGHT BROTHERS: CONCEPT OF GENIUS

Bilstein, Roger. *Flight in America: From the Wrights to the Astronauts*. Baltimore: Johns Hopkins University Press, 1994.

Crouch, Tom D. *The Bishop's Boys: A Life of Wilbur and Orville Wright*. New York: W. W. Norton, 1990.

Freedman, Russell. *The Wright Brothers: How They Invented the Airplane*. New York: Holiday House, 1991.

Howard, Fred. *Wilbur and Orville: A Biography of the Wright Brothers*. New York: Dover, 1998.

Jakab, Peter L. *Visions of a Flying Machine: The Wright Brothers and the Process of Invention*. Washington, DC: Smithsonian Institution Press, 1990.

Kirk, Stephen. *First in Flight: The Wright Brothers in North Carolina*. Winston-Salem, NC: John F. Blair, 1995.

Parramore, Thomas. Triumph at Kitty Hawk: The Wright Brothers and Powered Flight. Raleigh: Division of Archives and History, North Carolina Department of Cultural Resources, 1995.

Video: *The Wright Stuff* (The American Experience. Tel: 1–800–645–4727). *Wilbur and Orville: Dreams of Flying* (A&E Biography. Tel: 1–800 469–7977).

Website: www.wright-b-flyer.org.

## YELLOW FEVER: "A COMMON CAUSE FOR A DISEASE ALL TOO COMMON"

Bean, William A., M.D. *Walter Reed: A Biography*. Charlottesville: University Press of Virginia, 1982.

Epstein, Beryl Williams and Samuel Epstein. *William Crawford Gorgas: Tropic Fever Fighter*. New York: J. Messner, 1953.

Gibson, John Mendinghall. *Physician to the World: The Life of General William C. Gorgas*. Durham, NC: Duke University Press, 1950.

Hill, Ralph Nading. *The Doctors Who Conquered Yellow Fever*. New York: Random House, 1957.

McCullough, David. *The Path Between the Seas: The Creation of the Panama Canal 1870-1914*. New York: Simon & Schuster, 1977.

## YELLOWSTONE: OUR FIRST NATIONAL PARK

Anderson, Nancy K. *Thomas Moran*. Washington, DC: National Gallery of Art and New Haven, CT: Yale University Press, 1997.

Hales, Peter B. *William Henry Jackson and the Transformation of the American Landscape*. Philadelphia: Temple University Press, 1988.

Jackson, William Henry. *Time Exposure*. New York: G. P. Putnam's Sons, 1940.

Kinsey, Jean Louise. *Thomas Moran and the Surveying of the American West*. Washington, DC: Smithsonian Institution Press, 1992.

Video: *The Story of Yellowstone National Park*. Tel: 1–800–544–8422.

## YOUR SHOW OF SHOWS: A LEGACY OF LAUGHTER

Kisseloff, Jeff. *The Box: An Oral History of Television, 1920-1961*. New York: Viking/Penguin, 1995.

Sennett, Ted. *Your Show of Shows: The Story of Television's Most Celebrated Comedy Program*. New York: Da Capo, 1977.

Sullivan, Mark. *Our Times: America Finding Itself*. New York: Charles Scribner's Sons, 1927.

Fox, Margalit. "Lucille Kallan,76, Writer for Show of Shows, Dies." *New York Times*, 21 January 1999.

Website: www.emmys.org/archive. www.lib.umd.edu/umcp/lab.

## WEST POINT

Ambrose, Stephen E. *Duty, Honor, Country: A History of West Point*. Baltimore: Johns Hopkins University Press, 1966.

Steward, Robert. *The Corps of Cadets: A Year at West Point*. Annapolis, MD: Naval Institute Press, 1996.

# photo credits

## title page

Charles Coiner, Hoover Institution Archives image #US6042

## contents

**l** Keenland Library; **t** © Lee Tanner Photography; **b** Photograph by Scott Aichner; **t** San Diego Aerospace Museum; **m** © David Douglas Duncan, Freezing Marine, Korea, 1950. HRHRC; **b** Anchorage Daily News; **t** Warner Brothers (Courtsey KC); **m** C-B; **b** Photographer unknown / NYT Pictures; **t** Special Collections and Archives, Wright State University; **m** C-B; **b** Noir Tech Research.

## text

2, 4 C-B; 6-7 Kettering/GMI Alumni Foundation Collection of Industrial History; 8t Laura Wilson. *Barb Wire.*; 8b Laura Wilson. *West Texas Landscape*; 10 © Stephen Green Photography; 11 National Baseball Hall of Fame Library, Cooperstown, N.Y. Reproduced with permission of Spalding Sports Worldwide, Inc.; 12 C-B; 14 John J. Audubon, *White-Headed Eagle,* c.1830 from *The Birds of America*. SMA; 16 John J. Audubon, *Great Blue Heron*, 1834 from *The Birds of America*. SMA; 17 John J. Audubon, *Blue Jay*, 1831 from *The Birds of America*. SMA; 18 John J. Audubon, *Grey Fox*, 1843 from *The Viviparous Quadrupeds of North America*. SMA; 19 John J. Audubon, *Long-billed Curlew*, 1838 from *The Birds of America*. SMA; 20, 22-23 Noir Tech Research; 24 MOMA, Gift of Arnold H. Crane, 1972. (1972.742.2) © Walker Evans Archive, MOMA; 26 © 1996 ErrolGraphics USA, 17

S.E. Third Avenue, Portland, Oregon 97214, 503-244-7262. Coordination / Art direction: E. Michael Beard, Artist: Craig Holmes; 28 Photographer unknown / NYT Pictures; 30 Photograph courtesy Glaxo Wellcome Inc. Research Triangle Park, North Carolina; 32-35 Bill Lyons, Courtesy C-SPAN Television; 36 Alexander Calder, Model for East Building Mobile, Gift of Collectors Committee, Photograph © Board of Trustees, National Gallery of Art, Washington. Artwork © 1999 Estate of Alexander Calder / Artists Rights Society (ARS), New York; 38-39 Carnegie Corporation Papers, Rare Book and Manuscript Library, Columbia University; 40 Artwork by Patricia Curtan and James Monday; 43 Artwork by Patricia Curtan; 44 LOC; 46 Photographs and Prints Division. Schomburg Center for Research in Black Culture. NYPL. Astor, Lenox and Tilden Foundations; 48, 50, 52 Copyright 1999 Michael Witte; 54, 56 BB; 57 C-B; 58, 60 Copyright 1978 General Motors Corp. Used with permission of GM Media Archives; 61 Cheverolet Photos; 62,65 Detail, © Hatch Show Print, a division of The Country Music Foundation; 63-64 BMI Photo Archives; 66-69 © Lee Tanner Photography. All rights reserved. The Jazz Image 1563 Solano Avenue Berkeley, CA 94707; 70 U.S. Department of the Interior, National Park Service, Edison National Historic Site; 72 From William Strunk Jr. & E.B. White, Elements of Style 2/E © 1972 and 3/E © 1979. All rights reserved. Reprinted / adapted by permission of Allyn & Bacon. Single copies may be ordered from Allyn & Bacon 1-800-278-

# acknowledgments

The essays in this book have profited from the assistance of numerous people. For their help in providing information and materials, our thanks go to:

David Hunt and Laura Bowler, Stark Museum; Ron Tyler, Texas State Historical Association; Bill Holleran, Kettering/GMI; Peter Arturi, Spalding Sports Worldwide, Jim Gates and Patricia Kelley at the Baseball Hall of Fame; Peggy Riddle, Legends of the Game Museum; Larry Lester, Noir Tech Research; Mike Beard, Errolgraphics; Tammy Gabert, Rensselaer Polytechnic Institute; Dr. Marty St. Clair and Bill Chapman at Burroughs-Wellcome; John Maynard at C-SPAN; Nancy Stanfield, National Gallery of Art; Alyson Dinsmore; Jean Ashton and Brenda Hearing, Rare Book Library, Columbia University; Lyn McRaney, Chicago Historical Society.

Also providing invaluable assistance were Mike McFarland, Margaret Johanssen; Steve Eckelman; Van Hayes; Frances Conroy; Danielle Mattoon; Bobbi Carrey; Jill Bloomer, Cooper-Hewitt Museum; Ronnie Pugh and Mark Medley, Country Music Hall of Fame; Pam Morris, GM Media Archives; Doug Tarr, Edison National Historic Site; Lawrence Stark, Washington State University Library Special Collections; Laura Linke, Cornell University Library Special Collections; Bonnie Tower, Allyn-Bacon; Dr. John Sellars, Library of Congress; Harmony Haskins, White House Historical Association; Peter Kunhardt and Joan Caron, Kunhardt Productions; Pat Loud and Anne Adams, Kimbell Museum; Cheryl Hurley, Library of America; Roy Flukinger, Mary Luzious, and Linda Briscoe at the Harry Ransom Humanities Research Center; A.J. Lutz, San Diego Aerospace Museum; Mark Day, Teledyne-Ryan Aeronautical; Ann Sindelar, Western Reserve Historical Society Library; Amy Pettit, Keeneland; Kent Farnsworth; Ev Cassagneres; Wallace Best; George Elsey; Joe Nardone; Holly Anderson; Michael Witte; Scott Harbin; Pam Zaremba; David Hannah; Thierry Demont; Sarah McGrath; Lee Tanner; Alexandra and Augusta Aston; Rudy Reece and Christopher Ryan Reece; Nnogo Obiamwe; Joseph Olisaemeka Wilson; Peter Bogdanovich; and Nan Talese.

Others who helped us find images or supplied needed information included Diedre Cevington Attardi and Margurite Hunsiker at the National Geographic Society; Betty Monkman and Lydia Tederick of the Curator's Office at the White House; Karen Baumgartner, Brandywine Museum; Janet Wolf, CTW; Brendan Murphy, Gracie Films; David Sanjek, Hatch Show Prints; Stan Hoig; Susan Burrows, Bowdoin College Library Special Collections; Bob Prescott; Chad Wall, Nebraska State Historical Society; Ellen White and Herb Scher of the New York Public Library; David C. Burgevin, The Smithsonian Institution; Strawberry Luck, Vanderbilt University Library Special Collections; Hank Davis, Sun Records; Linda Scipione, Volkswagen of America; Jason Murray, *Surfer* magazine; Shane Bernard, archivist, McIlhenny Company; John Pampalone and Kathy Dawkins, City of New York, Department of Sanitation; Donaly Brice, Texas State Archives; E. Philip Scott, LBJ Library; Cathy Streuss, Eisenhower Library; Diane Meuser and Phyllis Collazo, *New York Times Pictures*.

Also supplying assistance to us were Ellen Gartrell at the John Hartman Center, Duke University; Adam Karp, Arnold Communications; Andrea Hamburger and Theresa Ali, West Point Public Affairs Office; Aisha Ayers, Oakland Musuem; Antony Toussaint, Schomburg Center for Research in Black Culture; Dawne Dewey, Wright State University Library; Mike Rhode, archivist, National Museum of Health & Medicine; Jon Dahlheim, Curator, Yellowstone National Park; Kathleen Moenster, Jefferson National Expansion Memorial; Jeff Rosenheim and Mary Daugherty, Metropolitan Museum of Art; Sid Shiff, Limited Editions Book Club; Christine Montgomery, State Historical Society of Missouri; Benita Washburn, Anchorage Daily News; Johnnie Luevanos, Universal Studios; Christopher Holm, Lucasfilm; Shelley Mills, Eames Office; Jim Lapides, International Poster Gallery; Jeff Dosik, Statue of Liberty National Monument; Don Clampitt and Barbara Wardlow, Clampitt Paper; Stephanie Theriot and Joe Issak, Potlatch; Carol Butler, Brown Brothers; Mara Fuentes, Corbis; Liz Durkin, Hamilton Projects.

# index

The text of *American Greats* is set in 21st Century Roman, created specifically for this book, and based on the typeface Century, drawn by Linn Boyd Benton for Century Magazine in 1900. His son, Morris Fuller Benton, later redrew Century for book publication, known as Century Schoolbook, which is the standard for school texts to this day. Far more prolific than this father, Morris made a career of typography, and among his accomplishments was the creation of typeface for the New York department of Roadways, Franklin Gothic, which appears on the cover of *American Greats* and nearly every traffic sign in North America.

Book and jacket design by Joe Goodwin and Staci Teague, Wilson Associates, Dallas, Texas. Additional design and composition by Mark McGarry, Texas Type & Book Works, Dallas, Texas. Production management by Della R. Mancuso. Color separations prepared by Color Associates, St. Louis, Missouri. Book jacket printed by Coral Graphic Services, Inc., Hicksville, New York. Text printed on Potlatch 80lb. Northwest Dull. Printed and bound in the U.S. by RR Donnelley & Sons Co., Willard, Ohio.